RURAL DEVELOPMENT AND EDUCATION

RURAL DEVELOPMENT AND EDUCATION

(In 2 Volumes)

Rural Development Priorities

(Volume-2)

Editor

Dr. M.L. Dhawan

ISHA BOOKS

DELHI-110 033

Rural Development and Education

ISBN: 81-8205-055-3 (Set)
ISBN: 81-8205-057-x (Vol. 2)

Published in 2004 in India by
Isha Books, D-43, Prithviraj Road,
Adarsh Nagar, Delhi-110 033

Laser Typesetting at : Shree Vaishnavi Creations, Delhi
Printed at : Chawla Offset Press, Delhi

Contents

Preface

Rural areas constitute a larger part of the world. About three-fourth of the total population of the world are living in these areas. So that rural development is central to the development efforts of any nation. A substantial volume of assistance has been provided to rural authorities by government and non-governmental agencies for the development of key areas like agriculture, food security, natural resources management, economic development, banking, habitation, health, sanitation, education, etc.

This volume presents a cohesive and comprehensive scenario of the changing dimension of rural development process. The problems of infrastructure to rural development and poverty alleviation have been viewed in relation to agricultural and economic growth. The sustained efforts made by government and voluntary agencies are also described in detail.

The book suggests that there remains a lot to be done to brush up these attempts, because infrastructure disparities between rural and urban areas have accentuated the income disparities. Written in a simple and lucid style, it will prove highly informative to policy makers, academicians, students and research scholars.

Editor

1

Goals of Rural Development

The mission of Rural Development is to: Enhance the ability of rural communities to develop, to grow, and to improve their quality of life by targeting financial and technical resources in areas of greatest need through activities of greatest potential. Following are the goals of rural development programme:

1 *Good Jobs and Diverse Markets*: Rural Development will improve the quality of life in rural America by encouraging the establishment and growth of rural businesses and cooperatives.

2 *Quality Housing and Modern Community Facilities*: Rural Development will improve the quality of life of rural residents by providing access to technical assistance, capital, and credit for quality housing, and modern, essential community facilities.

3 *Modern Affordable Utilities*: Rural Development will improve the quality of life of rural residents by promoting and providing access to capital and credit for the development and delivery of modern affordable utility services.

4 *Community Capacity Building*: Rural Development will provide information, technical assistance, and, when appropriate, leadership to rural areas, rural communities and cooperatives to give their leaders the capacity to design and carry out their own rural development initiatives.

5. *Effective, Efficient Service to the Public*: Rural Development will develop the staff, systems, and infrastructure needed to ensure high quality delivery of its programs to all rural residents.

Good Jobs and Diverse Markets

Rural Development will improve the quality of life in rural America by encouraging the establishment and growth of rural businesses and cooperatives. Data comes from a variety of sources including: an internal management system, the Rural Community Facilities Tracking System (RCFTS); two internal accounting systems; the Program Loan Accounting System (PLAS) and the Guaranteed Loan System (GLS) and Department of Labor employment estimates.

Determining the number of jobs saved and created for the IRP is much more difficult. These are loans made to an intermediary lender who then uses the funds to make loans to entrepreneurs. As the loan is repaid to the intermediary, the funds are used to make new loans to other entrepreneurs. Since virtually all IRP loans to the intermediaries have a loan term of 30 years, the funds revolve 3.4 times during the term of the loan.

Development of the Rural Development Application Processing and Tracking System (RDAPTS) is underway which will provide a basis for approving and measuring the progress of projects. The RDAPTS will allow integration of information from multiple systems in a data warehouse thereby improving the integrity of the data used for reporting of policy targets, loan applications, obligations and servicing actions. Development of this common computing environment will eliminate the redundant data entry and provide the data in a location that can be easily consolidated, transitioned and loaded into the data warehouse.

Screens are being developed to collect information on characteristics of ultimate recipient loans made under revolving loan fund programs such as IRP. This is expected to provide more reliable jobs and leveraging data for revolving loan fund programs. Improvements in procedures for collecting technical assistance data for State Rural Development Offices are planned. Leveraging of research expenditures will depend upon availability of cooperative agreement research funds.

While data from RCFTS and state surveys is considered soft, it is considered sufficiently accurate to be used for management decisions. Information regarding the Rural Economic Area Partnership (REAP) zones was added to this statement because REAP zones were combined with Empowerment Zones and Enterprise Communities (EZ/EC) for FY 2000.

RCFTS is a non-accounting management system, which contains a variety of data related to Business Programs, such as the number of jobs created or saved. Data in RCFTS is input by the field staff and does not contain edits to verify the accuracy of the data. Manual reports from State Directors will be used to obtain data regarding several of the performance measures. This information will be less reliable because it is obtained manually and its accuracy cannot be verified. However, confidence in this data is high enough to be acceptable for the purposes for which it is used. Therefore, the information is considered sufficiently accurate to be used for management decisions.

Quality Housing and Modern Community Facilities

Rural Development will improve the quality of life of rural residents by providing access to technical assistance, capital, and credit for quality housing and modern, essential community facilities. The goal overall and most targets were met for the direct loan program but were not met for the guaranteed loan program. According to the Mortgage Bankers Association of America, more than 50 percent of those refinancing their mortgages have taken out equity in the process. RHS will continue to monitor performance progress quarterly and take necessary and appropriate actions in the event performance is less than expected.

Modern Affordable Utilities

Rural Development will improve the quality of life of rural residents by promoting and providing access to capital and credit for the development and delivery of modern affordable utility services. The increase in loan guarantees and the advance of loan funds was in direct response to the uncertainty of the wholesale power market and the need for borrowers serving rural areas to manage their electricity supply portfolio to ensure reliable electric service at a competitive cost. RUS responded quickly to the demands placed on the nation's energy supply and delivery system.

Community Capacity Buildingm

Rural Development will provide information, technical

assistance, and, when appropriate, leadership to rural areas, rural communities and cooperatives to give their leaders the capacity to design and carry out their own rural development initiatives.

With the emphasis being placed on the third round of the EZ/EC program, Rural Development anticipated much lower numbers. However, due to extraordinary efforts by all involved, we were able to exceed the goal. It was consistently found that there was a direct correlation between those communities that are successfully implementing their strategic plans and the commitment, skills and abilities of the Rural Development staff charged with assisting these communities. However, inconsistencies were found among Rural Development State offices as to how the community development staffs are organized, trained and allocated to the community development functions.

Effective, Efficient Service to the Public

Rural Development will develop the staff, systems, and infrastructure needed to ensure high quality delivery of its programs to all rural residents. Following are the objectives:

— Create and sustain a work environment that develops and fosters partnerships, cooperation, full and

— open communications, teamwork, mutual respect, and maximum individual development.

Rural Development exceeded the target for civil rights training. This was achieved by aggressively contacting states with less than 100% completion rates. Those states were encouraged to contact all employees who had not taken the training. The Civil Rights staff reduced its backlog of EEO complaints by focusing most of its resources in the informal process to increase the resolution rate.

Leave and other common policies are currently on hold at the direction of the National Food and Agriculture Council (NFAC) pending review and guidance from policy officials of the new Administration.

Develop information systems which support cost-effective delivery of programs and maximize the availability of information to all employees. There is no variance to consider and the assessment of results is accurate. The assessment of results, although not audited, is considered by management to be reliable. A new performance indicator for the effort previously included as the "Fully support the utility programs" will be redefined as the "Implement the Rural Utilities Loan (RULSS)".

Based on Rural Development's FY 1999 financial statements, guaranteed loans represent approximately 16% of the dollar value of Rural Development loan portfolio. The results of the FY 2001 indicators related to 100 percent of the Credit Reform programs having a clean opinion are pending final testing of the Credit Reform model that calculates subsidy for the direct single and multi family housing programs, and OIG's approval of the of the model.

Software has been implemented to disburse funds electronically (EFT). Rural Development did not meet the 60 percent target for EFT disbursements. However, it is anticipated the percent of EFT disbursements will increase as programs continue to expand the practice of using EFT. Additionally, the established target for obtaining a management decision within 6 months on 90 percent of the audits was not met for FY 2001. Rural Development succeeded in achieving the 90 percent target for FY's 1999 and 2000 and the target will remain at 90 percent for 2002.

Rural Development also anticipates meeting the indicators

related to Credit. Reform and receiving a clean opinion on the financial statements. Rural Development is one of a number of agencies struggling to develop more reliable Credit Reform models required to calculate subsidy rates. Overall, Rural Development, Procurement Management Division believes that the performance-based service contract goals have been met.

In US, the Rural Business-Cooperative Service (RBS), the Rural Housing Service (RHS), and the Rural Utilities Service (RUS) constitute the Rural Development mission area. The mission area's efforts support Goal 4 of the USDA Strategic Plan - "Enhance the capacity of all rural residents, communities and businesses to prosper." The staffs of these agencies have been, and will continue to be, important providers of financial and technical assistance to rural communities. Their efforts in the past have helped millions of rural Americans achieve a higher standard of living and have enabled them to live healthier, more productive, and more enjoyable lives. Much, however, remains to be done.

The development of rural America is a difficult and complicated task in the best of circumstances. The mission area is charged with being the lead Federal entity for rural development in an era of dwindling Federal resources and in the face of rapid changes in the global economy. Substantial challenges exist for both rural America and the mission area. This plan covers fiscal years 2000 through 2005. It is an update of the mission areas' first Strategic Plan published in September 1997. The plan will be reviewed annually and updated every 3 years.

Rural America is diverse and complex. The thousands of communities which make up rural America are at different stages in their adjustment to the forces which impact US national economy. Some communities have adjusted well and are prospering. There are, however, regions of the country, and pockets in every State, where unemployment and poverty are widespread. Between these two extremes are numerous individual communities, throughout the country, with major unmet needs.

Until these needs are met, these communities have a very limited ability to attract the job-creating businesses needed for the community to grow and prosper in the future. Even though rural communities are very diverse, with each one having its own unique needs, most of them share a common problem - difficulty in obtaining financing for needed improvements. This problem is exacerbated by the limited number of available users to support the repayment of debt, the high cost per user of rural projects due to their small scale, and the lack of expertise in many rural communities in the technical aspects of project development and management.

Most small rural communities do not have bond ratings, which makes it nearly impossible for them to obtain private sector financing. Rural residents and businesses encounter similar problems in obtaining financing. Financing for homes or businesses in small rural communities is often very limited due to the small number of interested lenders in the area.

There may also be a high potential for loss in case of financial failure due to a number of factors including the lack of economic diversity in the community and the limited number of people who might be interested in assuming the debt or buying the property securing the debt. Rural Development programs are designed to meet the diverse needs of rural communities and to help them obtain the financial and technical assistance needed to improve the quality of life in rural America and help individuals and businesses compete in the global marketplace.

These programs consist of a variety of loan, loan

guarantee, and grant programs, plus technical assistance, in the areas of business and industry; cooperative development; rural housing; community facilities; water and waste disposal; electric power; and telecommunications, including distance learning and telemedicine. Rural Development loan programs, with an outstanding portfolio of approximately $79.6 billion, are delivered through a National Office for each agency, 47 Rural Development State offices and a network of other field offices.

The mission of the Rural Business-Cooperative Service is "to enhance the quality of life for all rural Americans by providing leadership in building competitive businesses and sustainable cooperatives that can prosper in the global marketplace." RBS accomplishes this mission by investing its financial resources and technical assistance in businesses and cooperatives, and by building partnerships that leverage public, private, and cooperative resources to create jobs and stimulate rural economic activity.

The Rural Housing Service' mission is "to improve the quality of life in rural America and help build competitive, vibrant rural communities through its community facilities and housing programs." Two of the key components of a healthy community are decent and affordable housing and the availability of essential community services such as fire protection and health care.

RHS has financed over 2 million single-family homes since the inception of its home ownership program. The rural housing programs are an essential part of the President's National Homeownership Initiative. In the last 20 years, the community facilities program has enabled over 7,000 communities to provide basic community services for their citizens.

The mission of the Rural Utilities Service is "to serve a leading role in improving the quality of life in rural America by administering its electric, telecommunications, distance learning-telemedicine and water and waste programs in a service-oriented, forward-looking and financially responsible manner."

RUS programs provide rural residents access to modern, affordable telecommunications, distance learning-telemedicine, water, waste water disposal, and electric service. In addition to financial assistance, the agencies provide technical assistance to help rural communities deal with both day-to-day management and operational problems plus long-term problems, such as developing contingency plans for droughts, floods, and other natural disasters.

These infrastructure systems are essential for the health and safety of rural Americans and are vital if they are to be participants in the global economy. The mission area administers, through its Office of Community Development, the rural portion of the Administration's Empowerment Zones and Enterprise Communities (EZ/EC) Initiative.

Its mission is "to create self-sustaining, long-term economic development in areas of pervasive poverty, unemployment, and general distress, and to demonstrate how distressed communities can achieve self-sufficiency through innovative and comprehensive strategic plans developed and implemented by alliances among private, public, and nonprofit entities."

This program is seen as the first step in rebuilding poverty-stricken communities in rural America. It is designed to empower people and communities to work together to create jobs and opportunities. The mission area also houses and provides support to the National Rural Development Partnership, a nationwide network of rural development leaders and officials committed to the vitality of rural areas.

The legislative authorities for the mission area programs

are found in the Consolidated Farm and Rural Development Act, as amended; Title 5 of the Housing Act of 1949, as amended; the Cooperative Marketing Act of 1926, as amended; and the Rural Electrification Act of 1936, as amended. The mission area is also impacted by other legislation, such as the Food Security Act of 1985, as amended; the Federal Agricultural Improvement and Reform Act of 1996; the Telecommunications Act of 1996; and the Energy Policy Act of 1992.

A basic mandate of many of the mission area's programs is that they are not to compete with private credit, but rather supplement that credit. If the individuals or entities can obtain affordable credit to meet all, or part, of their needed funding from other sources, they are expected to do so. Another legislative mandate is that priority should be given in the delivery of programs to the smallest and poorest communities.

The partnerships and coordination with other organizations required for program delivery varies between agencies and by programs within the agencies. Most of the coordination with rural development partners occurs at the state level or local level. This plan serves as the basis for the development of State/Tribal strategic plans required by the Federal Agricultural Improvement and Reform Act of 1996.

The Rural Development State Directors develop their plans with their various public and private partners to support the coordinated delivery of all resources, both financial and technical. These partners include other Governmental agencies at the Federal, State and local level; small farm operators and organizations that represent small farm interests; minorities organizations; and community-based and nonprofit organizations.

While coordination with other agencies are not required for program delivery, close coordination with the Farm Service

Agency and the Natural Resources Conservation Service is required for the Department's Service Center initiative. This initiative focuses on the effective and efficient delivery of programs of the three agencies at the local level. This coordination involves not only the sharing of office space but also the development of common automated systems and administrative policies and practices.

Other Departmental agencies which the mission area works with are the Economic Research Service; Forest Service; Foreign Agricultural Service; Agricultural Marketing Service; Cooperative State Research, Education and Extension Service; and National Agricultural Statistics Service. Outside of the Department, coordination occurs, as needed, with the Department of Housing and Urban Development; Department of Commerce; Environmental Protection Agency; Small Business Administration; Department of Labor; Department of Energy; Federal Deposit Insurance Corporation; Federal Home Loan Bank; Federal Communications Commission; Federal Energy Regulatory Commission; and Nuclear Regulatory Commission.

The ability of the mission area to achieve the goals of its strategic plan can be impacted by a variety of factors beyond its control. Primary external factors affecting all programs are:

Macroeconomic influences - Changes in the economy, including the global economy, can have a major impact on financial programs and the ability of customers to meet their obligations. Rural businesses need to be competitive in the global economy if they are to succeed.

A rise in unemployment generally impacts low-income families first. Inflation can impact the disposable income of low-income families and may also adversely impact the ability of small communities and businesses to meet their obligations if their operating expenses are increasing faster than their income.

Changes in the cost of money have the greatest impact on the mission area.

As interest rates rise or fall, there is a clear impact on the cost of the financing provided by the mission area and the ability of new customers to afford the assistance they need. For instance, high interest rates reduce the ability of existing direct loan borrowers to graduate to private sector credit. Changing interest rates will impact the subsidy rates of each program.

Lower interest rates reduce the subsidy cost of direct loans, and increase the subsidy cost of guaranteed programs. Rural Development can partially ameliorate the impact of adverse economic conditions by increasing its loan servicing activities to minimize delinquencies.

Reductions in funding - Reductions in level of funding provided to the Rural Development agencies will reduce their ability to help rural America and to achieve their goals. Likewise, reductions in funding for Salaries and Expenses will limit the ability of the mission area to provide the staff and other resources needed to deliver the programs or achieve the anticipated level of performance.

Reductions in program funding can be partially offset by efforts to increase the leveraging of agency funds with other sources of funds. Reductions in Salaries and Expenses can only be offset by the elimination of lower priority work efforts which may, in the long run, be to the detriment of the Government or its customers..

The mission of Rural Development is to: "Enhance the ability of rural communities to develop, to grow, and to improve their quality of life by targeting financial and technical resources in areas of greatest need through activities of greatest potential."

Rural Development will improve the quality of life in rural

America by encouraging the establishment and growth of rural businesses and cooperatives. Rural America is currently experiencing an economic and population revival, after the declines of the 1980's. Yet rural America continues to face significant challenges. Income and earnings from non-farm jobs in rural areas continue to lag behind those in urban areas.

Structural changes in production agriculture have been, and will continue to be, significant. There is a strong continuing need for more diversified sources of income for farm and non-farm workers in rural areas. The need is not just for jobs, but for jobs that pay a livable wage. Less than one in four rural jobs are in farm or farm-related industries.

During the 1990's, the rural-urban gap in real per capita annual income remained approximately $7,000 or greater, while rural non-farm jobs in 1996 paid over $9,000 per job less than urban jobs. The rural-urban gap in real earnings per non-farm job is wider now than it was in either 1980 or 1990. There is also disparity in the poverty rates between rural and urban areas. In 1996, 15.9 percent of rural residents were in poverty compared to 13.2 percent of urban residents.

Objective 1: Increase the availability and quality of jobs in rural areas.

Strategies for Achieving the Objective:

— Build leveraging partnerships with State, local and private sources to expand total resources going to rural areas.

— Work with local communities to ensure funds are directed to projects with the highest job creation potential.

— Coordinate with the Foreign Agricultural Service to promote product development in rural areas which have a foreign market.

— Involve 1890 and 1862 land-grant universities in providing technical assistance to minority-owned businesses and entrepreneurs in training, credit acquisition, and business plan development.

— Amend the Business and Industry (B&I) Guaranteed Loan Program regulations to eliminate agricultural production when it is part of an integrated business also involved in the processing of agricultural products as an eligible purpose.

— Utilize existing regional and national conferences and workshops to inform potential lenders about Business Programs and how these programs can be used for locally based market development for small farmers.

— Strengthen business and cooperative performance strength and growth through appropriate research and non-financial technical assistance.

— Develop and maintain a series of educational and informational publications targeting the cooperative knowledge needs of small and disadvantaged farmers, including Spanish translations of the core publications in that series.

— Train appropriate staff to recognize the unique needs of small farmers by FY 2002.

Objective 2: Encourage and promote the use of marketing networks and cooperative partnerships to increase marketing opportunities and market access for farmers and rural residents.

Strategies for Achieving the Objective:

— Coordinate efforts with the Foreign Agricultural Service to utilize cooperatives to promote, in rural areas, the development of products which have a foreign market.

— Research and develop models of cooperatives that address the barriers facing small and beginning farmers and marketing challenges facing all farmers.

— Improve access to cooperatives for small, beginning, women, and minority farmers.

— Partner with public, non-profit, and educational institutions to heighten awareness and understanding of cooperatives and marketing opportunities in underserved rural areas.

— Provide field level training and technical assistance to cooperatives and developing cooperative groups.

— Give priority to development of cooperatives which will primarily benefit small arm operations including women, minorities and beginning farmers.

— Research and develop cooperative models that address the barriers beginning farmers face, particularly models that address the barriers.

— Research and develop means for cooperatives to enable new small farmers to join cooperatives, to ensure that control remains dispersed.

Objective 3: Direct Rural Development program resources to those rural communities, and customers with the greatest need.

Strategies for Achieving the Objective:

— Support Rural Developments' Appropriate Technology Transfer for Rural Areas Program (ATTRA) by developing a clearinghouse of available equipment and systems and a means to identify unmet needs.

— In ranking projects for funding consideration, discretionary points authorized under the various Business Programs loan/ grant regulations will be considered for projects involving value-added cooperative development and other business activities that support marketing and supply service needs of targeted groups including small beginning farmers.

— Ensure accessibility of Rural Development programs for Native Americans.

— Set aside B&I Guaranteed Loan Program funding for cooperative development financing. Priority within the set aside will be given to projects involving farmer-owned, value-added cooperatives.

— Conduct a program of outreach to inform minorities, women, and small or beginning farmers of the availability of Business Programs loan/grant programs.

— Conduct outreach to State Rural Electric Cooperative Associations to leverage available loan and grant funds for agricultural development to create local value-added agricultural businesses for the products produced by small farms.

— Invest 20% of the B&I Guaranteed Loan Program funding for cooperative development. Priority will be given to locally owned, value-added cooperative farm-product-related businesses or small farm business operations.

Objective 4: Manage the loan portfolio in a manner that is efficient and effective.

Strategies for Achieving the Objective:

— Acquire software that will assist National and Field Staffs in analyzing financial statements, comparing their standard ratio trends to make a more informed decision on the credit or servicing review.

Rural Development will improve the quality of life of rural residents by providing access to technical assistance, capital and credit for quality housing and modern, essential community facilities. Vibrant communities are critical to the success of rural America. One of the key components of a healthy community is decent, safe, sanitary and affordable housing.

Another fundamental foundation for strong rural communities is the availability of essential community facilities, such as fire stations, health care clinics, and child care facilities. These facilities often provide the bedrock for economic development in the community and provide a sense of security and well being to the residents. The need for homeownership in rural areas is continuous as new families are formed and rural residents move from one community to another.

In addition, with an estimated 1.6 million rural households residing in substandard housing, there is a need for families to move to decent, safe and sanitary housing. Available mortgage credit has always been more limited in rural areas, especially for those families with very low to moderate incomes. Since 1950, RHS has helped more than 2 million families become homeowners.

Rural communities also need decent, safe, and sanitary rental properties to house those members of the rural population who cannot obtain homes of their own or may not want to be homeowners. Although RHS's housing programs have been successful, many rural residents still live in substandard housing.

According to the Housing Assistance Council's recent report, The State of Rural Rental Housing, more than 900,000 rural rental households, 10.4 percent of the total, live in either severely or moderately inadequate housing. More than one million rural renter households are "worst case needs" households, which the Department of Housing and Urban Development defines as being below 50 percent of the area median household income, extremely cost burdened or inadequately housed, and receiving no federal housing assistance.

Of those rural renters with worst case needs, 92 percent pay more than one half of their income, about $6,000, for housing costs. Together, RHS's Section 515 Rural Rental Housing (RRH) program and Section 521 Rental Assistance (RA) program provide decent, safe, and affordable housing to those families who need it most. The Section 515 program provides loans at 1 percent interest rate to build affordable housing, while the Rental Assistance program ensures that tenants pay no more than thirty percent (30 percent) of their income for rent.

Many rural communities lack the basic services needed to provide the residents with a good quality of life. Although over 20 percent of Americans live in non-metropolitan areas, only 11 percent of patient care physicians practice there. In a recent survey, there were 243 rural counties which had no primary care physicians practicing in the county.

Rural Development has provided funding for more than 80 different kinds of projects, from child care centers to hospitals to fire trucks. These projects, while vital to the residents, also help communities attract businesses that provide jobs and services for their residents.

Objective 1: Improve the quality of life for the residents of rural communities by providing access to decent, safe, affordable housing.

Strategies for Achieving the Objective:

— Build leveraging partnerships to expand resources going into rural areas.

— Direct resources to the neediest families and communities.

— Work with rural communities to ensure housing funds are wisely invested.

— Expand self-help housing to all 50 States.

— Provide leadership for the President's Homeownership Initiative in rural areas.

— Request $50 million of RHS funds annually for the Farm Labor Housing (LH) Program.

Objective 2: Improve the quality of life in rural America by providing essential community facilities.

Strategies for Achieving the Objective:

— Build leveraging partnerships to expand resources going to rural areas.

— Direct resources to the neediest projects and communities.

— Work with local communities to ensure funds are wisely invested.

— Support Welfare Reform by promoting development of day-care facilities.

Objective 3: Maximize the leveraging of loan funds to increase the number of rural residents assisted by Rural Development programs.

Strategy for Achieving the Objective:

— Develop joint funding agreements with partners.

Objective 4: Manage the loan portfolio in a manner that is efficient and effective.

Strategies for Achieving the Objective:

— Improve portfolio and debt management by enhancing the Dedicated Loan Origination and Servicing (DLOS) system.

— Utilize the existing partnership with the Office of the Inspector General to identify and correct any fraud or abuse in the management of the RRH projects.

— Improve coordination with the other agencies and departments involved in detection of fraud, waste and abuse cases and the enforcement of corrective actions related to those cases.

— Preserve and maintain the existing stock of rural rental housing projects for low-income families and ensure the projects are well managed and maintained.

— Reinvent the Multi-Family Housing (MFH) Program, including completion of automation projects to improve program management.

Rural Development will improve the quality of life of rural residents by promoting and providing access to capital and credit for the development and delivery of modern, affordable utility services. Access to safe drinking water and modern, sanitary waste facilities is critical if a community is to prosper. An estimated 2.5 million rural Americans have a critical need for safe, dependable drinking water, including approximately 1 million residents who do not have water piped into their homes.

The telecommunications program provides capital,

establishes telecommunications standards, and provides policy guidance for rural telecommunications in the Administration's National Information Infrastructure Initiative. The Information

Superhighway can provide rural residents access to libraries, training centers, vocational schools, and other institutions located in metropolitan areas and support rural businesses. It also provides improved health care through linkage with other rural health care providers and urban medical centers for clinical interactive video consultation, distance training of rural health care providers, and access to medical expertise and library resources.

As part of the restructuring of the electric utility industry, Rural Development is ensuring the continued availability of reliable, high-quality electric service at a reasonable cost to rural consumers. Many rural electric and telecommunications systems are aging and the obsolete infrastructure must be replaced and improved.

Objective 1: Improve the quality of life in rural America by providing technical assistance and financing for modern, affordable water and waste water services in rural communities.

Strategies for Achieving the Objective:

— Utilize leveraging partnerships to expand resources going to rural areas.

— Direct resources to the neediest projects and communities.

— In the spirit of Water 2000, continue to pursue the achievement of its goals by bringing safe,

— clean drinking water to every rural household.

— Ensure accessibility of Rural Development programs to Native Americans.

Objective 2: Improve the quality of life in rural America by providing technical assistance and financing for modern, affordable telecommunications services, including distance learning and telemedicine facilities, in rural communities.

Strategies for Achieving the Objective:

— Continue to build leveraging partnerships to expand resources going to rural areas.

— Where applicable, direct resources to the neediest projects and communities.

— Work with borrowers and grantees to ensure funds are wisely invested.

— Implement the President's National Information Infrastructure Initiative thereby increasing educational and health care levels in rural areas

Objective 3: Improve the quality of life in rural America by providing technical assistance and financing for modern, affordable electric service to rural communities.

Strategies for Achieving the Objective:

— Continue to build leveraging partnerships to expand resources going to rural areas.

— Where applicable, direct resources to the neediest projects and communities.

— Work with borrowers to ensure funds are wisely invested.

Objective 4: Where applicable, direct Rural Development program resources to those rural communities and customers with the greatest need.

Strategies for Achieving the Objective:

— Improve accessibility to Rural Development programs for Native Americans.

— In the spirit of Water 2000, continue to pursue the achievement of its goals.

Objective 5: Maximize the leveraging of loan funds to increase the number of rural residents assisted by Rural Development programs.

Strategy for Achieving the Objective:

— Where possible, increase the leveraging of RUS funds with borrowers and supplemental lenders.

Rural Development will provide information, technical assistance, and, when appropriate, leadership to rural areas, rural communities and cooperatives and provide to their leaders the capacity to design and carry out their own rural development initiatives.

The preceding goals recognize that rural development involves the provision of financial assistance. This goal adds the understanding that a successful comprehensive community development process also involves technical assistance to build leadership capacity and community development skills. Mission area staff provide technical assistance to rural communities and cooperatives, often in partnership with public and private organizations.

Two key avenues for providing this assistance are the

Empowerment Zone/Enterprise Community (EZ/EC) initiative and the Rural Economic Area Partnership (REAP) initiative. EZ/EC focuses on poverty communities and builds upon earlier rural development efforts at the Federal and State level by including tax credits and other supply-side incentives for business development in the neediest communities.

The difference between the two designations is the level and type of assistance provided to them by statute. Eight rural communities have been designated as Enterprise Zones, including one Native American tribe. Fifty-one rural communities have been named as Enterprise Communities, including 4 Native American tribes.

The REAP program is designed to address a different, but significant, problem in rural areas—declining populations and job opportunities. These communities are often characterized by historical dependence on agriculture, geographic isolation with communities separated by long distances, an aging population, and a lack of access to major transportation routes. Four multi-county zones have initially been designated for the REAP initiative.

Strategies for Achieving the Goal:

— Use local and state coordinating bodies, such as planning districts, Resource Conservation and Development Councils (RC&D) and the State Rural Development Councils, to identify alternative sources of funding for rural projects.

— Provide assistance and training to rural leaders on strategic planning and other sources of technical assistance, which are available to help them assess community strengths, plan for the future, and prepare applications for assistance.

— Implement collaborative rural economic and community development training for rural organizations, involving other Federal, State, and local agencies, and organizations.

— Expand the base of knowledge and understanding of the Rural Development mission area employees in economic and community development, evaluation methods and operations, and analyzing the social/economic dynamics of rural areas and communities.

Rural Development will develop the staff, systems, and infrastructure needed to ensure high quality delivery of its programs to all rural residents. Rural Development is dependent upon the ability and skills of its staff for the effective delivery of its programs. The staff must be adequately trained and have the resources needed if it is to accomplish its job.

The mission area's administrative resources have been reduced as a result of the Administration's and Congress' joint efforts to balance the Federal budget, while program resources have increased. This has resulted in reductions in staff and field offices needed to deliver the programs plus an even greater reduction in administrative staff. A reduction in human resources increases the need for automated systems which can help staff work more efficiently, while still maintaining their effectiveness..

Reductions in resources also requires that Rural Development be innovative in identifying new ways of doing business while being ever mindful of the need to provide high quality service to the customers. Rural Development will utilize a management approach and encourage a workplace environment which values employees and involves them, as partners, in the management of the mission area. The environment of the workplace will ensure that all customers and employees are treated fairly, equitably, and with dignity and respect.

Objective 1: Create and sustain a work environment that

develops and fosters partnerships, cooperation, full and open communications, teamwork, mutual respect, and maximum individual development.

Strategies for Achieving the Objective:

— Develop a workforce capable of delivering a full range of financial and non-financial services in support of rural development activities.

— Foster, and continually strengthen, an internal culture that focuses on and is driven by customer needs, both internally and externally.

— Increase the use of Alternative Dispute Resolution (ADR) as a tool for resolving workplace and external customer disputes.

— Enhance the work environment by developing policies and adopting processes which are friendly to the employees and their families.

— Instill the value of cultural diversity in all Rural Development personnel and develop a workforce which is representative of the diversity of the areas in which they work.

— Provide Civil Rights training to all employees.

— Support USDA service centers by developing common administrative policies and processes with other USDA agencies.

— Maximize the use of automated systems to ensure consistency in work processes and as a replacement for staff lost in downsizing efforts.

— Include in the recognition and rewards system a linkage to the accomplishment of the goals and objectives of the strategic plan.

Objective 2: Develop information systems which support cost-effective delivery of programs and maximize the availability of information to all employees.

Strategies for Achieving the Objective:

— Support the establishment of USDA Service Centers and develop processes and automated systems which maximize their effectiveness.

— Focus information and technical infrastructure development on enhancements which improve service delivery and maximizes the availability of data for all employees.

— Make data more accessible by utilizing WEB technology.

— Develop a data warehouse to ensure current data is available to all employees and to support the ability of the mission area to better manage and analyze its delivery of programs.

Objective 3: Improve financial management to ensure fiscal accountability.

Strategies for Achieving the Objective:

— Enhance Rural Development's ability to track and monitor administrative funds appropriations and provide accurate reports to all internal customers.

— Implement the electronic funds transfer (EFT) requirements of the Debt Collection Improvement Act.

— Work with the Departmental OIG and OCFO to resolve issues related to credit reform and obtain a clean opinion on Rural Development's audited financial statement.

An annual performance plan will be prepared each fiscal year to accompany the Rural Development budget request. The plan will consist of annual performance measures directly linked to the general goals, objectives and strategies contained in the strategic plan. It will outline an annual increment of the key strategies called for in the strategic plan and any additional strategies that are required to implement Rural Development objectives and achieve current performance goals. It will also contain baseline data for the measures for the two fiscal years prior to the budget year.

The data systems used by the Rural Development mission area contain elements responsive to many needs other than this plan. The performance measures included in this plan are selected indicators of success in achieving the goals and are based on data currently available in the existing systems. As new systems are developed and refined, additional data will be available for measurement of future performance.

Most of the performance measures used in this plan will also be used in the annual performance plan. However, additional or different measures may be used in any given year to report on priority concerns related to the Goal or to make use of new data that has become available.

As a result of Congressional mandates, Administration initiatives, and internal studies, a variety of program and management concerns have been identified and were considered in the development of this plan. Future internal studies planned are:

Multi-Family Housing Preservation Needs - a study to determine the resources needed to preserve the multi-family housing stock. The Role of Cooperatives in Supporting and Enhancing Farm Policy and Contributing to the Health of Rural Economies - an examination of how farm cooperatives can be most effectively used to improve the health of the farm and rural economies.

Rural Development will evaluate the impact of these strategically driven changes through Management Control Reviews, State Internal Reviews, and findings in future audits. Stakeholders provided significant contributions in the development of the earlier plan through their participation in focus groups and listening forums held at the State and national levels.

Rural Development State Directors held 39 listening forums with partners and stakeholders to identify their concerns and obtain their input. Since 1997, Rural Development staff has held numerous meetings with stakeholders on a variety of issues and the feedback from those meetings have been considered in the development of this plan.

2

Rural Development Intervention

In developing countries rural people have often not been able to obtain formal credit, leading many writers to see credit as a panacea, the missing ingredient, for rural development. The famous modernisation theorist, Walt Rostow, spoke of modernisation causing compound growth that would move continually forward and never backward. Echoing similar optimism Mohammed Yunus, founder of the famous DFI, the Grameen Bank, spoke of the establishment of a virtuous circle, "....low income, more credit, more investment, more income".

Mohammed Yunus heads the mostly World Bank financed Consultative Group to Assist the Poor (CGAP), to "propagate his vision worldwide". With the rise of neo-liberal development ideology in the early '80s a great deal of emphasis has been placed on the development of micro enterprises.

State sponsored development initiatives have been characterised by neo-liberals as inefficient. This has generated a great deal of interest in the prospect of rural micro enterprises, which has in turn focused on the question of credit provision to rural micro entrepreneurs. The vast majority of developing countries have formal lending institutions such as commercial banks.

However these are often inappropriate for providing credit to rural micro enterprises. Before examining the reason for their inappropriateness, we need to be clear on the distinction between formal and informal credit institutions. The distinction is often hazy. Definitions of formal and informal finance and trade It is perhaps misleading to speak of two distinct forms of credit institutions, formal and informal.

Any distinction between formal and informal credit institutions needs to be fairly flexible. For one thing, the definition needs to be country specific, as in one country, some formal credit institutions, for example pawnshops, may be a registered formal credit institution, while in another they may be illegal and informal. Indeed a single country may even contain both registered and unregistered pawnshops.

The most accurate distinction between formal and informal credit institutions could be made in respect of the way in which they operate. Informal credit institutions are characterised by flexible small operations, and they operate mostly in a circumscribed area or a specific niche of the market. They tend to deliver personal service very close to the locátion of the borrower. They tend to be non-bureaucratic and much more flexible in respect of loan purpose, interest rates, collateral requirements, maturity periods and debt rescheduling.

Developed countries have developed capital markets that rely on formal credit institutions. Formal credit institutions have on the whole failed to provide credit to the poor. Von Pischke in his book, *Finance at the Frontier* gives reasons for their failure. Firstly formal financial institutions are removed, in a number of respects, from the lives of rural people. One need simply enter the foyer of any commercial bank to get an immediate sense of this.

For instance, formal financial institutions tend to require literacy and often have little knowledge of how business operates in rural areas i.e. the complex interaction of business and social obligations. For the rural poor, transacting with formal financial institutions often involves time consuming journeys away from the village and transactions conducted during office hours with unfamiliar faces in unfamiliar surroundings.

When the formal financial institution is a state run or parastatal organisation, it may be driven by a range of sociopolitical considerations, in addition to considerations of the clients' ability to repay. Credit provision for the development of rural micro enterprises may not be an appropriate way of facilitating rural development, and if the provision of credit is determined mostly by factors other than ability to repay the loan, it is unlikely that the micro-enterprise will be self-sustaining.

In such a circumstance the state or parastatal is likely to cease providing credit. The transaction cost of the provision of credit to rural micro enterprises may prove prohibitive to large formal financial institutions. Rural micro enterprises are often dispersed over large areas. Transactions involve relatively small amounts and they require relatively large amounts of non-interest earning cash to serve their clients.

Von Pischke claims that, "Obligations to formal institutions may not be accorded very high priority.....especially when institutions are not responsive to clients". In some instance, the opposite may be true. For example, when a non-government organisation (NGO) that was known in the past for providing grants moves into providing loans, the recipients often see the NGO as a soft target. Loan recipients recognise that the NGO would be unwilling to put pressure on lenders who defaulted and would certainly be unwilling to force the sale of collateral.

Formal credit institutions deal frequently with a large number of clients who are often unknown to them. They rely on well developed financial and legal markets to obtain information about their clients, for example, institutions that collect information on bad debts and organisations that give credit ratings. Such institutions do not exist in rural areas where information about credit worthiness needs to be extracted on a more personal basis.

In assessing an enterprise, formal financial institutions tend to rely on financial profitability and cash flow analyses. These are expensive and are often inappropriate ways of assessing rural micro enterprise projects. They do not take account of social factors influencing production and distribution in rural enterprise projects in developing countries.

Unlike their larger formal counterparts, entrepreneurs who start micro enterprises typically lack assets, especially marketable ones to use as collateral for loans. Many rural micro enterprise projects tend to be agricultural enterprises, and are dependent on such vagaries as the weather and are therefore risky. The loans are often used in purchasing seeds, fertilisers, pesticides and herbicides which cannot be recovered if the crop fails.

Thus formal credit institutions have tended to stay clear of lending to rural micro enterprises. Two broad responses have emerged in response to this failure. The first response, a neo-liberal one, was to remove government legislation preventing informal credit institutions. This usually involved the removal of those laws that restricted trade in credit e.g. lifting the usury laws, removing state subsidised credit, etc. The second response was to facilitate the development of more innovative DFIs to overcome the problems outlined above.

The vast majority of societies with money economies have, or have had, some form of informal money lending. Very often the money lender has been a despised member of the community. In all societies with the malicious money lender myth, the money lender is usually believed to extract exorbitantly high interest rates because of the weak bargaining position of the borrower. Highly publicised cases of high interest rates have very often prompted governments to outlaw informal money lending through the passing of usury laws which set the ceiling on interest rates.

Von Pischke and other theorists of what has become known as the Ohio School, have argued that the high interest rates often charged by money lenders are a real reflection of the opportunity costs of the loan. Lending to poor rural people is an extremely risky business. Loans to rural people frequently tend to be for agriculture, a very risky enterprise dependent on climatic conditions. Rural people tend to be very mobile between rural and urban areas, which can facilitate debt evasion.

Rural people often have a low life expectancy. While this is not a problem with formal lending where personal loans are taken in conjunction with life insurance policies, such financial instruments are generally not available to rural money lenders. Finally Von Pischke believes that people tend to overlook the rural lenders' relatively restricted loan portfolio. He writes:

"First, the number of borrowers they can accommodate is limited by the amount of funds they have to lend. A lender with a loan portfolio of 50 loans of roughly equal size would lose two percent of his loans if one borrower did not repay. To cover this risk, the lender would have to raise the annual rate of interest on the 49 remaining loans by about two percentage points. If ten borrowers failed to repay the capital loss would amount to 20% of the portfolio, and the compensating rate increase for the remaining 40 loans would be about 25%. Slow repayment because of a poor harvest, for example, also absorbs funds that the lender would want to recycle into new loans in the next season. Inability to continue to lend would jeopardise relationships with established borrowers, diminishing their incentives to repay outstanding amounts and raising the risk exposure on their entire portfolio."

Other research, by Tun Wai has shown that the seemingly high rates of interest often include payment for a range of non-financial services provided by the money lender. Tun Wai cites storage of produce and payment of market taxes as services provided by money lenders. Thus essentially Von Pischke and members of the Ohio School argue that government intervention generally, and usury laws more specifically, have prevented many rural people from obtaining credit.

The simple solution is, for a start, to repeal the usury laws. This would allow different money lenders to compete openly for clients, which, through market forces, would cause the interest rate to reflect the undistorted opportunity cost of capital. The Ohio School relies on some very shaky ontological assumptions. Firstly, they assume perfect competition. They implicitly present a picture of a myriad of money lenders competing with one another for clients.

While stories of monopolistic informal credit lenders are perhaps exaggerated, it is wishful thinking to assume they do not exist. There are countless examples, spanning centuries, from all over the world where credit markets exist or existed, of monopolistic money lenders, to the extent that the monopolistic money lender has almost become an archetype in European and South Asian literature.

A small farmer in Africa or Asia who does not have access to a state sponsored credit institution, may not have the option of choosing between one of the many competing informal money lenders because informal money lending may not be profitable. To recapitulate, this could occur for a number of reasons:

1. Investment funds may be scarce

2. The risks of nonpayment may be too high - most rural micro credit is lent for agricultural production. Agricultural production is very risky in developed countries and it is even more risky in developing countries with poor infrastructure, corrupt marketing boards, etc. The lender cannot reduce these risks through taking out insurance because it is often not available.

The Ohio School focuses almost exclusively on economic growth with little attention to equity. Where informal credit markets exist, being risk averse they are likely to prefer to lend to larger, better established, wealthier and, in short, less risky enterprises. This leaves the poorest section of the population unable to obtain credit. As with the familiar "infant industry" argument, it is likely that government intervention will be necessary to help the poorest establish infant micro-enterprises.

The Ohio School implicitly assumes perfect competition. But the school decontextualises the lives of rural people to a much greater extent. It ignores the complex socio - political environment of rural people. In particular it ignores the distribution of power in rural societies and the impact of this distribution on the success of credit markets. Many state or donor sponsored DFIs seem to have proved successful in assisting rural people to start and profitably maintain rural micro enterprises.

The difficulties that formal financial institutions experience in supplying credit to rural micro entrepreneurs, can be divided into three categories - access, screening and incentive. The problem of access is not so much a problem faced by formal financial institutions in lending to poor people, but a social development problem.

The second problematic category is that of screening loan applicants. How does one screen loan applicants for bad borrowers, where borrowers do not have formal business plans or even written records? The third category relates to the incentives to repay. In respect to access problems, two methods evolved to ensure that the poor were targeted. The first was to supply very small loans that only the poor would be interested in borrowing.

The second was to only allow loans on the basis of a minimum amount of assets and/or income. This approach was taken by a number of DFIs, most notably the Grameen Bank. Three screening methods have evolved to assess the borrowers' credit worthiness. The most common is to lend to members of a group who are jointly and severally liable for the repayment of loans made to each member of the group. Screening is facilitated by self selected groups.

This ensures that only people who the rest of the group take to be credit worthy are allowed in. Such groups have been euphemistically called 'solidarity groups'. This is by far the most common approach, although of course this does not necessarily attest to its efficacy.

The success of both the Ohio School and the innovative DFIs is difficult to assess. For one thing, what constitutes success is dependent on how one defines rural development, e.g. either as growth or equity. The results of an empirical analysis of DFIs seem to indicate that there is a trade-off between growth and equity. This could be caused by a range of factors, including the fact that poor people were less likely to undertake certain potentially lucrative, but risky, investments, because the consequences of failure would be much more severe than it would be to wealthier borrowers.

In order to assess the effectiveness and/or limitations of

micro credit as a development intervention, one needs to define development. The debate around what constitutes development is a highly contentious one. In practice, a range of very diverse strategies, from apartheid separate development schemes to Oxfam gender development programmes, have laid claim to bringing about development.

Although there is much dissent in the definition of social development in the writings of the founding figures of Western social theory - Durkheim, Weber, Marx and Talcott Parsons - they all subscribe to the notion that social development is about long term and sustained improvement in human well-being. Two broad schools of thought on development emerged over the last century - idealistic and materialistic.

Of the idealistic approaches to development, perhaps the best known is the hermeneutic one, where development is viewed as the restoration of meaning to individuals. It is compatible with a very participatory approach to development. It sees individuals defining their own meaning and assigns to the development practitioner the role of restoring that meaning to their lives.

As such, this approach does not specify development priorities, but allows the individuals in the community to specify their own development goals and then assists them in realising their goals. The major difficulty with such an approach is that it decontextualises individuals. It fails to see individuals as part of a wider society with an intricate web of power relations which circumscribe or facilitate their development.

Materialist notions of development see power as a central part of the development equation. The materialist school encompasses a broad range of approaches. One of the most common definitions and measures of development explores increases in levels of per capita income. This approach is useful because it provides a quick and easy measure of development levels. In extreme examples it can be useful - it is clear that Sweden is more developed than Ghana, mostly because of the higher per capita levels of income in the former.

But it is only really useful at extremes: For instance, in what sense is South Africa, which has a higher per capita income than Cuba, more developed than Cuba, with its higher HDI ? Although the per capita levels of income are much higher in the former, the quality of life with respect to life expectancy and education is much higher in the latter.

Economic growth measured in rises in per capita income fails to capture income distribution. If the benefits of economic growth are captured by a small segment of the population, improvements in (material) well-being are only likely to accrue to that segment. There are countless definitions and measures of development. A meaningful critique of the HDI or any of the other measures is beyond the scope of this dissertation.

The approach taken here is to define development broadly, focusing on improvements in levels of income and income distribution. In respect of income distribution, it focuses on the distribution of income between and within classes i.e. between the wealthier of the poor and the 'poorest of the poor'.

This approach gives an indication of changes in a factor that is universally taken to contribute centrally to individual 'well-being' i.e. levels of income. By taking this broad approach, it is not suggested that definitions of development that include other measures of well-being are somehow incorrect. All measures and definitions of development that attempt to gauge improvement in 'well-being' are correct.

The success of any rural micro enterprise is dependant on a range of factors, of which access to credit is one. The micro finance evangelists create a vision of the rural poor as a collection of budding entrepreneurs, waiting for salvation from credit agencies, who, on receipt of credit, will develop successful micro enterprises and leave poverty forever. Their promotional activity gives rise to the worrying spectre of a return to a 'blueprint' approach to rural development. The very idea of a blueprint, implicit in the new micro finance approach to development, seems at once antithetical to the complex, localised, dynamic world of rural micro enterprise.

Micro credit is not a sufficient condition for rural development, because it is not a sufficient condition for ensuring the success of rural micro enterprises. Infrastructure, human capital, information and social factors can make or break rural micro enterprises. Infrastructure Micro finance proponents are right to stress the importance of an appropriate infrastructure for credit provision. Credit is, however, one of many infrastructural needs in developing countries.

To respond to a potential demand for a good or service a rural micro-entrepreneur may require access to one or more of the following: transport, communications, power, water, storage facilities, a legal system for enforcing contracts and settling disputes etc. Infrastructural factors may be less important for non-agricultural rural entrepreneurs, for example, for bicycle repair and sewing shops.

However they are very important for agriculture, one of the most significant rural micro enterprise in developing countries. No amount of accessible credit could induce a sub-Saharan subsistence farmer to cultivate land for cash crops, if for instance, there is no place to store the crops or there is no marketing authority to market the crops or there is no way of getting the crops to the market place.

The history of postwar rural development is littered with examples of where one or more missing factors were provided by donors, who crudely assumed that the provision of one factor would be sufficient to get rural enterprises to succeed. In developing societies with lows levels of formal education and a rational aversion to risky enterprises, such ingredients may not always be in abundance.

Literacy, numeracy and formal education levels in most developing countries are extremely low. Non-numerate people struggle to start enterprises by themselves as it is extremely difficult for them to keep track of the flows of income in their enterprise. Those entrepreneurs who are numerate but not literate can often go some way in developing their enterprises, but their enterprises are severely limited.

For example, they do not have access to information from the print media, they cannot enter into written contracts and have to act on trust and they cannot easily engage with the state and formal private sector who normally work with written documents. Incentives to start new rural enterprises or develop existing ones may be unaffected by the existence of cheap or more accessible credit for two reasons.

Firstly, in rural areas in developing countries, the market for any good or service is, compared to developed countries, highly imperfect and unstable. For instance, small farmers in developing countries may not want to change from subsistence crops to cash crops and become entrepreneurs, even if cash crops could provide a significantly higher income, because doing so is very risky.

Transport systems are fragile, farmers do not have access to legal systems if marketing authorities breach agreements etc. Not only is it very risky to become a rural micro entrepreneur, but the consequences of failure - potentially starvation, are severe. Secondly, the incentive to become an entrepreneur - higher levels of income - is not significant if there are no consumer goods to buy with the new income. With the non-availability of consumer goods, the marginal utility of additional cash earnings is close to zero.

A combination of low levels of formal education, the remoteness of rural areas and poor communications networks often mean that rural entrepreneurs are the last to be informed of changes in market conditions. The case of the Power Station initiative, a South African, Oxfam-funded rural income generating project illustrates how critical information of market conditions is to rural entrepreneurs.

Many social factors can prevent the establishment of enterprises or, at least, mitigate against their chances of success. Not all groups of people have values central to entrepreneurial success -competitiveness, the need for achievement, the pursuit of profit or strong notions of private property.

In some parts of rural India, for example only, certain castes are allowed to act as moneylenders. If there is only one member of this caste in a particular isolated rural village, then that person will have a monopoly that will be maintained through social norms. Indeed there are even societies that do not use money in their transactions and do not have a great deal of private property.

The Khoisan people, in the deserts of Northern Namibia, or at least those of them who have not yet urbanised, are traditionally migratory. They do not use money or any other equivalent to facilitate their barter relationships. They do not have any culture of accumulation and live through traditional hunting and gathering. It is highly unlikely that access to credit will solve any of the development needs expressed by this community. A less extreme example of the significance of social factors in determining the success of rural micro enterprises.

In 1991 a South African development project which

bought a farm for the use of farm workers who were dismissed from commercial white-owned farms. It was assumed by the project designers that it was simply apartheid legislation that had prevented these former farm workers from becoming successful farmers.

The project provided free land to the former farm workers and access to credit. All the elements for the farm to run successfully were apparently in place. The new farmers were highly skilled, had access to extension officers and were highly motivated, the marketing network for their product, wool, was highly developed, the wool price was high, etc. The project, however, failed. Being former farm workers they were part of informal networks of support designed to survive the tenure insecurity of farm workers on white owned farms during the apartheid years.

This involved, among other things, supporting the unemployed and/or recently evicted households. Because of the insecurity of a farm workers life this, was, and still is, a very important way of reducing risk. When the former farm workers were given land and access to credit, they were immediately flooded with requests from evicted farm workers to allow their cattle to graze on the project's farm. They were unable to refuse the requests and the land could not support their own stock as well.

In this case the new farmers acted not as profit maximisers but utility maximisers. Where there is such a strong divergence of profit and utility, there is little scope for successful rural micro enterprise projects, irrespective of how much credit is available. The list of factors that can cause the failure of rural micro enterprises projects is by no means exhaustive.

They capture some of the most significant categories of reasons why rural micro enterprises can fail. One could go on at length providing reasons - geographical, macro-economic (inflation, trade tariffs) etc. The point of this chapter is simply to illustrate that credit is not a sufficient condition for rural development; it is not even a sufficient condition for ensuring the success of rural micro enterprises.

If some notion of equity is part of the definition of development, then the question of which segments of the rural population are affected by a micro credit intervention becomes central to assessing the success of micro credit as a development intervention. The establishment of the World Bank financed Consultative Group to Assist the Poor (CGAP), will facilitate the development of an enormous number of micro credit schemes that set themselves up to be judged by their impact on the 'poorest of the poor'.

The results of the few empirical studies that have assessed the impact of micro credit schemes on the 'poorest of the poor' seem to suggest that they benefit the richest segment of the poor. Before examining the results of the research, the problems that arise when one attempts to quantify social impact need to explored. The measurement of any social intervention is inherently difficult. Unlike the natural world where one can often readily establish closed systems, and conduct experiments using controls, the social world is an open system and it is difficult to separate out one set of causal factors from another.

Aside from this methodological problem there are also a number of problems that arise in collecting information. For example, respondents to an impact assessment who have received loans have an incentive to lie about their impact if they hope for more credit, or if they have used the loan for a purpose other than the stipulated one.

Perhaps the most important difficulty, and one that arises repeatedly in development studies, is defining well-being. When we talk of the equity impact of a development intervention, we are speaking of the distribution of improvements in well-being among a target group. There is a tendency to reduce well-being to material well-being, which arises in part because material improvement are easier for the social scientist to quantify than non-material improvements.

Non-material improvements in well-being are difficult to quantify because they involve inter-personal comparisons of utility. Such comparisons are difficult to make. In the context of a developing country where the provision of basic needs cannot be assumed, material needs are primary, in that one has 'to be before one can well be'.

In many developing countries people earn a living through a variety of formal and informal pursuits, many of which result in non-cash benefits that are difficult to quantify. It is not possible to quantify such income generating activities in absolute terms, and the result of the research should be seen as showing trends rather than absolutes.

The most recent comprehensive study of the impact of a variety of micro credit schemes on the 'poorest of the poor', is provided by Hulme et al in their book *Finance against poverty*. The conceptualisation of poverty as living below a poverty line, leads to promotional strategies that emphasise credit provision for income generation activities. Alternatively, poverty reduction can be viewed with respect to dampening fluctuations above and below the poverty line.

Income fluctuations above and below the poverty line are experienced frequently by many in developing countries, for example, in the period prior to a harvest, illness in the wet season, etc. Such a conceptualisation leads to greater emphasis on saving schemes. Savings provide a buffer against the vagaries of income fluctuations. The impact of 13 micro credit schemes in Asia, Africa and South America in improving incomes, indicate unanimously that the benefits of the micro credit schemes under study were not scale neutral - the upper and middle income poor tended to benefit more than the 'poorest of the poor'.

There is a trade-off between the financial success of micro finance institutions and the number of clients they draw from the 'poorest of the poor'. Perhaps the most worrying find of the study was the trend by many of the micro finance institutes to exclude the 'poorest of the poor', in spite of all the lip service paid to serving this group. Other interventions are necessary to target these groups. It would be tragic if all the micro finance hype persuaded governments and donor agencies to change their spending from programs which have a tried and tested (and often contested) impact upon the 'poorest of the poor', such as food aid, health care and other welfare transfers, to micro finance schemes, which unambiguously target the middle and rich poor.

Failure of Micro-finance Scheme

Many development academics in the Seventies would have been astonished by the claims made by politicians, academics and journalists (and reported at the beginning of this dissertation) as to how micro finance would solve world poverty. Where just twenty years ago development academics were writing about dependency and local elites capturing the benefits of development projects, today these academics and politicians who promote micro finance as a panacea either choose to ignore those power relations or pretend they do not exist.

Inflation and unemployment began to rise steadily throughout the 1970s. Increases in money supply caused inflation to rise dramatically in Western Nations. Milton Friedman argued that the state needed to reduce its role to ensuring the minimal function of maintaining external security and enforcing voluntary contracts. He believed that state run industries were not only inefficient, but were inherently less efficient than privatised industry. He argued for privatisation of state industry, and proposed that the private sector take up many of the functions of the state.

Taxes were to be reduced because they would not be needed on the same scale, and to give consumers more choice over their consumption. Markets were to be freed of factors that were said to 'distort' them like tariffs, pressure groups and licensing boards. Like the Modernisation theorists before them, the neo-liberals transposed the problems of the developed world, and what they took to be their causes, onto the developing world.

By 1985 the World Bank declared."....the record of development and the growing store of empirical research have heightened the recognition of the importance of markets and incentives - and of the limits of government and central planning. The new vision of growth is that markets and incentives can work in developing countries. But they are filtered through government policies and agencies, which, if inappropriate can reduce or even negate the possible benefits. Second, physical investment is only one determinant of the spread of development. Human development is at least as important and sound government action remains at its core. Third, the economic policies of governments, and the distortions they induce are now a major focus of the analysis of development policy".

This statement contained a summary of principles of the neo-liberal development school, these being:

— Reducing the size of the public sector: neo-liberals claimed governments had over-extended themselves (related to the

Chicago School notion of appropriate government action). In particular the neo-liberals took nationalised industry to be inefficient and ineffective.

— The over emphasis on physical capital formation: the 'break' with Keynes and Modernisation theorists. Governments were thought to have spent too much time and money on physical capital formation and neglected human capital formation.

— The proliferation of distorting economic controls: aside from the stated objection to government-imposed barriers to trade, for example licenses, neo-liberals objected to the proliferation of government policies which were motivated by egalitarian/humanitarian objectives e.g. consumer food subsidies, but resulted in dead-weight efficiency loses.

Neo-liberals reject the idea of growth with equity. The neo-liberals stressed the freeing of markets from government intervention. Indeed a central criticism of the neo-liberals is their continual attack on government actions, for example vaccination programs and free primary school education, which can result in a more egalitarian society, and their conspicuous lack of criticism of the vast national defence programs of many LDCs.

The promotion of micro finance as a development intervention lies comfortably with the neo-liberal philosophy developed by Lal, Friedman, Bauer and others and promoted by the World Bank and the governments of the United States and the United Kingdom, in that micro finance:

— develops new markets and promotes free market culture.

— involves minimum state intervention.

— creates entrepreneurs who are in touch with local markets.

— provides loans and not grants, consistent with notions of reducing grant entitlements.

Micro finance promises to deliver self-financing poverty reduction. Finally, and perhaps most significantly, the promotion of micro finance as a development intervention is consistent with theories of methodological individualism, in that it presents a picture of lone individuals, operating in a vacuum who, but for a lack of credit, would be able to be successful entrepreneurs.

Like much neo-liberal theory it is based upon the idea that society consists of nothing more than a collection of individuals. Neo-liberal theorists justify their position, by arguing that there is no such thing as society, because we cannot see an entity called society. However this is rather a narrow perspective. There are many things which exist even though we cannot see them.

In the very same way society can be said to exist. It exists in that it facilitates or circumscribes individuals behaviour through social rules and conventions. The micro finance evangelists dislocate the recipients of micro finance from the web of social power relations in which they are inextricably entangled. The poor are often poor not because they do not have access to credit but because of their relative powerlessness.

In attributing the cause of poverty to insufficient access to credit, micro finance evangelists obscure the generative mechanism behind much poverty - an unequal distribution of power at all levels - international, national and local. Underdevelopment and poverty has often been attributed by so-called dependency theorists and others to the unequal power relations between rich and poor nations.

Many theorists writing during the 1960s and 1970s attributed underdevelopment to the unequal relationship between developed and undeveloped countries. Dependency theorists took underdevelopment to be the result of colonisation. The relationship was and is (argue dependency theorists) sustained by unequal terms of trade through tariffs and other forms of protection imposed by stronger developed countries on their weaker counterparts.

In its weakest form, few but the most ardent free-marketers could fail to recognise that developed countries have a massive advantage in having developed first. Their industries produce goods at much lower costs than developing countries because of bigger economies of scale. Developed countries can pressurise weaker developing nations into accepting terms of trade that are not in their interest through a range of devices for example, indebtedness.

National politics can entrench poverty and undermine the success of micro finance interventions. The British-based donor organisation, Co-operation for Development, together with Palestinian NGOs and the Bank of Palestine, established a micro finance project in Palestine. The national political situation in Palestine militated against the success of micro credit lead development intervention. On the local level in certain conditions, those with social power can ensure economic returns to their social power by appropriating all the benefits obtained from micro credit schemes.

In rural Baluchistan, most of the land is owned by a few feudal landlords . There is almost no market for land as sales of land are extremely rare. In addition the transaction costs involved in a tenant farmer moving off the land are by and large prohibitive, partly because of indebtedness and partly because they have not been able to accumulate enough to afford to move. Thus a few landlords act as oligopolists, enjoying a captive market.

A micro finance project was established in the area in the early 1990s. The project lent money to tenant farmers to finance the purchase of high yield variety crops. While the project successfully allowed high yield variety crops to be grown, there were few benefits for the farmers because all additional profit was simply appropriated by the landlords who increased the rent. The tenant farmers could not resist the rent increases because the transaction costs of moving were too high and there were no competing land owners to rent or buy land from at a cheaper rate than the "feudal" landlords.

Thus micro finance did little to improve the lot of the tenant farmers since all extra profit was appropriated by the landlords. The aboves example illustrate how at all levels (international, national and local) the success of a micro finance scheme hinges critically on the social context and the particular set of power relations that prevail.

Micro credit is increasingly promoted, not only as a positive rural development intervention, but in some instances as a rural development panacea. This frenzied promotional activity derives in part from the putative success of prominent DFIs, most notably the Grameen Bank. The rise of neo-liberalism has facilitated a distorted perspective of the prospects and possibilities of micro finance as a rural development intervention.

The promotion of micro credit as a rural development intervention has tied in neatly with neo-liberal development ideology. As mentioned, it develops new markets and promotes a culture of entrepreneurship; it involves minimal state intervention; and provides loans, not grants, moving away from welfare type interventions; finally and perhaps most importantly, it shifts the locus of attention away from society towards the individual.

The limits of micro credit as a rural development

intervention have been lost in the promotional frenzy. Essentially, the limits arise from the individualist focus of the intervention. Micro credit as a development intervention requires an enabling environment for it to be successful. By an 'enabling environment', reference is made to those conditions which have been outlined as necessary for the success of micro enterprise.

The provision of micro credit is a necessary but not sufficient factor in ensuring the success of rural micro enterprises. Sufficient infrastructure, skilled entrepreneurs, access to information and culture conducive to micro enterprise are necessary conditions for the success of micro enterprises and hence micro credit. Even where micro credit does succeed in stimulating the growth of micro enterprises, the developmental impact of this on the poorest members of the target communities varies.

The wealthier the individual or household the greater the range of investment opportunities. The richer poor have the ability to take on riskier, more rewarding investments, without threatening their minimum need for survival. The wealthier the individual or household the greater the range of investment opportunities. Aside from better returns to wealthier investors, the 'poorest of the poor' often exclude themselves from larger loans, "not wanting to jeopardise their access to future credit by gaining a reputation for being uncreditworthy".

The impact of a micro credit scheme is limited by the political framework in which it is implemented. Political forces at the local, national and global level can undermine the success of micro credit. On a global level, developing countries are often in weaker bargaining position than developed countries. In such situations, developed countries have the capacity to impose terms of trade on developed countries that may be detrimental to micro enterprises in developing countries.

On a national level, the Palestinian example demonstrated

how a myriad of seemingly unrelated laws can curtail the success of a micro credit programmes. The example of a failed micro credit scheme in Baluchistan is perhaps the most stark example of economic returns to local social power. While lack of access to credit is undoubtedly a factor in some instances of rural poverty, the causes of rural poverty are complex and dynamic. They cannot simply be reduced to lack of credit.

The lack of recognition of the limitations of micro credit as a development intervention is likely to have a range of unfortunate consequences. Already we are witnessing the promotion of micro credit where other solutions (infrastructural, educational, political) may be more appropriate. A great deal more sober reflection and investigation into the limits of micro credit as a rural development intervention is urgently needed to counter the frenzied lobbying of micro finance evangelists, and reallocation of development funding likely to follow in its trail.

Financial Landscape Metamphor

The metaphor is not only used to indicate the physical features of the financial landscape such as the offices of banks, cooperatives, credit unions, traders, pawnbrokers, self-help groups, NGOs, and whatever other financial or quasi-financial institutions there may be. With the metaphor we wish to emphasize regional diversity and historical change in financial ecosystems. At the same time it stimulates us to explore what relations, norms, actions and processes influence, directly or indirectly, the transactions of savers, borrowers and lenders.

The landscape metaphor leads to expect variety: lowlands and mountain ranges, broad rivers and little streams, fertile regions, deserts and muddy swamps, urging us to adopt a view on a totality, and to ground the institutions and social processes we study in space and time. The metaphor points at the planned or spontaneous growth of financial intermediaries and relations as well as their predictable, unforeseen or even unnoticed decline - explaining the ever changing composition of financial ecosystem that do not evolve in one particular direction.

Furthermore, landscapes remind us of the physical infrastructure of a region, with different ways to travel from farm fields to market places, from houses to offices, from village markets to wholesale markets, and of poor roads connecting distant villages with capital cities. This leads one to explore the other interesting avenue of financial landscapes: the connections and disconnections between different kinds of savers, borrowers and lenders.

The metaphor directs the attention to "networks" of moneylending traders, money guards, banks and savings clubs, but also to deliberate non-use of financial services and short-circuits between financial intermediaries. For instance, inflation causes people to find refuge in "inflation hedges" in the form of golden necklaces and cattle, while political manoeuvres might keep savings clubs and money guards from entrusting even a single penny to a bank.

The metaphor refers to the complex dynamics of changing ecological conditions and human intervention, that include soil conditions, natural vegetation and crops, but also fertilization, salinization, and deforestation as well as natural phenomena like hurricanes, drought and floods. Diversity of landscapes is a result of different and frequently contradictory efforts at planning by individual and institutional actors who face and adapt themselves to specific ecological conditions and changes.

The metaphor of financial landscapes cautions us right from the start against too easy assumptions about the dynamics of financial intermediaries and relations between borrowers, lenders and savers. The quality and effectiveness of the maps of financial landscapes are very much dependent on the uses one needs them for.

The landscape metaphor allows to develop different contextual approaches for the analysis and evaluation of financial services in interlinked processes related to the development of state administrations, markets and communities. One approach might be to look at evolving social-economic relations between mutually dependent traders and farmer-borrowers, or at moral standards governing lending behaviour of village shopkeepers in crisis situations.

Soaring inflation and monetary instability can cause disintegration of the landscape, frustrating the accumulation of domestic funds in banks or self-help groups. Policies that promote the pouring of easy money into thirsty economies are yet another example: they can easily result in the destruction of financial intermediation structures - only increasing the number of graveyards in financial landscapes. Equally significant are measures that inadvertently influence the emergence and retreat of certain intermediaries, such as land reforms causing landlords to withdraw from the sphere of agricultural credit and traders and input suppliers to step in and fill the void.

Many financial self-help groups mirror social-economic changes and demonstrate their enormous adaptive capacities under macro-economic and political-administrative reform. There are countries in which the government is viewed as the sole grand designer of the landscape, in which every financial intermediary is licensed and controlled, his actions regulated, and the flow of funds directed towards prescribed sectors, in prescribed quantities to a prescribed number of clients; a landscape in which people deposit their savings with the officially recognized and approved banks.

Unregulated curb markets and their representatives are

seen as a disturbing factor that should be eliminated. Conviction becomes reality. The maps drawn by official Indian and Thai statistics are a case in point. They depict a very substantial reduction of the share of informal credit in total cash debts of cultivating households from 70 percent in 1961 to 23 percent in 1981 in India; in Thailand the share of informal loans has "officially" declined from about 90 percent to 30-50 percent between 1965 and 1991.

The official leaning towards discolouring of financial maps is reinforced by the fact that planners and consultants of development agencies persistently ignore the existence of financial curb markets. If we want to explore the rich variety of interrelations between different financial intermediaries, we need to question, however, the analytical value of the dualistic concepts of "formal" and "informal". These rather clumsy concepts not only violate the empirical diversity of financial intermediaries, they also assume the absence of direct or indirect links between traders, commercial banks, savings clubs, development banks, NGOs, and so forth.

There are financial sector specialists, commercial bankers and economists from international development agencies who view the "invisible hand" as the best designer of the landscape. They like to see the financial landscape as one great market, in which every financial intermediary is free to expand his services geographically and to set interest rates that will regulate the supply and demand for capital; a landscape without subsidies that will only ruin financial market places; a landscape in which people are preferably saving in financial assets that can easily be mobilized by commercial banks, subsequently investing their money abroad, in large industrial enterprises and/ or in government bonds issued to finance the state deficit, that is, a landscape in which funds flow automatically to rewarding and secure opportunities.

Again, informal financial agencies and arrangements are

considered a disturbing factor because they reproduce "segmentation of financial markets", take care only of consumption needs and keep the national economy stagnant. Unfortunately, the promotion of market mechanisms to structure relations between savers, lenders and borrowers is often based on a one-dimensional map of financial landscapes.

Credit transactions and financial services are evaluated in terms of interest rates or transaction costs only, ignoring other stipulations of contracts between borrowers and lenders or barriers to credit access. Credit relations that are embedded in wider social-economic relations are studied in isolation. The rise and decline of different financial intermediaries and specific financial arrangements is not analysed against the background of location-specific agro-ecological, economic, socio-legal and/or institutional conditions.

The use of dualistic or black-white symbols to depict financial landscapes, such as "formal versus informal" and "consumption versus production loans", allows many bankers to marginalize the development role of "informal lenders". However, these distinctions are false and misleading. Loans for so-called consumption purposes can be of great importance for income-generating activities.

Fridges are useful to make and sell ice; radios to listen to news of extension services; bicycles to transport chickens to the market; and medicines to cure the labour force. Not surprisingly, consumption loans do not necessarily represent a greater risk to lending agencies than so-called production loans. Besides, it is rather narrow to consider the use of loans for social security purposes, like housing, education, health and food, as counterproductive for "development".

Likewise, to speak of "segmentation of financial markets" is not only to ignore possible links, either direct or indirect, between financial intermediaries, but also to underestimate the importance for savings clubs, traders, farmers or market women to limit their contacts with banks and co-operatives when the latter impose rigid rules or are simply not dependable. For a long time it has mainly been economists who have drawn the maps and coloured the contours of the financial landscape.

However great their skills, this has brought us maps of a very specific signature, now coloured with the projections and symbols of liberalism, then of Marxism, then again of neoclassical and new institutional economics. Such maps can only be of limited use. The reconstruction of financial landscapes mirroring interlinked developments of state administrations, markets and communities, cannot and should not be the domain of one single discipline.

Of necessity, its tools are inadequate to picture the immense variety of the landscape, Multi-disciplinary approaches are called for to analyse and explain the diversity in forms of financial intermediation and the interrelations existing between them, in regulatory frameworks of financial intermediation, in scale and volume of operations and the variations that occur in time and space.

Whatever financial landscapes were before, they changed drastically in the twentieth century, more particularly in its second half. Early in this century colonial administrations, greatly impressed by the success of the cooperative movement in the Western hemisphere, began to introduce the cooperative model in the colonies. It marked the beginning of the plight of rural households, and of what Polly Hill sees as "a colonial obsession with debt".

With the exception of the informal agents, financial intermediaries were - and have always been - reluctant to extend their services to rural areas. Financing rural development was mostly limited to the estate sector; providing financial services to small farmers and other participants of micro-economies was an almost alien concept and was left to export firms working through intermediaries.

Such financing could now be left to cooperative savings and credit societies. Setting this co-operative movement on its feet became the self-proclaimed task of colonial authorities. Progress was slow, and interrupted by two World Wars and the Great Depression. But between the 1950s and 1970s, when the former colonies became independent, rural development became a hot issue among major donor agencies and governments of Third World countries.

The All India Rural Credit Survey of 1951 set the tone, when it revealed that over 90 percent of the rural population depended on the services of what since has been called the informal finance sector, while cooperative and government credit together accounted for a meagre seven percent. The resulting political indignation - somewhat hypocritical, considering that earlier Commissions of Enquiry had reported practically the same situation - sparked a long debate on finance and development that has strongly affected the contours of the present-day financial landscapes, not only in India, but worldwide.

McLeod argues that two views on rural finance have dominated academic and political thinking in the post-colonial period. The first is a certain antipathy to informal finance, the second is "the notion that economic development can be encouraged by promoting financial development".

Different battles had a profound influence on the views of financial landscapes. One was a political-ideological battle between adherents of capitalism and Marxist socialism, while some parties championed an intermediate "third way" and promoted cooperatives to structure social and economic life. The other was a battle between economists regarding the effects of official regulation and deregulation of financial systems, or respectively the Keynesian and the Shaw-McKinnon models of growth.

In the first few decades of the post-colonial period, adherents of official control of financial systems dominated policies and projects in the financial landscape, thereby shaping its contours. The cheap credit creed was one of their most dramatic brain-children.

The population explosion in the newly independent states, the consequent diminution in the size of farms and gradual pauperization of the rural population, caused a rural exodus of hitherto unknown and frightening proportions that had to be stopped. Development of these countries became now equated with rural development, and this, in turn, with increasing agricultural output and rural incomes of small farmers in particular.

Although the Green Revolution promised bumper harvests, it required the application of costly new technology. According to adepts of neo-marxism, the fruits of the Green Revolution bypassed the small farmers due to their lack of capital, their victimization by moneylenders and traders, and the overwhelming influence of large farmers, landlords and other powerholders, who usurped all potential surpluses.

Although often wary of this diagnosis, politicians and planners in developing countries as well as donor agencies agreed that the small farmer should be helped, and the logical remedy seemed to be to provide him with the necessary capital in the form of cheap loans. Since the informal finance sector was obviously the wrong circuit, it became the mission of formal institutions to do this.

The financial landscape became dotted with rural banks, cooperatives, and specialized farm credit institutions, while hundreds of billions of dollars were poured into countless projects that all claimed to have the well-being of the poorer strata of rural society at heart. It was the era of "small is beautiful", when low-priced small farmer credit became the major tool of rural development.

The cheap credit policy soon largely dominated the reconstruction of financial landscapes, not only in the physical sense through increased numbers of finance institutions, but also through changes in regulations regarding financial intermediation, manipulations by financial authorities, and the domination of research and political and scholarly debate.

The world of students and planners of rural development became divided between antagonists and proponents of cheap farm credit, of "financial liberalization" versus what Shaw and McKinnon critically described as "financial repression". The now dominant views and issues of this debate are described by Seibel: many financial markets have now been deregulated and interest rates are no longer artificially kept low, but allowed to reflect so-called market conditions.

This brought an increasing number of students of rural sociology, legal anthropology, social geography and development economy to study the actual relations between savers, lenders and borrowers at micro level. Studies of financial intermediation in the curb market not only emphasized the ubiquity and universality of financial self-help groups, but revealed also that the Green Revolution had ushered in new categories of lenders: rich farmers, having themselves profited from the Green Revolution, input suppliers, traders, millers and white- and blue-collar workers with a regular monthly income and access to banks - all acting as part-time moneylender and replacing the former professional moneylender of ill repute.

Rural (and urban) financial landscapes in the 1970s and 1980s have thus undergone a major metamorphosis. Pawnshops have become second-hand goods stores selling unredeemed pawns, and financial self-help groups have diversified and grown - some of them handling millions of dollars - taking care of social security, insurance, local and regional investments, and improvement of infrastructure.

Linkages between these groups and banks have been established and new ones proposed. The emphasis has shifted from the rural to the urban scene and from farms to non-farm micro enterprises. Now that commercial banks are no longer forced to finance small businesses and farmers, a task for which they are ill-equipped and which left a trail of degenerated financial ecosystem, others are coming forward to fill the gap.

The 1980s and 1990s are becoming the decades of the Non-Governmental Organizations (NGOs). A countless number of NGOs have taken up where others have left and continue a policy of cheap credit. In a report for the Conference on NGOs in October 1992 in The Hague, the number of NGOs in India alone is put at several millions!. In the Philippines, the number of NGOs has grown to 17,000, while over 12,000 cooperatives were registered between 1987 and 1992.

Although most NGOs are indigenous, many are supported by foreign donor parties from all spheres of life, representing a cross-section of society. Many of these donors are NGOs themselves. During the past two decades, NGO policy has undergone a major shift in emphasis, from welfare and relief orientation to a policy centered on income generation. Provision of financial services for the poor - somewhat misleadingly called credit for micro enterprises - is one of the mainstays of this policy.

Sometimes such provision is embedded in what is termed

an "integrated development approach", encompassing "awareness building", training in all sorts of education that includes "skills", and health and housing programs. But increasingly, financial services are now provided without such extras and are labelled "minimalist programs", although technical training and management advice figure prominently in the brochures of quite a number of NGOs.

Since most NGO staffs cannot boast of any such skills themselves, these brochures have to be taken with a grain of salt. Although most NGOs profess to aim at long-term viability and sustainability - magic words that are often heard but rarely addressed seriously by NGOs - the sad truth is that almost no organization or NGO could survive without heavy subsidies and grants from sympathetic, but ill-informed donors.

The nagging doubt how long the efforts at filling a bottomless pit can last, has been vividly expressed by Abugre, arguing from personal experience that very few NGOs know anything about handling money, having always channelled but not managed funds. The concept of the cost of money is still a strange one for many NGOs, including the big ones.

Many times one comes across large credit funds managed by entirely unprofessional and untrained staff, the schemes themselves carelessly conceived, designed and implemented, generating an enormous waste and actually leading to either the indebtedness of the poor or their increased dependency on external support.

Many NGOs have drawn fresh inspiration from the experience of the Grameen Bank (GB), the archetype of successful financial intermediation for the poor. One could rightly argue that the success of the GB in Bangladesh has had a devastating effect elsewhere, in the sense that many NGOs have copied and are still trying to replicate the GB model.

In the excitement about the GB success, an almost lone jewel in a series of mostly dismal failures, it is easily forgotten that this bank is, indeed, run by professionals, and yet is, after almost two decades of experimenting, still dependent on outside funds to survive. Moreover, replicationcontains its own dangers of introducing "dormant viruses" and adoption of a model "without a grasp of the substance that animates and sustains it".

And, most importantly, the graveyards of public institutions and banks that toiled under the illusion that the poor could effectively be reached with cheap credit projects, have apparently never been visited by most NGOs. Besides concern over the lack of expertise of NGOs in the field of finance, sincere doubts are warranted about the proficiency of banks to alleviate poverty by providing credit to the poor.

In case of ecological crisis, political turmoil, economic decline but also financial and monetary instability, the indigenous systems might be very important devices of low-income people to restrict mobility of scarce financial funds. It would then not be very wise to pursue a development policy directed at integration of financial markets in which the allocation of financial resources is determined by the marginal productivity of capital. This might shift away scarce financial resources of marginalized groups who need and prefer to invest in subsistence security, education and housing.

A contextual approach to the promotion of financial self-help organizations implies a greater emphasis on the creation of an environment that enables them to flourish and shape their own development. With regard to financial and monetary instability, for instance, the organization of finance at the fringes might be best served when at the core of financial systems there is established a competitive banking system placed under the effective control of a properly managed central bank.

When banks become dependable institutions that gain people's trust, linkages between financial self-help groups and nearby banks will evolve automatically. When the local currency is quite stable, participation in ROSCAs and ASCRAs to finance funeral expenses, house construction material or working capital, can be more attractive. After having witnessed the destruction of financial landscapes through an overkill of credit by international donors, government organizations and NGOs - getting in each other's way, even competing with each other with too liberal doses of cheap funds - it is time now to study finance in context and to develop policies and projects that mirror region- and location-specific circumstances and grant much more respect to financial self-regulation.

Intervention of Rural Finance

In the early 1950s, we have become masters in the art of underdevelopment: at the levels of experts, institutions, governments and donors. Underdevelopment in large parts of the world has been expertly prepared, government-made and donor-supported. Of course, there are exceptional cases of successful development. Yet by treating them as such, there is little to be learned from them.

We are now rich in experience and hope to have learned from it—like the proverbial banker who invariably gains from making a loan: either in monetary terms, when the loan is paid back, or in experience, when it is not. Inspired by the poverty-alleviating impact of the industrial revolution and, later on, by the effect of the Marshall Plan on the reconstruction of Europe, policy makers and experts during the 1950s and 1960s embarked on the gigantic experiment of technology and capital transfer from the rich to the backward countries of the world.

Social scientists constructed a modernization theory and

argued that the whole social, economic and financial system of industrial societies was to be transplanted, including values, motivations, educational and legal systems. As a preparatory step, this required a tabula rasa strategy, destroying, or ignoring, the obstacles to development embedded in indigenous economies and traditional social systems.

As this did not leave much of an entrepreneurial base, the government took it upon itself to act as entrepreneur and banker. The good effects of their deeds were to trickle down to the poor and eventually lead to progress for all segments of the population. On a global level, whatever differences in approach existed, as between capitalism and socialism, Eastern and Western or Northern and Southern cultural systems, they eventually were to converge on a single industrial development model.

A corollary to modernization theory was the vicious-cycle-of-poverty hypothesis, which added to the poor-country approach a corresponding poor-people approach. Eighty to 90 percent of the population in poor countries are poor. They were portrayed as illiterate, improvidential, superstitious, undernourished and of ill health - a mix of facts and fiction. Without further examination, they were assumed to be too poor to save, unable to organize themselves and incapable of self help.

According to that theory, countries are poor because people are poor and helpless; and people remain poor as long as their countries are poor. The two theories are similar in etiology but different in operational approach. Modernization theorists aim at growth and attack poverty at the national or macro-economic level; poverty theorists aim at a dignified life and attack poverty at the individual or micro-entrepreneurial level.

There is no abating of the controversy, as indicated by the ongoing Poverty Lending versus Financial Systems approach carried by influential lobbies even into the American Congress. Capital transfer, the poverty hypothesis, the trickle-down effect and government banking all entered into a complex equation, the solution of which was cheap credit. To offset the effects of overtaxing agriculture and to speed up the trickling-down of expected industrial growth effects, governments intervened with subsidized targeted credit.

The crucial strategy adopted was credit disbursement rather than savings mobilization. Credit dependency - instead of self-reliance through self-financing - was one of its immediate effects. When governments took it upon themselves to develop agriculture, they assumed the combined roles of planner, banker, supplier and marketing agency. Among their main financial instruments were interest rate ceilings and subsidies, credit targeting, credit rationing and agricultural price controls.

Institutionally, governments fostered specialization, creating separate savings banks, credit institutions, agricultural development banks, etc. Subsidizing interest rates on loans and directing subsidized credit to priority borrowers and crop-related activities became major development strategies, with agricultural production, rather than rural development, the objective.

Institutions were instrumentalized as conduits of government funds, hampering the growth—and sometimes even the emergence—of institutional financial intermediaries and the functioning of rural financial markets. This in turn hindered rural development, including the growth of agricultural production. As credit was only available for government-imposed and sometimes ill-defined purposes, farmers tended to take advantage of the fungibility of money.

They substituted the funds for activities which they would anyway have undertaken or diverted them to other purposes. While this was frequently a rational strategy from the point of view of the farmer, it subverted project additionality. As a result, projects had little or no impact. Due to inevitable limitations in the availability of subsidies, subsidized lending projects were narrow in scope and void of growth. Given a wide discrepancy between supply and demand for credit and a price far from equilibrium level, credit rationing was one of the principal strategies in credit allocation.

Frequently, the wrong recipients obtained the wrong quantities of credit for the wrong objectives. Government officials and experts substituted their own rationality and decisions for those of the farmers and of the market. This led to crop and project failures, sometimes on a large scale. Farmers were practically forced into diversion of funds. Factor allocations were distorted. In some cases, the impact of development projects was negative. Ceilings on interest rates, usually combined with targeted subsidies, prevented financial institutions from charging interest rates that covered transaction costs.

As transaction costs tend to be constant per loan independent of loan size, interest rate ceilings and credit subsidies led to concentrations in the loan portfolio, allocating relatively large loans to a few big farmers, to the exclusion, or neglect, of small farmers and tenants. In addition, the transfer of transaction costs to borrowers (i.e., the non-interest component including transportation costs, legal expenses, opportunity costs and also illicit charges) tended to price small farmers out of the market.

Borrower transaction costs also added to the burden of the fortunate few big borrowers, frequently bringing their actual expenses close to what would have been a market rate. As banks acted as conduits of government funds, rather than developing and applying credit policies of their own making, subsidized credit created its own high risks and associated default rates. Undercapitalization and contractions in the lending volume were virtually inevitable concomitants, gradually diminishing the scope and impact of projects.

In some cases an inverted interest rate structure, with interest rates on deposits above lending rates, discouraged banking, as practiced for extended periods, e.g., in India, Vietnam and the Philippines. Subsidized funds were usually channeled through credit institutions specifically created for that purpose. Agricultural development banks and special projects are the most prominent examples. Many of them were barred from deposit mobilization. As a result, institutional facilities for the depositing of savings in organized financial institutions were notably absent in many rural areas.

Specialized savings institutions, on the other hand, such as government or post office savings banks, offered negative real rates of return and lacked the sophistication to develop attractive and convenient deposit facilities. In many countries, the rural population created their own informal financial institutions on a self-help basis. Without access to refinance, these were restricted in their capacity for generating the necessary resources for growth. Subsidized and targeted credit negatively affected loan recovery on several grounds:

1. Farmers tended to consider the loans as free presents attained through government patronage and had no intention to repay;
2. Or they diverted them to other purposes and found themselves unable to repay;
3. Or they complied with ill-founded government directives, invested into activities that were perhaps productive but not profitable due to price controls, and were equally unable to repay;

4. Financial institutions were forced to accept non-bank criteria in credit decisions, perhaps allocating the wrong loan sizes at the wrong time to the wrong customers for the wrong purposes. This inevitably led to high default rates;

5. Because banks were unwilling to take risks not covered by an adequate reserve for bad debts, governments instituted credit guarantee funds or agencies absorbing all or part of the risk. This, in turn, discouraged banks from collecting loans in arrears and further increased defaults.

In many developing countries government interventions, subsidies, loan targeting, reliance on government or foreign rather than domestic funds, misappropriation and diversion of funds, defaulting, price distortions, institutional specialization and a host of related policy and operational factors have been closely related to the underdevelopment of market mechanisms, financial institutions, agriculture and the rural economy.

In some cases subsidized credit did have positive effects on production, though invariably at high cost. Estimates are difficult as no country has monitored its costs and benefits. With regard to Indonesia, which until January 1990 ran a number of large subsidized credit programs, the following information may be indicative.

Several decades of experimenting with development have taught a powerful lesson: rigid regulation of the economy, in combination with an all-encompassing role of government in all spheres of the economy, leads to underdevelopment. This has stifled the growth of money, production, income and employment. Production is the motor of the economy, finance is its fuel. Unless there is a functioning fuel injection system, the motor will not run. The faster the motor is to run, the more fuel it needs.

It is the financial system which has to pump the money

into the economy: it has to mobilize savings, provide credit and assure an adequate growth of the money supply. An undersupply of money will stall the engine, thus halting the economy; an oversupply will lead to inflation, thus choking the engine. While the government adopted the role of a donor, the banks were unable, or restricted, to act as financial intermediaries between savers and borrowers. The financial system remained repressed, in many cases inoperative.

During the first two development decades, the role of the financial system in economic development was virtually ignored. The theory of the day was modernization through technology transfer with external capital. Domestic capital formation and resource mobilization did not enter into that theory. Well into the 1980s, many developing countries were held in its grip.

The logical consequence from the recognition that cheap credit undermines development appears to lie in the policy recommendation to deregulate and introduce market rates of interest, with the triple objective of mobilizing domestic resources, covering the costs of credit and achieving a balance between demand and supply of money. This raised the question of the definition of market rates.

Some countries, among them the Philippines, have introduced what they call market rates for final borrowers. While rates to bank and non-bank (including NGO) intermediaries continue to be subsidized, there is now a tendency to require end-user rates to approximate commercial (sometimes: prime) rates of interest. This is, of course, not the market rate in rural lending, nor can there be a single market rate. The market rate is that rate of interest which covers the costs of funds, administrative costs, risks and an adequate profit margin.

For practical purposes, costs of funds may be equated to

three-monthly fixed deposit rates. Administrative costs and risks vary widely, depending on type and location of customer, availability of information, services rendered (e.g., doorstep services), collateral, etc. If governments require their banks to lend to farmers or micro-entrepreneurs at undifferentiated commercial rates, they are, in fact, demanding subsidized lending, with the same consequences as any type of subsidized credit.

The second issue concerns the source of loanable funds, whether they are domestically mobilized or supplied by donors and governments. Even when subsidies have been stopped, donors and governments frequently continue liberally to supply liquidity, which discourages banks from mobilizing their own resource base. The rise in interest rates to market level, therefore, does little in dampening the banks' demand for liquidity credit, and there is little evidence that the usual negative consequences of subsidized credit have been alleviated.

A policy of easy money represses the financial system just as much as a policy of subsidized credit. The impact on adverse borrower selection, loan apportioning, moral hazard, etc., is hypothesized to be similar to that of subsidized credit. Its worst impact is on the financial system, which it prevents from developing at its own. By increasing the money supply without recourse to domestic resource mobilization, it is also a major factor in budgetary deficits and inflation.

When refinanced by international loans it becomes a long-term liability which is not matched by gains in productivity. Once easy money is available, it becomes difficult for individual banks to escape its attraction. It is too convenient a source of funding. While some bank managers see its limiting effect on the institutional growth of their banks, their board members may be less enlightened. When combined with government credit guarantees, it appears to be a low-risk operation.

Banks are lured by governments, and governments by donors, into credit dependency. In that respect there appears to be little, if any, difference between GO and NGO donors. Market rates alone will not lead to financial systems development. Reconstructing - just as undermining -financial landscapes is most effective when tackled at all systems levels.

For development to occur it takes more than the experience of underdevelopment. A systematic analysis of underdevelopment, and financial repression in particular, from a systems perspective is therefore but a starting point. There are several systems levels of financial repression. In many countries, the government as banker, entrepreneur, policymaker, planning and executing agency has taken control over the total system. This has resulted in a breakdown of accountability.

Regardless of their ideological leaning, governments in many developing countries have implemented central planning - an unexpected form of convergence between socialist and non-socialist countries. As a side effect, this has given powerful individuals in government the opportunity of transferring the wealth of their country abroad - much of this at the expense of later generations.

On the policy framework level, regulation or deregulation of respectively, the real and financial sectors are closely interrelated. Through prices and quotas, government takes control over exports and imports of real sector goods. Overvalued domestic currencies make imports cheap, including technology. As a free flow of imports is unaffordable, government has to resort to rationing.

This leads to under-the-table trading of import licenses. Import substitution becomes the guiding principle of industrial policy, rather than export promotion of finished products. Agricultural prices are controlled, to the advantage of the urban wage earners. Much of the proceeds of agriculture is taxed away directly to finance the government budget and indirectly to stimulate industrialization.

Low prices, however, discourage the farmers from producing food and cash crops. This is then partially offset by food imports at subsidized prices, which further distorts local agricultural markets. The banking law has been a powerful instrument in suppressing financial growth. Here are some of its tenets:

1. All power to the government, none to the central bank;
2. Nationalize all banks;
3. No foreign banks, no joint ventures, which bring in alien influence;
4. Allocate the turf, eliminate competition;
5. Prohibit branching out;
6. Restrict the services of each bank, eliminate universal banking;
7. Restrict deposit mobilization to a few institutions;
8. Define collateral requirements narrowly, which may exclude up to 90 percent of the population from borrowing;
9. When the financial system turns terminally ill, concentrate on curing the symptoms, e.g. using targeted subsidized credit as one of the remedies.

Given the overregulation of the financial system, many governments regarded it as superfluous to impose further bank supervision through differentiated supervisory institutions. A repressed financial system does not require a differentiated institutional infrastructure. The primary objective of this infrastructure is to serve the purposes of the government as defined in the development plan.

Under conditions of repressive finance, banks are required to follow administrative procedures set by government. Banks do not learn from each other or from experience, nor is there any learning from local or informal financial institutions. Loans are uniformly allocated according to defined production goals, which leaves little room for loan appraisal or creditworthiness examination.

Administrative delays in credit delivery have no impact on lending decisions. There is minimal, if any, monitoring, and loan collection is passive, with no recourse to social controls, enforcement of repayment or litigation. No efforts are made to actively collect savings.

Loan terms such as sizes, maturities and grace periods are not individually determined. They are also undifferentiated within a series of repeat loans. In production credit, collateral requirements are usually waived. Instalments tend to be in long, with quarterly or seasonal intervals, ignoring individual repayment capacities deriving from other sources of income.

Loans are generously rescheduled, and new loans granted before the old ones are repaid. Penalties are not enforced, nor are there incentives for timely repayment. At election time repayment may be waived altogether. The world of credit-driven, supply-leading finance and social banking uses its own language, displaying a predilection for beneficiaries and target groups of channelling institutions, handling banks or conduits.

In contrast, there is the savings-driven world of demand-leading finance and competitive financial intermediation with its own language: there are savers and deposit takers, lenders and borrowers, customers or clients and banks. In fact, the customers or saver-borrowers may own financial institutions, as in the case of cooperative banks.

Subsidized targeted credit for beneficiaries defined by government undermines institutional viability and systems sustainability - this is the principal lesson of the past. But how can effective financial services for all segments of the population be attained, together with institutional viability and systems sustainability? Micro-entrepreneurs and the poor have not benefited from financial repression.

In fact they have paid most of its price. It is now being realized that a full range of financial services to micro-entrepreneurs and the poor as well as all other sections of the population depends foremost on the quality and effectiveness of financial intermediaries, and their viability in turn depends on the sustained health and growth of the overall financial system.

The optimal provision of financial services will ultimately depend on the successful development and integration of all levels of the financial system. In actual practice decisions are required on ground rules for interventions and strategic entry points. The landscape of finance is not adequately captured by the concept of the structure of the financial sector, which has been the object of most financial sector studies in the past.

It now appears that a static concept of structures and component parts only befits a situation in which governments, rather than markets, possess the power of resource allocation, with a tendency to administrative definition of financial contracts and structural frameworks, as is in fact the case in many developing countries. From a strategic viewpoint, governments in these countries have shielded the structure of the financial sector from external influences, preventing adaptation and creating an artificial stability in a world of flux and turmoil.

Those developing countries which have undergone a process of gradual and prudential deregulation and have submitted their financial institutions to market forces require a new conceptual approach to finance: an approach which emphasizes process rather than structure, dynamic rather than static interrelations, interactive rather than prescriptive decision-making. In a systems approach, the world of finance is envisaged as a complex open system in which the component subsystems are dynamically interrelated, with a change in one resulting in a change in all others, yet a stable equilibrium remaining an elusive state, and with satisficing rather than optimal problem solutions.

From a strategic viewpoint, governments in these countries have typically exposed the financial system to external influences from within and without, thus contributing to continuous adjustments on local, national and global levels. It is therefore not feasible to arrive at an identifiable optimal financial system, and even less so at a single definite set of steps of transition. Instead, there may be process ground rules that have to be observed for interventions to have a chance of market acceptance and success:

1. Any intervention can only depart from the state of the system as a whole at a given point in time. This also includes the cultural, social and political setup, to which interventions have to be properly adjusted;
2. The acceptance of interventions depends on interactive rather than prescriptive approaches;
3. In a complex interrelated system, all interventions have unintended results. Careful impact monitoring is therefore necessary, which must not lose sight of other subsystems and secondary effects;
4. Interventions will at best lead to satisficing, not optimal results;
5. In evaluating the results of interventions, it is more important to envisage the overall process of change initiated than

narrowly focusing on performance criteria;

6. Interventions can only succeed with the market, not against the market. This also means that the market, not the government or donor, decides over its acceptance.

In the field of micro-finance, appropriate strategies for financial infrastructure development may offer entry points for strategic interventions, with a particular emphasis on local financial institutions, member-based or community-based. At least four different strategies may be discerned: (1) adapting formal financial institutions to the local environment (downgrading), (2) upgrading informal or semiformal financial institutions, (3) linking formal and informal financial institutions, and (4) creating new institutions (infrastructural innovation).

None of these strategies is universally applicable, nor does any single one offer an optimal approach. Their appropriateness depends on local circumstances and conditions, which need to be carefully assessed. In a subsequent stage of intervention, infrastructural development may be followed by measures on the levels of financial product innovations, procedures and terms and conditions.

This also requires coordination with measures of financial infrastructure development. Many of the institutions that may provide the strategic entry point for interventions require institution-building and capacity-enhancing inputs which they are not able to finance from their own profits. Furthermore, if a new infrastructure is to be developed at the grassroots or village level, which may be necessary in many developing countries, considerable financial infrastructure investments are required which may not immediately pay off.

Institution-building may thus become a major field for subsidies. Financial subsidies undermine micro-finance, but institutional subsidies may contribute to the development of a micro-financial infrastructure. A friendly policy environment will greatly facilitate such an approach. In a less than friendly or hostile environment, two supportive strategies may be examined: (1) niche-seeking in the short run, and (2) supported by a joint donor effort, policy reform in the medium or long run.

3

Rural Financial Development

During the 1980s, there has been a fundamental shift from a supply-leading to a demand-oriented approach to the development of rural financial markets in developing countries. The rationale of providing credit for production purposes was simple: credit, used to enhance the productive capacity of the borrower, will increase his future income, which, in turn, will allow him to pay interest and repay the loan.

The actual performance of agricultural credit programs in many developing countries, particularly in Sub-Saharan Africa, seems to suggest that borrowers failed to follow this rationale on both accounts: the economic efficiency of credit use has often been low; the repayment performance has been poor. Many agricultural lending institutions operated with losses, and some collapsed when governments became unable to sustain them financially.

Cheap credit policies, often implying negative real interest rates, have been seen to be an important contributor to institutional collapse. Low interest rates make it difficult for commercial banks to mobilize savings. They tend to lower the margin on lending, causing banks to ration credit to a few and generally the larger and wealthier borrowers. Market determined interest rates are likely to reduce the lending bias towards large borrowers and to support the availability of credit for consumption purposes.

Providing production credit is only one of the three needs financial markets must address at the micro level. Failure to address the other needs will hamper financial market development. Besides loan services, rural households show strong preferences for savings opportunities. It is also apparent that rural households look at financial markets as providing important insurance functions. Financial markets serve three important functions for rural households/farms. All three functions can principally be served by formal as well as informal institutions.

Production credit is extended for the purpose of increasing the borrower's production capacity and income. This function has been the centre of attention in literature and research on financial market development. Too often, it has been found, agricultural production did not expand and loans were not repaid. Also, only a small segment of the rural population was reached and the institutions providing such loans became increasingly weak and some even collapsed under the burden of loan defaults. It seems that the failure of production credit and the faltering of rural formal financial institutions are inversely related to the income level of a country.

Rural bank failures particularly in the poor countries of Sub-Saharan Africa. This may simply be explained by the fact that the poorer countries are not able to subsidize unprofitable financial institutions for any extended period. It may, however, also reflect the rural population's relatively greater need, in poor countries, for the other services of financial markets, i.e. consumption credit, savings, and insurance.

Consumption credit is an important component of financial needs of rural households. The roles of rural financial markets in consumption stabilization are shown as being pursued by two possible strategies: the savings/dissavings process and consumption credit. Both are connected. If the food security of a household is at risk, various strategies may be chosen. In a situation of temporary food insecurity, entailing a short-term temporary shortfall of consumption below the needed level, households may diversify their income sources, sell assets or ask for support by others.

However, they may also resort to informal and formal suppliers of credit and savings services. Typically, the closer a household is, even in a "normal situation", to inadequate food consumption level, the greater the need for access to any of the food securing strategies; and the more limited the income diversification, asset sale and inter-household support strategies become, the more important will be the access to rural financial intermediaries and their services.

If a transitory food insecurity occurs repeatedly, the production and income base tends to get eroded, and the household may finally face a chronic food insecurity. Timely access to suppliers of credit and savings facilities may help prevent the occurrence of a chronic food security problem for a household.

Another function of financial markets is to improve a household's ability to cope with potential risk situations. In contrast to the first two functions, the immediate goal is not to directly influence income or consumption in a particular period, but to increase the range of options a household has at its disposal to cope with periods of income or consumption stress. Sources of risk in rural households are manifold, and the timing and intensity of risks and its impact on income are difficult to predict by households.

Formal insurance schemes are often not accessible to the rural population. Households, thus, pursue a range of strategies of self insurance: they save in the form of cash, deposits, food or other assets; they diversify production structure, cropping patterns and income sources; and they build networks of social relationships. However, in intense and extended risk situations, and particularly in the case of covariate risks, the self-insurance mechanisms may not be sufficient.

The mere access to credit, not the actual borrowing, can serve as an important insurance substitute. Having potential access to credit enables the household to transfer part of its risk to the financial market. Lacking access to formal finance and insurance schemes, rural households resort to indigenous informal savings and credit arrangements. Studies of African and Asian informal financial markets point out the variety of savings and credit options that these sources provide, but indicate also the insurance, co-insurance and risk pooling services these markets provide.

Ensuring potential future access to credit in an informal market requires, as the most vital element, the building of trust, reliability and confidence within the local community. It will be shown below that rural households in their participation in informal financial markets appear to be well aware of this need.

The integrated nature of production and consumption activities in rural households has been one of the fundamental reasons for developing the farming systems concept. Ruthenberg applied the traditional approach of continental European farm management theory to farms in developing countries. He saw rural farm households as a complex interlinked system of production and household activities, characterized by the common use of labour, land and capital.

In this system, consumption activities are inseparably

linked to the production sphere and vice versa. Expenditures for food, health and education are needed to maintain the most important production factor: labour. Social activities may serve to build a mutual support system. In the farming systems literature these interlinkages have been amply researched and documented, and development projects take this increasingly into account in their approach.

This cannot be equally said for the rural financial market literature and even less for rural financial market policy, where the "agricultural credit" project syndrome still prevails over "rural financial market" development. The failure to recognize these facts and to open the supply of financial services to all needs of rural households, hampers rural financial market development. It leads to approaches and programs that bypass important, and in emergency situations often the most important, needs of rural households.

In that way a large part of the rural clientele is alienated, particularly women and the poor. In a survey covering 160 rural households in the three Cameroonian provinces Adamawa, North West and West carried out between August 1991 and September 1992, 441 individuals were asked about their credit and savings activities.

Slightly more than half of the people interviewed lived in villages with a credit union office and thus could turn at low cost to a formal financial institution. Yet, only seven respondents took out a credit union loan compared to 146 taking a loan from a financial self-help group. 215 respondents lived in villages without such locally-based formal institution; to apply for a formal loan they had to travel significantly longer distances to neighbouring villages or towns.

Rural people's use of consumption credit was, however, much wider, as individual consumption loans were smaller (US$135 on average) and the number of these loans was more than three times the number of production loans. Consumption credit, especially from informal sources, was taken primarily to cover health, school, and food expenses. The main sources of both production and consumption loans were informal groups and individuals.

The presence of a formal finance institution appeared to have little impact on the number of clients reached; however, they contributed about half to the total loan amount extended. A loan was categorized as consumption loan when the percentage share of it spent for food, health, education, and social events exceeded the amount spent for production purposes. Similarly, a loan was considered a production loan when monies spent on agricultural/livestock/handicraft equipments and inputs, labour, and capital investments such as housing, exceeded the percentage share spent for consumption purposes.

Considering the type of funds used for the various purposes, the more or less subsidized loans from banks and development projects were used almost exclusively for production, while credit unions, informal groups and individuals financed predominantly consumption purposes. Gifts were partly used for production, but mostly for education. Noteworthy is also the size of the "gift economy".

In Cameroon household funds play a most important role financing consumption expenditures, particularly education but are also significant in production. In Benin production credit accounts for only 24 percent of total loan amount and 18 percent of the number of loans received by the rural households.

Rural Financial Market (RFM)

A new thinking about rural finance and its role in development, based on the concept of the Rural Financial Market (RFM), clearly demonstrated the shortcomings of the cheap credit policy. It enabled a more balanced understanding of the roles of rural banks, informal intermediaries and their (potential) clients in the supply of and demand for financial services.

The new thinking also resulted in a growing recognition that governments should refrain from direct participation in banking and concentrate on policies that establish and maintain confidence in financial institutions.* Such a new role of government in finance is a pre-condition for the provision of sustainable financial services by banks. Of course, this is not the only issue.

Various studies have explored other factors that strongly affect the provision of rural banking services. The calculation and monitoring of costs is of central importance when rural banks pursue the socially desirable objective of providing financial services to new clients. Emphasis on reaching new clients without due attention to costs, and the control of costs in particular, leads invariably to operating losses which sooner or later result in a reduction or termination of services provided.

From a long-term perspective, the objective to reach new clients should thus necessarily be linked with attention to costs, or in broader terms: with the objective to operate on a financially viable basis. Rural banks trying to achieve these two objectives simultaneously are faced with a host of questions regarding the demand for various types of financial services by their new clients, and their own organizational, operational and financial capabilities to meet this demand.

Rural financial markets consist of relationships between buyers and sellers of financial assets in a rural economy. Relationships develop between market parties through financial transactions, such as: lending, borrowing, saving, insuring, and the transfer of ownership participation in enterprises. Funds are exchanged in these transactions for other financial assets: debt claims or ownership claims.

Participants in the rural financial markets are the rural households and intermediaries operating between buyers and sellers of financial assets to bridge preferences for quantity, time, risk and space. Intermediaries are usually divided into informal intermediators such as traders, moneylenders, indigenous bankers, landlords and pawnbrokers, and formal intermediaries like banks, specialized credit institutions and cooperatives.

The specification of financial assets in terms of size, maturity or tenor, and additional conditions is linked to the type of financial transaction in which they are produced, and to the type of intermediary involved. It is therefore useful to speak of "financial services" and specify these services as short-term lending, insurance against risk, etc., possibly in combination with classifications of "formal" or "informal", to identify the types of financial assets.

The rural financial market can then be described in terms of demand for and supply of financial services. The potential demand for financial services, that is, the capacity of households to engage in financial transactions, is related to rural incomes, which in turn are related to the stage of development. This demand has two dimensions, a qualitative aspect including the types of services, and a quantitative aspect covering the size or scale of individual services.

The total demand for financial services in an RFM, specified by type and size, is thus related to the total household income in a rural area. Incomes of rural households have a certain distribution, and we may assume that the richer households have a demand for a wider range of services with a larger size than households with lower incomes.

The services which are potentially attractive to rural clients are not necessarily all available, or available in appropriate amounts, creating an unfulfilled demand for financial services in RFMs. Extension of services towards more clients, those further away and those with smaller financial capacity, dramatically increases costs of banks. Addressing the central issue thus requires careful balancing between costs, returns and the increased scale of operation in order not to endanger the condition of financial viability.

This is especially the case for an expansion of lending services because screening of applicants, monitoring of borrowers, and enforcement of repayment involve considerable expenditures. The provision of financial services such as money transfer and insurance might be worth considering as well, the former especially in areas where part of the population work elsewhere.

The expenditures and revenues of these types of services can be estimated with much less uncertainty than lending services, and their introduction does not involve major risks. These supplementary financial services might improve the profitability of a bank through economies of scope. The cost of lending is central to a bank's financial viability, and thus to its ability to provide services on a permanent basis.

The cost of lending is composed of (1) the costs of funds which include interest paid to savers, depositors and other suppliers of funds, and the administrative costs of handling savings accounts and deposits; and (2) the cost of providing loans which consists of administrative costs for screening, monitoring and loan recovery and the cost of default. Lending costs thus determine the bank's ability to attract funds and to allocate these to borrowers.

The large impact of loan tenor on lending cost is due to the fact that administrative costs and cost of default (expressed as proportion of loans not repaid) must be recovered in a much shorter period. The effect of small loans and loans of short tenor on lending cost is especially relevant for rural banks that want to extend their services to new customers, as their demand is initially for these types of loans.

The operational application of the formula to study the effects of present and new lending operations is, however, subject to two limitations:

1. The cost parameters available are stated in proportions that reflect the average present situation with regard to loan size and tenor; for an appraisal of new lending services-short term and small-the cost parameters need to be defined accordingly.
2. The volume of loans provided or expectedly to be provided is not taken into account. Volume is a vital issue for rural banks, because their fixed costs can be covered at a certain interest rate only if a sufficient volume of services can be provided.

Thc two limitations can be lifted simultaneously by incorporating lending operations in absolute terms in the formula. The lending operations of a bank in year t can be described by three parameters: loan volume (Lvt), loan amount (Lat), and number of loans (Lnt). Therefore, the sum of outstanding loans at the end of each month of year t can be used as a proxy for loan volume in year t expressed in Rpmonth. The loan amount Lat is the sum of new loans provided in year; the number of loans provided is Lnt.

With these three parameters lending operations formula (1) can be expanded to reflect lending costs more precisely, either as the interest rate on loans required to cover all annual expenditures, or as an absolute amount of annual expenditures. The total costs of funds is proportionally related to the loan volume (Lvt). The direct cost of default, the loss of funds, is related to the amount of loans provided (Lat). It is assumed that a bank makes provisions in year t proportionally to the volume of loans provided in that year. Later, when defaults on loans issued in year t appear, they can be written off against these provisions.

The effect of default on all cost components (the term 1/1-d) is related to loan volume (Lvt), as interest payments in year t must cover all costs in that year. Administrative costs can be divided into fixed cost (Aft) and variable cost (Avt), the latter related to the number of loans. Of course, in the long run all costs are variable, but the distinction is useful as banks have tendency to operate with a considerable amount of fixed costs for staff and building.

Rural banks are usually branch offices, and the cost resulting from supervision and guidance from the main office can be either stated as a separate term in the denominator (Aot), or included in the fixed and variable administration costs. A multitude of factors affects performance. Some are under control of the bank, others are not. The factors under the bank's control can be grouped under three main headings: organizational structure, method of operation, and services offered.

Decisions taken in these three fields determine the supply of financial services. Factors not under the bank's control are those governing the demand for financial services: the number, location and financial capacity of actual and potential clients. The relationship between a bank and its clients is expressed in the financial services provided. Therefore, the logical performance indicator for banks with the objective of providing financial services to more rural households consists of the types and volume of financial services provided over time.

For analytical purposes, type, volume and time aspects can be separated into two operational performance indicators: (1) the types and volume of financial services provided in a particular year, and (2) the bank's financial viability in that particular year as a proxy for the bank's ability to offer these services in the future. Financial viability has two aspects: profitability, or the balance between revenues and costs as stated in the profit and loss account; and the capital position which reflects the ability to attract capital and the ability to cover anticipated and unanticipated losses through reserves.

Profitability and capital position are usually stated in the bank's financial statements. The main factors in the supply of and demand for financial services and the performance indicators for the harmonization of supply and demand. The three main fields of the bank's policy decisions are organization, operations and services offered. These affect the cost structure through fixed costs for building and staff, and through variable costs determined by the volume of financial services provided to and accepted by the rural population.

Policies regarding the three main fields of bank decision making-organization structure, operations and services offered-and the two performance indicators-qualitative and quantitative-offer a comprehensive framework for the analysis of a bank's performance. This framework can be used by rural banks to analyse their present situation and the effects of possible policy changes.

It can also be used by researchers to analyse experiments to determine the feasibility of innovative organization structures and methods of operation aimed at providing formal financial services to small rural clients, such as, group loans within a two-tier financial organization, mobile savings and credit units, mobile credit officers, and various types of specialized, more or less formal institutions operating at low costs.

Comprehensive analysis with attention to all components of the framework and elaboration of the details of the innovative experiments will contribute to better insights into the possibilities and limitations of rural banks to serve the poor and to realize financial sustainability at the same time.

Changing Financial Landscape

In India, rural formal finance system have significant changes. First, the physical features of these landscapes have been radically changed with the estab-lishment of cooperatives, rural and semi-urban branches of commercial banks, land development banks and Regional Rural Banks: in total, just over 146,000 primary offices by 1986. Second, policies directed through these formal constituents of rural financial landscapes have combined both development and welfare objectives, by means of government directives concerning bank location and loan portfolios, and a series of poverty alleviation programs with subsidized, activity specific and target group specific credit as the main instrument.

Third, dramatic changes have been reported in the relative shares and importance of formal and informal financial intermediaries. More generally, Harriss, by comparing the results of macro (census and survey investigations) and micro (anthropological studies or small-scale surveys) research in Tamil Nadu, demonstrates the problems of "ascer-taining, aggregating and interpreting" through large-scale surveys, fundamental facts about agrarian change, given the complexity of labor force structure and economy in rural India. Collecting data on rural financial landscapes at the micro-level poses particular problems.

Although anthro-pological investigations emphasize the

wider economy and society in which credit relations are "embedded", such micro-level research, usually relies on clients for establishing basic facts concerning these landscapes, although, as Darling pointed out in 1925, these clients are always anxious to throw "the purdah" over their debts.

An example of a micro-level financial landscape in India, whereby the effects of entry and expansion of village bank finance upon pre-existing informal financial arrangements are assessed, by data collected from the lenders (both informal and formal) themselves. The principal comparison is with respect to the lending activities of an individual unlicensed lender (a shopkeeper) and the village bank.

The lending records of the informal lender are examined with respect to just before and six years after the bank was established in the village. The lending records of both these financial intermediaries are then examined over the course of a full year 1988-89; the role of informal mutual finance is also consid-ered. For Hindu households, the non-agricultural activities are largely caste-based. Jain house-holds dominate the commercial and financial services in the village. Migration to Gujarat and Bombay provides intermittent employment in the construction and service sectors.

The major sources of commercial informal credit were Jain shopkeepers, who in 1983, ran 20 of the 28 retail shops in the village. According to RBI data, the penetration of commercial banks in the rural areas of Rajasthan has brought about a fundamental shift of the financial landscape of this State.

Whereas the bank loans catered to a limited range of officially sanctioned loan purposes, the shopkeeper willingly advanced pawnbroking loans for an extensive range of needs. A very high proportion of the 1988-89 bank loans were secured through the Integrated Rural Development Programme (IRDP), whereas the shopkeeper advanced credit for a large number of cere-monial, domestic consumption and productive purposes. Compared to the bank's IRDP loans, a much lower volume of pawnbroking loans went to productive purposes: agriculture loans, loans to finance informal lending and business loans.

Thus, productive loans and loans for productive consumption purposes together account for 43.6 percent of loan volume, and 37 percent of number of loans advanced in 1988-89. Second, although proportions of loan volume for productive purposes were generally lower for the shop-keeper, analysis of individual loan purposes indicates more positive features compared to the bank. This is shown by reference to loans for agricultural purposes. Also, whereas the bank's agricultural loans were all IRDP livestock loans, the shopkeeper advanced pawnbroking credit for an extensive range of agricultural fixed capital (six loans) and seasonal needs (eight loans).

In addition, whereas 11 of the bank's 13 agricultural loans were advanced in March, the shopkeeper supplied loans for agricultural purposes, precisely when cultivators needed them, for as many as 10 months in the year.

Another category of informal finance, mutual finance, not specifically allowed for in the macro-level RBI data quoted by Pradhan and Dinakar and Gadgil, also shows signs of expansion rather than contraction since the establishment of a bank in this village. In addition, a micro-level analysis of group membership and lending records, points to significant differences, not just between mutual finance and specialist informal finance such as pawnbroking credit, but also between different mutual finance groups in the same locality.

More significantly, it was clear that by 1992 some mutual finance groups, through expansion of their capital base, were now advancing loans of a much higher value than those reported for 1988-89. For instance, the Mitra bank in 1989 reported a maximum loan size of Rs.1,500. Through multiple membership within and between the different savings and credit groups in the village, individual households could obtain greater access to mutual finance and thus secure larger amounts of loan capital.

Microcredit—Small Loans for Rural People

Microcredit is the extension of small loans to groups of poor people, especially women, for the purpose of investing in self-employment programmes . It is a way of improving the earning capacity and therefore the standard of living of the poor. Nevertheless, a poor woman who generates income through microcredit but who does not have adequate access to health care for herself and her family, who lacks essential information about health and nutrition and who is unable to send her children to school is still living in poverty.

There is a greater reduction in poverty when microcredit programmes are combined with increased access to basic social services than when the programmes focus on credit alone. When microcredit is linked with access to basic social services and key social development messages, the health and nutrition of borrowers' children - particularly girls - improves; school enrolment increases; safe water and sanitation use broadens.

This combined approach, therefore, is an important strategy for achieving the year 2000 goals for children. Microcredit also empowers women, by enabling them to make economic decisions and become the source of increased household income. Experience shows that with the empowerment of women come significant improvements in children's survival rates, health, nutrition and development.

Successful experiences with microcredit involve a combination of credit and savings. When borrowers are obliged to set aside a minimum amount of savings on a weekly or a monthly basis, this savings component reinforces the discipline of the borrower to make regular repayments of the borrowed money. It also creates a sense of 'ownership' on the part of the borrowers that is vital in ensuring the scheme's sustainability. Group-based lending has helped marginalized groups gain access to credit. Because the poor lack material collateral, group-based lending allows for the sharing of risks.

The group collectively works to ensure that all loans are repaid on time so that other members of the group are not deprived of credit if a member defaults. This creates a sense of joint responsibility and generates peer pressure to comply with the repayment schedule. Experience with microcredit has shown that the poor can be disciplined borrowers and savers, able to repay loans on time and to save.

If poor families are to pull themselves out of poverty, they need access to the successive loans that microcredit programmes provide. UNICEF is not new to microcredit, having supported the Grameen Bank's efforts in Bangladesh since the early 1980s. A number of country offices have also made credit an integral component of programmes designed to increase access to, and sustainability of, basic social services.

UNICEF-supported programmes are successful not only as measured by loan recovery rates but also because they have broadened access to basic social services and empowered women in a number of countries, including Bangladesh, Benin, Brazil, Cambodia, Egypt, Guatemala, India, Kenya, Nepal and Viet Nam.

In Bangladesh, the Grameen Bank, with UNICEF

assistance, integrated social development activi-ties into its credit extension services, adopting the now familiar 'Sixteen Decisions' that are recited in every weekly meeting of the Bank's borrowers. The decisions affirm, among other things, the need for health services, adequate nutrition, child spacing, safe water and sanitation and primary education, as well as the elimination of dowry in marriage.

In Nepal, UNICEF has linked the delivery of social services to credit and other support provided under the Small Farmer Development Programme (SFDP) since 1982-1983. Implemented by the Government, the programme reached 123,000 families in 422 villages and 75 districts by 1992. In areas where credit has been combined with support for basic social services, infant mortality is lower, school attendance for girls is higher and children's health, nutrition and education have shown greater improvement, than in areas where credit alone is given or where no credit is provid-ed.

In 1982, UNICEF began supporting the Production Credit for Rural Women (PCRW) programme by providing credit and training and supporting community development in five districts. In 1988, the programme was extended to 37 districts for which the International Fund for Agricultural Development (IFAD) supplied funds for credit. Since 1989, credit has been linked with social development messages, drawing on the experiences of the Grameen Bank and the Self Employed Women's Association in India.

The approach of combining credit and basic social services has been successful, attracting support from a number of donor and multilateral agencies. In Viet Nam, UNICEF provides loan funds for programmes administered by national non-governmental organizations (NGOs). These programmes combine credit with access to basic social services and information, using tools such as the basic health manual, Facts for Life, and opportuni-ties such as the national literacy campaign. The results are positive: In one programme, 97 per cent of daughters of borrowers attend school compared with 73 per cent of daughters of non-borrowers.

Dramatic improvements in household food security were also observed, with only 12 per cent of borrowers reporting food shortages of three months or more compared with 73 per cent of non-borrower households. Communities identified having water closer to the home as a major need that they would like to see fulfilled through access to credit. In Cambodia, since 1988 UNICEF has provided core funds for microcredit through NGOs.

Microcredit helps build the borrower's confidence: By completing successful rounds of credit with the NGO, the borrower is in a better position to apply for credit with commercial lenders or state-owned banks. The programme is now managed by commercial banks and government departments. UNICEF no longer provides funds for credit, directing support instead at capacity-building at the dis-trict level.

Since the programme's inception, over 15,000 women have received credit. The recovery rate of 70 per cent is relatively low because it has been affected by severe fluctuations in borrowers' incomes because of droughts, flood and war. Based on national experience and exchange visits to the Grameen Bank, a savings component and a fund for insurance against natural disasters have been instituted.

In Egypt, the UNICEF-supported Family Development Fund Project was set up in 1993 in coop-eration with the Government. The programme, growing rapidly, now has 3,600 borrowers and is being implemented through local NGOs in four poor rural regions. Loans are used for small-scale enterprises in cattle raising, retail trades, food processing, sewing and handicrafts. Another 2,700 borrowers are reached through a programme that was initiated with UNICEF assistance, but that is now managed and run by a commercial bank.

In another scheme, microcredit is helping to com-bat child labour in an urban slum area by making credit available to poor women whose children work, as long as the children also attend school. The recovery rates in the various schemes are all over 95 per cent. A commercial bank has recently committed credit of almost $6 million for the poor to be lent through group-based schemes along the lines of the Grameen Bank model, with UNICEF providing technical support.

In India, UNICEF has supported the Development of Women and Children in Rural Areas (DWCRA) programme run by the Government, which in some regions advances loans to women. In Nellore and Anantapur Districts in the state of Andhra Pradesh, for example, women pool their savings as a group: the money is then used as a revolving fund from which members of the group can borrow, at above market rates of interest but still below moneylender rates.

Once the borrowers have shown that they can manage the payments, additional resources for loans are provided by the Government and donors. In some villages, these funds have been rotated 22 times since 1988. The credit is linked to access to basic social services and social development messages and as a result, the children of borrowers are healthier - almost 100 per cent of children are immunized.

Families have improved their nutritional status, through the cultivation of kitchen gardens, and they follow clean sanitary practices. Women have been empowered through the programme, openly discussing domestic violence, alcoholism and village conflicts. They are treated with greater respect by men and are more aware of their health needs, seeking medical attention for ailments that would have been endured silently in the past. It is recognized that while the empowerment of women is a process that will not happen automatically, credit is an important component for accelerating that process.

The Small Farmer Development Programme (SFDP), implemented by the Government of Nepal, gives loans of up to NRs30,000 on a group-collateral basis to small groups of farmers for various income-raising, agro-based enterprises. By 1992, the programme had formed 19,307 credit groups for men and 4,837 for women, each with 5 to 10 members. The groups covered 123,000 families whose annual per capita income was below NRs2,500.

UNICEF has supported SFDP in some areas since 1982-1983 with interventions in health, nutrition, education and water and sanitation. The repayment rate for the loans is above 80 per cent in the women's groups and 60 per cent in the men's. The loan repay-ment rates are higher in those areas where social interventions are combined with credit than in areas where credit alone is given.

Social indicators also show greater improvement in areas where credit is combined with delivery of basic social services:

- school attendance of girls between 5 and 14 years of age was higher in families that received both credit and support for basic social services than it was in families that received credit alone and in families in areas where there was no SFDP;
- infant mortality rates were lower in areas with a combined credit and basic social services approach than in areas where credit was extended without social services and in those where no credit was provided;

— the average number of child deaths from diarrhoea was reduced by 33 per cent in the areas where credit alone was provided and by 37 per cent where credit was combined with basic social service interventions;

— immunization coverage for BCG (tuberculosis), DPT3 (diphtheria, pertussis, tetanus), polio and measles was higher in areas of combined credit and social development interventions than in areas where credit alone was extended or where no programme was operating at all (83 per cent, 71 per cent and 61 per cent respectively);

— more women of reproductive age were immunized against tetanus and had greater knowledge of nutritional needs in areas where credit and basic social services were combined;

— the proportion of households with latrines was twice as high in areas where credit and basic social services were linked, compared with the areas where SFDP was not operating.

In areas where UNICEF gave support, 70 per cent of households built latrines after receiving SFDP credit compared with only 45 per cent where only SFDP provided assistance; v the percentage of households using tap water doubled in areas where SFDP extended only credit, but it rose by a factor of four when credit was linked with basic social services.

The Production Credit for Rural Women (PCRW) programme began with UNICEF support in 1982 in five districts of Nepal. In 1989, a basic social services component was added, along the lines of the successful experiences of the Grameen Bank in Bangladesh and the Self Employed Women's Association in India. The scheme targets women with household incomes below NRs2,500 per annum, and the loans offered vary from NRs500 initially up to NRs10,000 in the most successful cases. The repayment rate is 70 per cent.

UNICEF has supported a microcredit and savings programme since 1989 in Viet Nam. Implemented by the Viet Nam Women's Union, the programme has provided credit to 33,584 borrowers in 16 provinces. Borrowers form groups of between 10 and 15 members, and loans are made on a group-collateral basis. All the loans are to women. Many social indicators have shown improvement:

— 97 per cent of the daughters of the borrowers attend school compared with 73 per cent of daughters of non-borrowers;

— a survey showed that 73 per cent of the non-borrower house-holds faced food shortages of three months or more compared with 12 per cent of the households that had borrowed money. Borrower households no longer attribute food shortages to a lack of land and capital; they attribute them instead to reduced time for food production because of the need to care for small children;

— the project has also increased animal husbandry as a source of income, with 36 per cent of the borrowers considering this as their main occupation compared to 16 per cent of the non-borrowers.

In another UNICEF-supported scheme in Viet Nam, 9,600 women have benefited from a microcredit programme combined with literacy and education. Loans go to groups of women comprised of 20 to 30 members each in four provinces. Evaluation shows that:

— a vast majority of the borrowers (97 per cent) have significantly increased their household production since the project began in 1994;

— prior to receiving credit, 86 per cent of the borrower households faced a food shortage of more than one month. After the scheme was introduced, only 33 per cent of borrower households experienced food shortages compared to 77 per cent of the non-borrower households;

— although credit has increased household production, it is not clear whether it has enhanced borrowers' confidence and their capacity for decision-making. The empowerment of women, from this perspective, is still to be assessed; v there is a high demand by non-borrowers to join the scheme - 93 per cent of non-borrowers interviewed wanted access to project loans.

Since 1993, UNICEF has supported a number of microcredit schemes in poorer regions of Lower Egypt and in some urban slum areas. In Alexandria, a microcredit scheme run by a local NGO combines cred-it for women with efforts to combat child labour. Each borrowers' group comprises five women, two of whom have working children. The condition for the women's loans is that all the children should go to school.

This scheme, in an area with adequate access to basic edu-cation, has proved that microcredit can reduce child labour and improve school attendance while at the same time improving the income levels of the participating families. It also shows that parents are willing to send their children to school once the economic condi-tion of the family improves.

In two districts of Andhra Pradesh, thousands of women come togeth-er in small groups. They each save 1 rupee a day, pool their savings and rotate the sum among them-selves for production and day-to-day needs and as a source of capital for micro-enterprises. The Development of Women and Children in Rural Areas (DWCRA) scheme, supported by the Government and UNICEF, then extends further credit to the women once they have demonstrated their ability to form groups and save.

Women are proud to display their passbooks and speak of their experiences. In one village in Nellore District, for example, women have acquired land titles in their names and taken Rs180,000 as loans towards construction of their houses. They have said that they will not tolerate wife-beating and have forced their husbands to stop drinking alcohol. The longest-standing group in the village has rotated the revolving fund 25 times and also has a savings deposit of Rs30,000 in the bank.

In another village, a group has saved Rs800,000. In total, the women of the district have mobilized savings of Rs60 million. The women have used the revolving funds for productive activities, emergency consumption, health needs, marriages and children's education. The Total Literacy Campaign launched in the district in 1991 has brought education and information, with the savings groups becoming important centres for disseminating infor-mation on health, education, water and sanitation.

There are visible changes in the health and nutrition of women and their children. Women have identified sanitation as a major problem and are exploring possibilities of financing sanitation improvements, with matching funds from the Government. Women in the credit groups have a positive self-image, recognize their own health needs better and find themselves consulted by men, who realize that credit and information can be accessed through the women's savings groups.

In 1992, in Anantapur district, 1.2 million families were desti-tute and another 1.3 million lived just above the poverty line. In this area, a women's savings group, which initially handled Rs500, developed its creditworthiness and capacity to handle Rs18,000 in just 18 months. There are now around 6,000 groups, 3,500 of which are functioning well. With minimal training, the women began managing their own money and after six to eight months had built up a small amount of savings and rotated the fund among them-selves.

DWCRA funds were then made available to the successful groups. Almost all the children of the borrowers receiving DWCRA support attend school. As water is a major problem in this region, almost 6,000 dams and percolation tanks were planned, with the objective of harvesting rainwater. Efforts were integrated into the credit scheme to empower communities to safeguard their own environment.

Supporting Microcredit Initiatives

Grants for establishing loan capital and covering initial administrative costs are necessary to launch a microcredit scheme. These funds usually come from donors, United Nations agencies, international financial institutions and governments. Experience has shown that some groups can also generate these funds through their own savings. Microcredit programmes must sustain themselves by charging interest rates that are above market rates to recover the operating costs associated with extending small amounts of credit.

A major concern to the poor is their limited access to credit, not the relative cost of credit. A successful microcredit scheme requires a long-term commitment from government authori-ties, donors and NGOs because time and effort are needed to establish the infrastructure and to build the necessary capacities. It takes even longer to develop the trust, group confidence and financial discipline on the part of borrowers to make such schemes sustainable.

Partnerships between NGOs, financial institutions, donors and UN agencies are also time consuming but are essential for developing sustainable schemes. Such partnerships allow for greater outreach, as well as better identification of, and support to, the most appropriate local NGOs to manage the schemes.

Systems for monitoring and evaluating the schemes' performance are also important, and borrowers must be helped to graduate to other systems of credit.

The nature and extent of UNICEF support for microcredit is determined at the country level through the country programme process. The lessons learned from many experiences suggest that in view of limited resources and capacity, UNICEF's role in microcredit is primarily to be supportive of national schemes, with a view to maximizing their outreach and impact.

In certain countries, UNICEF plays a catalytic role in microcredit by working with governments to stimulate national efforts through NGOs and socially conscious financial institutions. Where UNICEF provides direct financial support, it covers areas such as creating a core capital fund for lending, building national capacities, and monitoring and evaluating activities to learn from experi-ence and adapt the schemes to the specific situation at local and national levels. Management of the schemes is most often in the hands of a partner organization.

All microcredit schemes that are supported by UNICEF primarily target poor women. In almost all countries, UNICEF advocates for basic social services and social communication to be linked with microcredit schemes in order to maximize the impact on the survival, protection and development of children and the empowerment of women.

Microcredit is not to be viewed as a charity or welfare-oriented programme. It should be run on sound business criteria with the objective of moving towards financial self-sustainability. UNICEF experience shows that the lasting impact of credit in reducing the worst manifestations of poverty can be enhanced when it is combined with basic social services and key social development messages.

The combination of access to microcredit and basic social services is an effective and cost-efficient approach to enable the poor to pull themselves out of poverty. Repayment rates among poor women borrowers are high, and significant improvements are seen in the health, nutrition and education of the most disadvantaged children. Microcredit, combined with basic social services and key social messages, is a powerful tool for reducing poverty.

4

South Asian Credit Access

In India, cooperative marketing was aimed at eradicating middlemen "where they are exploitative". Regulated marketing sought to reduce transactions costs to codify transactional practice and reduce the power of merchants by making private agricultural markets more open and competitive. Storage and anti-hoarding laws had the purpose of reducing price fluctuations caused by mercantile speculation, as did controls over futures trading contracts.

State storage schemes were intended to reduce the concentrated control of inventory by merchants. None of these interventions was meant to benefit merchants. It is entirely consistent with this orthodoxy that public sector credit should be lent to traders only under the strictest conditions. The Reserve Bank of India (RBI) curtails loans to private trade by nationalized and state-owned banks in three ways. One is exhortatory. Banks were "advised to keep a strict vigilance on advances and to check any tendency to utilize bank finance for hoarding" with reference to circumstances when agricultural wholesale prices had risen despite "comfortable supplies".

The second is mandatory. The RBI can set restrictions on

the value of private traders' stocks on which loans can be given, and can specify interest rates to be charged, generally set at or near the formal sector maximum. The third mechanism of regulation is diversionary. Nationalized and cooperative banks are required to lend a majority of their deposits to priority sectors in which private trade is conspicuous by its absence. Of late, the orthodoxy about private trade has been questioned.

New institutional channels for credit are being experimented with. Financial self-help organizations, landless credit and savings groups on the lines of Bangladesh's Grameen Bank are one. That private agricultural traders be used as credit agents, is another. Two different but related sets of circumstances have led to the present challenge: (1) the chronic failure of public sector, particularly cooperative, production credit, and (2) pressures to deregulate domestic markets, as part of the package of structural adjustment conditionali-ties.

The general cases for deploying food product merchants as credit agents for onward lending from public sector or state-regulated banking institutions takes four forms. The first argument, based on the formal assump-tions of neoclassical economics, is that, since distortions in financial markets are the result of mismanaged state intervention, then deregulation will "undistort" this market.

The second reason assumes that financial dualism is eroded by the cooption of merchants and the use of their pre-existing transactional networks. The third argument arises from the inadequacies of capital formation to enable the development of privatized agricultural marketing systems. The fourth argument in favor of traders as credit agents is that this is the most cost-effective and feasible response to the contraction of bank lending caused by the collapse of nationalized banks.

By lending to traders for on-lending, banks reduce transaction costs. Traders represent a restricted clientele which could be cheaply screened according either to collateral or to license possession, and onto whom would be shifted the bulk of costs of loan repayment collection. Traders, in turn, possess low cost information about their clients, which reduces the costs of monitoring and enforcement.

Their borrower-producers also face lower transaction costs. Information costs, costs of documentation, of access and of repayment are lower because of different customs for screening and collateral and because market transactions are minimized in repayment. Associated with the onward lending of traders is a range of interest rates and of social forms taken by interest. In India, state regulated credit for agricultural production is part of a package of agricultural subsidies amounting currently to 3 percent of GDP.

It has been estimated that the subsidy on agricultural credit alone touches Rs30 billion. In India, the argument for selecting traders as credit agencies is part and parcel of a strong advocacy in favor of the liberalization of agricultural credit. This liberalization implies reducing subsidies by increasing interest rates, ceasing the targeted direction of credit and removing credit control on the finance of inventory.

To use traders as credit agents is a controversial proposal in Indian agrarian conditions. First, costs of the monitoring and enforcement of fungible credit are indeterminate but very high. Second, and related to this, the existing theoretical models of exchange relations under differentiated owner-occupancy and under sharecropping both predict that moneylending traders will encourage the pre-harvest indebtedness of small peasants on terms and conditions which tie their post-harvest sales.

The marketable surplus will be price unresponsive and include an element of the producer's subsistence requirements which then requires repurchase on credit. Thus traders ensure a type of commerce which is "forced", not voluntary; and marketing takes place under "distress". Technical change and innovation adoption may be slowed down as a result. The further implication is that, unless we have evidence to the contrary, small-scale production may be perpetuated not by dint of superior efficiency but because of compulsive debt relations with merchants, or because of a mixture of efficiency criteria and credit relations, the terms of which are thus crucial.

Two clusters of hamlets in southern Andhra Pradesh, one accessible and the other remote, have been studied by Olsen. The agricultural economy is dominated by irrigated paddy and dryland groundnut. Agricultural production and the marketed surplus is dominated by relatively small capitalists and petty commodity producers. Rice is sold only by capitalist farmers and merchants. Groundnuts sales are dominated by capitalists, who nevertheless receive average prices little above those of small scale producers and below prices got by stocking traders.

Village traders dominate neither in terms of fixed assets nor in terms of numbers. They control the wholesale, retail and inputs markets, however, and are the major source of consumption and production credit, with sharp variations between the clusters of hamlets. While in the accessible hamlets 14 percent of all money borrowed by petty commodity producers was from traders and 34 percent from banks, in the remoter cluster 63 percent was from traders and 4 percent from banks.

In the remote cluster with a monopolistic market structure, speculative sellers are lent money at zero interest but have no alternative but to transact in wholesale and retail markets with the lender. Petty commodity producers are charged a high interest rate on credit and are also bound to the lender for transactions on retail and inputs markets at higher prices than those for speculative sellers. That mercantile moneylending (1) reduces the freedom of debtors to borrow elsewhere, (2) results in higher retail prices than for unindebted purchasers, and (3) results in lower groundnut prices to producers combined with control over the timing of current commodity flows.

The latter have led to the development of a market for water, able to operate independently of the more limited one for land. The agrarian structure of this dynamic locality is a mix of landless laborers, petty commodity producers and capitalist farmers. The cropping system is one of increasingly less diversified rice cultivation.

Agricultural trading credit operates quite differently from that in the maps so far. Two types of contract have been found. In the first, consumption credit in kind is provided by petty firms, from periodic marketplaces, to the agricultural and industrial labor force for repayment in cash. It is forced commerce all right, but confined to the assetless and nearly assetless wage labor force. Repayment is regulated via the mutual interests of lenders in the sharing of information about high risk purchasers and the withdrawal of credit sales to such indi-viduals.

Nevertheless, this credit is risky to the lender. In the second case, traders' credit supplies a system of indebted agents at interest rates rising to over 36 percent at the base of the hierarchy where producers of irrigated agro-industrial crops, such as tobacco and cotton, meet traders. Contracts are marked not only by differentials in explicit interest rates, but by the less calculable costs of delayed, unsymmetrical and uncompensated payments for commodities by lenders to borrowers.

The striking feature about trading credit in this developed area, however, is that the tying of money to supplies is much rarer. The borrower is able to repay a cash loan in cash and may deposit savings with the merchant. Both of these two contractual arrangements are likely to obtain only under conditions of comparative freedom of wage labor on the one hand and capital on the other.

Although tenurial reform in West Bengal has consolidated petty commodity producer forms of sharecrop-ping, and major irrigation has improved environmental security, agrarian structures are still complex and heterogeneous. Changes in the modalities of surplus extraction leave small-scale producers little better off than before.

The pace of compulsive commercialization by sharecroppers was forced in the early part of the century by the necessity to pay land revenue in cash. The lowering of levels of indebtedness by the time of the Great Famine in 1943 is evaluated as the unintended result of two Acts designed to regulate moneylending and protect debtors. These Acts encouraged erstwhile moneylenders to invest directly in land. Meanwhile famine beneficiaries who had acquired land stepped into the breach left by the moneylenders.

Much later on in the 1960s, public sector credit, particularly from cooperatives, emerged as a challenge to the by then well estab-lished class of rich peasant moneylenders. But default and therefore mass ineligibility for cooperatives' credit helped this class to retain their preeminence in the loan market. These financial relations persisted until Operation Barga, presenting sharecroppers with the choice between recording their tenancies and foregoing landlord's loans, or foregoing their legal shares and taking these loans at high implicit interest.

At this point, the rich peasant and landlords' credit dried up and a new set of financial intermediaries, wholesale traders and brokers in paddy, plugged the gap. These moneylending traders control the paddy wholesale and inputs markets. It is estimated that over half the so-called Barga tenants have recourse to such credit. Loans stipulate the timing and price of kind payment.

A tentative estimate for a region in Burdwan puts traders' credit in 1989-90 at twice the volume of that from nationalized and cooperative banks. The forms of crop and money markets and relations of exchange certainly do not prevent technical change, but do affect the speed and social profile of adoption as well as the distribution of gains. Financial markets cannot be assumed to be competitive. Credit contracts are one part of the economic dimensions of social relations of exchange.

The empirical work reviewed here suggests that relationships of traders' credit might contribute to the urbanization of finance, which in turn increases the velocity of rural-urban flows of money and increases the economic and spatial concentration of finance, as trading firms combine to invest in "finance corporations".

Under these conditions, disadvantaged cultivators will enjoy lower returns to production and have disproportionately fewer resources. However, traders' credit cannot be generalized a priori either as exploitative or as developmental. The longitudinal study of agrarian change in North Arcot District of Northern Tamil Nadu, for instance, revealed a real expansion in agricultural credit from nationalized and cooperative banks of only 14 percent during 1973-83 when production doubled, while pawnbrokers and private finance corporations increased by factors of ten and more.

State credit to traders first began in Tamil Nadu in 1967, when American pressure was being applied to free the fertilizer distribution network from the stranglehold of the cooperatives. This required vigorous promotional marketing. Traders' credit started with kind advances at zero interest from public sector fertilizer distributing companies to private dealers, who then lent onward at interest. Private companies rapidly followed suit with credit borrowed from nationalized banks on concessional terms.

These fertilizer dealers were almost always paddy and rice wholesalers too, some specifically selected as such. Intra-seasonal paddy and rice storage, encouraged as much as was onward lending, was a strategy of low risk and assured return for the principals. But secondly, the state also funds grain traders through fungible loans for Small Scale Industry, through short term crop production loans and medium term livestock or land improvement loans: 80 percent of the traders studied in Coimbatore District and 75 percent in Burdwan district were landowners.

Thirdly, although trade is not listed as a priority sector for formal credit, an interesting feature of Priority Sector credit concerns that targeted at "small enterprise", the "tertiary sector", "services", "retailing business" and so, euphemistically, on. According to evaluations by Lead Banks in their Credit Plans, these particular targets for directed, subsidized credit always overachieve.

Merchants at the apex of the system of trading and credit, whose assets averaged 200 times those of the mass of licensed and unlicensed petty traders at the base, were able to obtain credit from the West Bengal Finance Corporation and the National Cooperative Development Corporation averaging Rs90 lakhs per firm. The eight largest firms in our survey had state credit equal to 20,000 Integrated Rural Development Programme loans.

Fourthly, state credit can also be got on concessional terms on the basis of private receipts for goods for which support price have been announced, stored with the Central and State Government Warehouse Corporations. Banks are asked to guard that the borrower is a bona fide farmer. Many of the latter are also bona fide traders. Lastly, nationalized banks can and do give financial guarantees to rice milling and trading firms to enable them to operate on contract to the Food Corporation of India.

This is a low risk, high capacity utilizing option and liberates traders' own working capital for other adventures. There are also a number of direct support mechanisms. Nationalized banks are strongly supportive of regulated marketing. Successfully regulated markets physically centralize trade and improve traders' access to banks. Nationalized banks have been investing in branches located in urban and rural regulated marketplaces. Also, nationalized banks extend unsubsidized credit to traders.

Further, the World Bank and IDA via the Agro Finance Development Corporation have financed the private ownership of an estimated 8 million tons of agricultural storage. The Indian state thus finances private trade on a massive scale. But the capacity of the RBI's machinery to check and regulate the lending of banks to traders was grossly inadequate. Traders have been formal sector credit agents in India on a large scale for at least two decades. But this credit agency has been unregulated by banks, dominated by the largest traders and secret from the banks' point of view.

It is ironic that the major assumed fault line between the so-called formal sector and the informal sector does not reinforce financial dualism but instead is highly permeable. But it does reinforce complex social and economic relations through interlocked contracts. This onward lending has a number of highly desirable features for state sector lenders. Most importantly, although their borrowings are often at subsidized interest, mercantile borrowers can operate in a production environment with high co-variate risk but at low default risks and at the interest ceiling.

Further, from a social banking perspective, traders can

lend for consumption as well as for production at lower transaction costs than do banks since they exploit the informational transparency that results from social embeddedness. Traders' onward lending might also have undesirable features for precisely the social classes to the develop-ment of which nationalized banks are stated to be committed.

These classes, while being numerically strong, are economically weak and supply little of the marketed surplus. The terms and conditions of traders' credit cannot be explained only in terms of administrative costs and risks (even though the latter are practically incal-culable). Indian agricultural trading firms are not necessarily risk averse and are likely to be opportunistic in relations with small suppliers and in backward regions with a low density of banks.

Thus, the major challenge is to describe existing transactions and networks of traders in different socio-economic environments. Such an effort might be helpful to better appraise the possible effects and side-effects of the use of traders as credit agents. However, such information is not easy to obtain, and, provided traders repay loans, banks have no incentives to collect such costly information. Nor can they necessarily enforce, given the necessity of banks to lend, the likely prevalence of triadic sanctioning relations (if they cannot enforce all misdemeanor, they are unlikely to enforce any), and the common subversion of the legal process.

However, the use of smaller traders as credit agencies would make the Regulated Markets Acts even more difficult to implement, because the physical centralization of the first post-farm commodity transaction is unimplementable under conditions of decentralized traders' credit. Traders' credit does not invariably have an adverse impact especially when compared to conditions in its absence.

Credit Access in Rural Sri Lanka

For more than two decades, analysis of borrowers' transaction costs has served as the analytical tool to investigate decisions of borrowers pro or contra informal and formal lenders. Sri Lanka's Central Bank compares interest rates in its various surveys of rural credit markets. The 1976 survey among paddy farmers showed that a large number of loans in the informal sector carried a high interest rate, but also that this apparently did not deter customers.

Fernando comprehensively describes interest rates of informal lenders in Sri Lanka and the perception of these rates among borrowers. However, focusing on interest rates alone is not sufficient to explain borrowers' choices for or against a particular financial intermediary. To a borrower, the interest rate represents but one of a set of total loan costs, that also comprises opportunity costs of foregone labour, the costs of travelling to the lender, and administrative costs such as paying for loan application forms.

The various stages that the farmers have to pass through before they finally get their loans from the banks are beset with a number of obstacles. Running after guarantors and struggling to cut through official red tape are to mention two of the many handicaps that the farmers have to guard against. An internal report of the IFAD-supported Integrated Rural Development Project in Badulla suggests that loan transaction costs of informal sources are 14 percent lower than those of banks, opportunity costs of labour providing a decisive cost component.

Ranking lenders according to interest rates and transaction costs only, implies that borrowers most likely will make use of those lenders with lowest rates and costs. But borrowers' decisions to accept or reject are influenced by other factors as well. The following barriers may prevent potential borrowers from applying for a loan:

1. Prohibitions on lending to former defaulters;
2. Collateral may not be available, especially when land titles are required;
3. Guarantors may be difficult to find, especially for people without connections in the higher strata of village society. Even when this is the case, there is a problem if a regular tax payer is required as a guarantor. Borrowers in urban areas have found a way out of this. A secondary market for guarantors has emerged with brokers bringing borrowers and a guarantor together. This can easily be included as a transaction cost for the borrower, but in the villages an applicant without the right friends may have to abandon a credit application altogether if no wealthy guarantor supports his request for a loan;
4. Some people have psychological barriers against using banks, or cannot cope with the complex procedure of a credit application typical of many institutional lenders;
5. Social proximity and personal knowledge between creditor and debtor. On the one hand, lack of close personal ties can constitute a barrier to entry. On the other hand, a borrower might not choose the most cost effective loan source, but the lender with whom he feels most comfortable in requesting a loan;
6. One may be excluded from borrowing because of political reasons.

Many borrowers are not able to overcome these barriers irrespective of the transaction cost level. An analysis explaining decisions for or against certain loan sources should take these barriers into account. Even if there are no barriers to entry into the rural credit market, borrowers' decisions may still be influenced by factors other than those usually typified as transaction costs for borrowers, such as:

1. Flexibility of repayment: moneylenders are an attractive source of loans because they often do not demand any specific date for repayment of the principal as long as the interest payments are serviced;
2. Mismatch of credit offered and actual loan needed;
3. Sanctions in case of non-repayment can deter credit applicants even from credit sources with low transaction costs;

It is interesting to observe that the bias towards a ranking order in the transaction cost analysis is self-deter-mining because transaction costs are only calculated for customers who already have entered a credit transaction. Potential applicants, not able to overcome the barriers of entry, are not included in the analysis. But how can a method highlight decision patterns, when the approach only encompasses actual borrowers, and neglects rejected applicants or those with the rational expectation to be rejected should they try to utilize a certain source?

In summary, the transaction cost approach not only fails to address important factors influencing entry into the credit market, but also reinforces this bias by the methods it employs. Low transaction costs are therefore not admission tickets to financial services. Only if access barriers of different sorts are overcome will transaction costs play a role as a useful tool for explaining decisions of borrowers for or against certain financial intermediaries.

The analysis of borrowers' decisions has nevertheless benefitted from the introduction of transaction cost calculations. Instead of focusing on the interest rates of a loan only, other components are included as well. The following method to analyze borrowers' decisions attempts to cover all relevant components of a loan contract. As a first step, these loan components are identified. Their relative importance to rural borrowers is then assessed in two field studies. These loan contract components are:

1. Average distance of lenders to borrowers;
2. Sanctions in case of late or non-repayment;
3. Conditions of lender for use of loans;
4. Interest rate levels;
5. Timely provision of loans;
6. Loan amounts;
7. Repayment periods;
8. Securities required;
9. Guarantor arrangements demanded by intermediaries.

The village of Mabodale in the Gampaha district, about 50 kilometers north of the Sri Lankan capital Colombo, was selected as characteristic of a semi-urban location in the immediate vicinity of the Katunayake Free Trading Zone.

Mabodale consists of 716 households. Six months were spent in this village to implement the field survey. The second village, Makkaduwawe, was chosen in a purely agricultural setting in a remote location, the Northern Kurunegala district. The village consists of 204 households.

The village Mabodale is located in the low country wet zone. Mean annual temperatures of this zone vary between 27 and 29 degrees celsius, with a relative daytime humidity of about 70 percent. The annual rainfall of about 2500 mm peaks during April-May and October-November, and determines the two cropping seasons, Maha and Yala.

Villagers work in Colombo or in the adjacent Katunayake

Free Trading Zone. Consequently, part-time farming is widespread. Cropping patterns are dominated by coconut, unirrigated paddy and fruits and vegetables that thrive in the humid tropical climate. Animal husbandry plays a minor role only.

Small industries in the village comprise two handloom weaving shops. Micro-enterprises are operated alongside a nearby through road or within the houses. Seasonal agricultural work is common. A period of violent political conflict caused by a Singhalese guerilla movement, the Janatha Veramukti Peramuna (JVP), came to an end in 1989. Villagers were seriously affected by the prolonged period of political instability and civil unrest: loss of life was minor, but income losses were considerable.

Makkaduwawe village borders the Sri Lankan dry zone. It is situated in a remote and isolated part of the Northern Kurunegala District, with only one small town nearby. Agriculture predominates in Makkaduwawe, where almost all heads of households are full-time farmers. Farming in the village with mean annual temperatures of 30 degrees celsius, and less than 1000 mm precipitation, relies heavily on irrigation. Rainwater is collected in catchment basins.

Water shortage allows regular cultivation only in the Maha cropping season. Paddy is the predominant crop, largely for subsistence needs. The climate does not allow the cultivation of coconuts. Necessary products like coconut leaves, nuts or trunks have to be imported from the southern part of the district. Micro-enterprises are restricted to shopkeepers, carpenters and a laundry business run by a family of the low dhobi (washermen) caste.

The village is very impoverished; 70 percent of the adults are food stamp recipients and incomes from farming are much lower than in the semi-urban village. Farmers suffered extensively from the period of political unrest. The JVP ordered bans on farming which decreased the already small incomes to critical levels. Borrowing in this village is mainly to ensure a minimum food supply.

The threat of a possible denial of a future loan seems a sufficient incentive for high repayment rates in the informal sector. Conditions of Lenders for the Use of Loans. Banks and NGOs 2 generally require loan applicants to state the intended loan purpose. Exceptions are advances against the deposit of a pawn or the small instant loans from NGOs. Field officers of banks inspect the use of loan capital when large loans are involved.

Studies in Sri Lanka generally emphasize the existence of very high interest rates in the informal sector, but Fernando notes that only a relatively small proportion carries an exorbitant rate of interest. The lower the interest rates the higher the probability that low risk investments are undertaken with low economic rates of return and consequently detrimental effects to the economy.

NGOs charge higher rates, because they do not subsidize loans. NGOs in the remote village charge the higher rates, since they had to add an extra risk premium for defaults stemming from the prolonged political unrest in this village. The interest rate structure of banks, particularly in the remote location, indicates market distortions: the spread between average deposit and lending rates is too small to operate profitably, especially in the light of higher default rates in this location.

Borrowers from informal sources face a wide range of interest rates. Loans from friends and relatives are interest-free. Traders provide loans to strengthen relationships with customers. Shopkeepers advance small amounts free of interest. The competition for customers is so strong in the small shops in both villages that shop owners are often forced into credit arrangements.

Many traders-cum-lenders in the semi-urban location are produce buyers. In the remote village, no trader engages exclusively in the marketing of agricultural produce. Some shopkeepers buy rice and dried pepper from the farmers as a side line. The erratic supply and subsistence orientation of farmers in the remote location limits advances against future supply of produce.

Moneylenders charge the highest rates of interest, averaging about 160 percent if calculated on an annual basis. But such calculation distorts the picture. If the loan amount is small and repaid after only a short period, borrowers are willing to pay these rates even when having access to other, but less flexible, credit sources.

Villagers who did not borrow stated that high interest rates of bank loans would explain the popularity of other credit sources. Actual borrowers, however, judged differently. Generally speaking, the lower the interest rate level, the longer the waiting time and the more demanding the requirements that have to be met. The pioneering effort of the People's Bank, which included advances for pawned jewellery, stands out as a successful innovation in rural finance in SriLanka.

Vidanapathirana estimates that pawning loans have become the single most important credit type offered by rural banks. The banks reap the profit, as pawning loans bear high interest rates, as do the customers, who have quick access to institutional advances. Speedy advance of loans is a common feature of all informal finance systems and another crucial variable that explains the popularity of informal financial intermediaries in rural Sri Lanka.

Respondents from the wider sample, not necessarily

themselves indebted, did not mention untimely disbursal or lengthy credit procedures as a major problem of rural borrowers. But asked why many people use sources other than banks, 30 percent in the semi-urban village and 20 percent in the remote location explained this with delayed credit disbursals and lengthy application procedures for institutional loans.

The volume of a loan plays an important role in the overall success of a business investment or a consumption loan. The analysis of loan amounts in the Sri Lankan context reveals some interesting insights into the lending philosophy of informal and formal financial intermediaries.

High standard deviation values point to highly variable loan amounts. Loans taken from friends and relatives are the second most important informal source of loans. In both villages the average loan size from this source comes to about two thirds of that of moneylenders. Traders give the smallest loans, especially village shop owners. Shop owners often use credit ceilings. Small farmers, occasional customers, and customers without safe income prospects get smaller advances.

Customers with regular incomes, in particular salaried people, get larger loans and are expected to settle outstanding claims at pay day. Farmers are granted longer repayment periods, until they have harvested their crops. No other formal or informal loan source in the survey villages extends credits of the size of Sri Lankan banks. In the remote village, banks offer average amounts almost four times higher than those of NGOs and moneylenders.

Banks apparently have a strong competitive advantage in this respect. NGOs, like the Sanasa credit cooperatives, set fairly limited credit ceilings which vary from group to group. Consequently, bank borrowers do not complain receiving only part of the amount demanded, as is the case with loans from informal intermediaries. Data from the semi-urban village illustrate an identical ranking of credit sources, but on a higher overall transaction level.

The higher loan amounts are mainly attributable to higher incomes and therefore better repayment potential in agricultural and non-agricultural professions. Further, the booming and dynamic economic environment promises higher returns on invested capital.

Moneylenders in the remote village do not insist on firm repayment schedules as long as the interest is paid regularly. This practice was also common in the semi-urban location. However, 17 percent of the loans granted by moneylenders in this location had fixed dates. Banks and NGOs have clearly defined loan maturities. They do, however, readjust agreed repayment schedules if events beyond the control of borrowers affect debt servicing. Average repayment periods of bank loans in Kurunegala and Gampaha are 44 months and 38 months respectively.

NGOs, who distribute much smaller loan amounts, operate with shorter repayment periods: seven months in the remote village and 15 months in the semi-urban village. Borrowers from banks and NGOs, asked whether repayment periods should be different than as stipulated in the loan contract, approve of these repayment schedules.

The views of actual borrowers on repayment periods of formal lenders somewhat differ from those of respondents in the total sample. In the remote location, seven percent of the villagers thought that repayment periods of banks are too short, against only three percent in the semi-urban location.

The idea of playing with someone else's money is an appealing one: if the borrower's investment project is successful he gains, but if it fails, someone else loses. By requiring security, the lender encourages the borrower in the most direct way to carefully judge the likely success of his proposed investment. However, banks operating in rural areas of low-income countries are often state-owned and have the specific mandate to extend loans to the rural poor.

The People's Bank and its network of Cooperative Rural Banks in Sri Lanka are a typical example. Many poor applicants do not dispose of land titles or similar securities and are therefore in danger of being excluded from the institutional credit market. From the opinions expressed in the wider sample of villagers, it becomes clear that the lack of suitable collateral constitutes indeed a major barrier for would-be borrowers. The inability to find securities was cited by 20 percent of the respondents as a major problem and a reason for resorting to lenders other than banks.

Traders, i.e. village shopkeepers and produce buyers, also operate without tangible securities, although produce buyers lay claim on the future crop. The personal relationship between borrower and lender is seen as sufficient guarantee for repayment of the loan. But moneylenders in the two villages do demand securities for loans extended, although the percentage that does is far below the figures in the nationwide survey of credit and indebtedness of 1976 when a reported 47 percent of the moneylenders secured their loans with some kind of tangible collateral.

In the remote village, the percentage is 25, as against only 16 percent of the moneylenders in the semi-urban village. The items range from bicycles to tape recorders, registration papers for motorcycles and cars to jewellery. From interviews with moneylenders it appears that securities increase the repayment morale of credit customers.

The most successful moneylenders in both survey areas were the ones with variable and sometimes sophisticated security arrangements. Banks resort to a wide mix of security and guarantee arrangements. Provisions differ according to the loan scheme and even for the same type of loan, different branches of the same bank asking for different securities, relying on personal judgement of bank staff rather than on rigid rules.

NGOs operate without collateral arrangements. The Sanasa credit cooperatives outperform other NGOs in terms of business outreach and repayment rates in both villages. Primary credit cooperatives advance loans largely from member deposits. Loans are granted individually.

Apart from small sized instant loans, credits are advanced only when two group members guarantee repayment of a credit applicant with their savings deposits. Other NGOs operate similarly with guarantee arrangements as collateral substitutes. Depending on the level of cohesion in the group, the repayment results differ. Wherever a group is on the verge of disintegration, the guarantor scheme no longer ensures the recovery of outstanding loans.

The village study underscored the problem of guarantee arrangements. This factor, not considered in a transaction cost approach, is of crucial importance in loan contracts in the two villages. About 55 percent of bank loans in both villages require guarantee arrangements. Loans from credit cooperatives are also mostly secured by guarantors. In the semi-urban village, a sizeable portion of loans from NGOs are small sized instant loans without requirements for third party guarantors.

ICT as a Development Instrument in Rural Nepal

The importance and potential of information and communication technologies in sustainable development and poverty reduction contexts is being slowly recognized in Nepal. These technologies to achieve sustainable development goals by creating knowledge based society and leveraging the power of ICTs to help extend the outreach of public service delivery to the people living in remote rural areas of Nepal.

While poverty and development do have definite cognitive dimensions where ICT's can theoretically have a substantial role, the issues regarding application of these technologies in addressing these dimensions effectively and efficiently still remains a gray area in that it involves a complex array of variables involving policy, institutional, demographic and infrastructure dimensions. This underscores the need to analyze real potential of these technologies to support good governance and poverty reduction initiatives and develop proper social-appropriation models of the application of ICTs aligned with ground realities of Nepal.

Given that ICT's are only means and not an end in themselves, best model of their application in development and poverty reduction contexts have to be premised around the ways of integrating these technologies into development strategies that have proven to be effective. The idea of building capabilities of rural hinterland areas so as to create better conditions for their integration into urban market systems has been practiced as an effective working model of development by Rural-Urban Partnership Programme (RUPP) in Nepal.

The study on *Assessing feasibility of ICTs as a development instrument for rural-urban linkage in Nepal* looks into the prospects of leveraging the power of ICT's to further catalyze RUPP's on-going efforts in the area of strengthening rural-urban linkage. The RUPP approach produces rapid and tangible results because it shows how urban centres, by enhancing the mutual interests and linkages between rural and urban areas, can stimulate the dynamics of trade linkages between them: creating conditions for enhanced economic and social exchanges for mutual benefits - a prospect that stands to be further catalyzed through proper application of ICTs. This defines the context for the current SPPD project which encompasses three distinct activity components:

a) developing a refined feasibility study on the use of ICT as an instrument for facilitating and promoting social and economic development, with particular focus on e-governance and e-commerce in rural-urban setting,

b) developing a strategic plan of action for pilot-testing for RUPP and then implementing ICT as an instrument for facilitating e-governance and e-commerce to stimulate pro-poor rural-urban linkages and

c) developing a refined strategic plan of action incorporating recommendations and lessons learnt through outcomes of piloting.

The pilot implementation will be collaborative initiative with RUPP acting as one of the principal collaborators and serving as a springboard to launch the pilot. At the central level, the implementation of pilot will be managed through PMU of RUPP. A joint MOU will be signed between SPPD, RUPP and partner municipality to carry out the pilot activities at the municipal wards and RMC.

At the municipality level, the pilot activities will be implemented through Implementation Management Committees formed to implement activities of RUPP. The pilot activities at a municipal ward level include establishment of Community Resource Centres (telecentres) in a particular ward selected for piloting. Such activities will be carried out through the formation Telecenter Users Committees (TUC) in the selected ward.

The pilot activities at Rural Market Centres (RMC's) will be launched through Implementation Management Committees of RMC. Market Centre Facilitators (MCF) recruited through RUPP will also function as the telecentre manager for RMC level telecentre. The pilot activities will be monitored and supervised by central level Steering Committee functioning as an apex body. For this purpose, existing Steering Committee of RUPP will be expanded to include representation from Ministry of Science and Technology, National Information Technology Centre (NITC) and United Nations Centre for Human Settlement (UN-HABITAT).

It has been expected that the strategy of building upon the initial headway made by RUPP in the area of e-governance and e-commerce with additional professional inputs and expanded scope in terms of expanded accessibility to ICT resources through establishment of Community Resource Centres (telecentres) and refinement of ICT based development models through SPPD support will generate important policy feedback with macro-level implications specially with regards to the developmental role of ICTs in rural-urban settings.

Urban Information Centres (UIC's) located within municipalities will serve as important institutional outfits that could facilitate local efforts aimed at harnessing digital means to achieve local development objectives. Analyzed on the basis of predefined monitoring and evaluation indicators, the findings and outcomes of pilot implementation of SPA will form the basis for its further refinement with policy implications with potentials to transcend RUPP's area of operations.

The proposed pilot implementation encompasses a comprehensive strategic orientation involving 3 key aspects of harnessing ICT's in good governance and poverty reduction contexts within a larger purview of development potential embedded in rural-urban continuum:

a) accessibility,

b) Institutional issues and local capacities and

c) development models.

Given current asymmetry in access to ICTs between urban and rural areas and even within these areas, any development model that seeks to leverage digital means to address key good governance and poverty reduction challenges must factor into account the accessibility issues. Under current pilot implementation, strategies aimed at working out development models and strengthening institutional capacities to harness ICT's to address these challenges will be complemented by establishment of Community Resource Centres - telecentres - in municipal wards and Rural Market Centres where RUPP programme has been launched.

These centers will provide access to ICTs to the immediate stakeholders and community members in selected wards of the municipalities and Rural Market Centres. More specifically, these centres will provide community access to e-Commerce and e-Governance (with urban governance orientation) around which this pilot implementation has been modeled. At least 17 such telecentres will be established in municipal wards and Rural Market Centres (RMC's).

Operating under a challenging environment characterized by relative novelty of the approaches in local conditions and the need to adapt and localize ICT based implementations accordingly, RUPP's activities in e-governance and e-commerce can be considered significant entry level initiatives which have served as logical extension of its efforts in the development of information systems and establishment of Urban Information Centres (UIC) in the 12 partner municipalities where the Programme has been implemented. Notwithstanding the fact that community based telecentres are primarily meant to provide digital means of further articulating rural-urban linkages and transforming these dynamics into tangible socio-economic gains for the intended beneficiaries, there is a need to devise a broad based footing for the pilot activities.

This underscores the need to factor in the roles of various institutions at the local level that define key elements of a synergistic framework for the creation of value through ICTs to the communities - more particularly e-governance and B2B e-commerce initiative launched by RUPP. Such institutions include:

— *Users committees in municipal wards and Rural Market Centres*: responsible for day-to-day operation of the telecentre by providing guidance, management and operational support for the centre

— *TLO*: forms telecentre user committee, hosts telecentres by providing physical facilities and sharing resources, uses telecentre resources for enhancing prospects productive economic activities and local development

— *Municipality*: Implements pilot at the local level including a selected municipal ward, shares resources and provides implementation and coordination support through IMC to launch the pilot activities in selected Rural Market Centre.

— *VDC (Rural Market Centres)*: Implements pilot through Rural Market Centre level IMC, provides physical facilities and shares resources, forms telecentre user committees involving members of TLO's.

— *Local Chapters of Chambers of Commerce*: Hosts B2B e-commerce portal, provides sustained operational support to B2B, works closely with local entrepreneurs Equally important from the sustainability perspective is the issue of capacities of these institutions in terms of being able to harness ICT resources to further their development objectives.

The pilot implementation envisages to carry out activities towards raising the level of awareness and building capacities of key partner institutions - municipalities, VDC's, Tole/Lane Organizations (TLO's) and CCI's. Under the pilot implementation, activities will be undertaken to ensure that the capabilities of Rural Market Centres (VDC's) are enhanced in such a way that they are able to sustain local level ICT based initiative without outside support.

The establishment of telecentres in Rural Market Centres (VDC's) also creates conditions for facilitating governance linkages between RMC's and the urban centres provided district level line agencies also wake up to the opportunity. Arrangements will be worked out to engage RUPP trained Market Centre Facilitators in piloting who, given their development orientation, would be best suited to furthering ICT and development agenda at the local level. Similarly, the municipality will assign a ward secretary to manage the telecentre.

The pilot activities will entail implementation of development models that constitute key elements of SPA under the larger framework of rural-urban linkages. Apart from a host of systemic issues, this includes analyzing current initiative of RUPP, isolating the gaps and strengths therein and extrapolating the same to map out macro-level strategies - in essence a road map - for application of ICTs as instruments of development in rural-urban setting in general and within e-governance and e-commerce framework in particular. On the level of specific activities, this includes refinement as well as development of e-commerce (eMarket Place) as well as eGovernance models.

5

Rural Development through Peoples Participaiton

Poverty and a degraded environment are closely inter-related, especially where people depend for their livelihoods primarily on the natural resource base of their immediate environment. Restoring natural systems and improving natural resource management practices at the grassroots level are central to a strategy to eliminate poverty. The survival needs of the poor force them to continue to degrade an already degraded environment.

Removal of poverty is therefore a prerequisite for the protection of the environment. Poverty magnifies the problem of hunger and malnutrition. The problem is further compounded by the inequitable access of the poor to the food that is available. It is therefore necessary to strengthen the public distribution system to overcome this inequity.

Diversion of common and marginal lands to 'economically useful purposes' deprives the poor of a resource base which has traditionally met many of their sustenance needs. Market forces also lead to the elimination of crops that have traditionally been integral to the diet of the poor, thereby threatening food security and nutritional status.

While conventional economic development leads to the elimination of several traditional occupations, the process of sustainable development, guided by the need to protect and conserve the environment, leads to the creation of new jobs and of opportunities for the reorientation of traditional skills to new occupations.

Women, while continuing to perform their traditional domestic roles' are increasingly involved in earning livelihoods. In many poor households they are often the principal or the sole breadwinners. A major thrust at the policy level is necessary to ensure equity and justice for them.

Literacy and a basic education are essential for enabling the poor to access the benefits offered by development initiatives and market opportunities. Basic education is therefore a precondition for sustainable development. A sizeable proportion (about 60 per cent according to some estimates) of the population is not integrated into the market economy. Ensuring the security of their livelihoods is an imperative for sustainable development.

With increasing purchasing power, wasteful consumption linked to market driven consumerism is stressing the resource base of developing countries further. It is important to counter this through education and public awareness. In several areas, desirable limits and standards for consumption need to be established and applied through appropriate mechanisms including education, incentives and legislation. Several traditional practices that are sustainable and environment friendly continue to be a regular part of the lives of people in developing countries. These need to be encouraged rather than replaced by more 'modern' but unsustainable practices and technologies.

Development decisions regarding technology and

infrastructure are a major determinant of consumption patterns. It is therefore important to evaluate and make development decisions which structurally lead to a more sustainable society. Technologies exist through which substantial reduction in consumption of resources is possible. Efforts to identify, evaluate, introduce and use these technologies must be made.

Subsidies often lead to wasteful and unsustainable consumption by distorting the value of a resource. The integration of agriculture with land and water management, and with ecosystem conservation is essential for both environmental sustainability and agricultural production. An environmental perspective must guide the evaluation of all development projects, recognizing the role of natural resources in local livelihoods. This recognition must be informed by a comprehensive understanding of the perceptions and opinions of local people about their stakes in the resource base.

To ensure the sustainability of the natural resource base, the recognition of all stakeholders in it and their roles in its protection and management is essential. There is need to establish well-defined and enforceable rights (including customary rights) and security of tenure, and to ensure equal access to land, water and other natural and biological resources. It should be ensured that this applies, in particular, to indigenous communities, women and other disadvantaged groups living in poverty.

Water governance arrangements should protect ecosystems and preserve or restore the ecological integrity of all natural water bodies and their catchments. This will maintain the wide range of ecological services that healthy ecosystems provide and the livelihoods that depend upon them. Biomass is, and will continue for a long time to be, a major source of fuel and energy, especially for the rural poor.

Recognizing this fact, appropriate mechanisms must be evolved to make such consumption of biomass sustainable, through both resource management and the promotion of efficient and minimally polluting technologies, and technologies which will progressively reduce the pressures on biomass, which cause environmental degradation. The traditional approaches to natural resource management such as sacred groves and ponds, water harvesting and management systems, etc., should be revived by creating institutional mechanisms which recapture the ecological wisdom and the spirit of community management inherent in those systems.

Globalization as it is taking place today is increasing the divide between the rich and the poor. It has to be steered so that it serves not only commercial interests but also the social needs of development. Global business thrives on, and therefore encourages and imposes, high levels of homogeneity in consumer preferences. On the other hand, for development to be locally appropriate and sustainable, it must be guided by local considerations which lie in cultural diversity and traditions.

Therefore recognition at the policy level, of the significance of diversity, and the need to preserve it, is an important precondition for sustainable development. In an increasingly globalizing economy, developing countries, for want of the appropriate skills, are often at a disadvantage in negotiating and operating multilateral trade agreements. Regional cooperation for capacity building is therefore necessary to ensure their effective participation in all stages of multilateral trade. Globalization is driven by a vast, globally spread, human resource engine involving millions of livelihoods.

Their security is sometimes threatened by local events causing global distortions. Mechanisms to safeguard trade and livelihoods, especially in developing countries, must be evolved and negotiated to make globalization an effective vehicle of sustainable development. War and armed conflict are a major threat to sustainable development. It is imperative to evolve effective mechanisms for mediation in such situations and to resolve contentious issues without compromising the larger developmental goals of the conflicting parties.

Human Health and Sustainable Development

Human health in its broadest sense of physical, mental and spiritual well-being is to a great extent dependent on the access of the citizen to a healthy environment. For a healthy, productive and fulfilling life every individual should have the physical and economic access to a balanced diet, safe drinking water, clean air, sanitation, environmental hygiene, primary health care and education.

Access to safe drinking water and a healthy environment should be a fundamental right of every citizen. Citizens of developing countries continue to be vulnerable to a double burden of diseases. Traditional diseases such as malaria and cholera, caused by unsafe drinking water and lack of environmental hygiene, have not yet been controlled. In addition, people are now falling prey to modern diseases such as cancer and AIDS, and stress-related disorders. Many of the widespread ailments among the poor in developing countries are occupation-related, and are contracted in the course of work done to fulfil the consumption demands of the affluent, both within the country and outside.

The strong relationship between health and the state of the environment in developing countries is becoming increasingly evident. This calls for greater emphasis on preventive and social medicine, and on research in both occupational health and epidemiology. Because of the close link, there needs to be greater integration between the ministries of Health and Environment, and effective coordination and cooperation between them. Basic health and educational facilities in developing countries need to be strengthened.

The role of public health services must give preventive health care equal emphasis as curative health care. People should be empowered through education and awareness to participate in managing preventive health care related to environmental sanitation and hygiene. Most developing countries are repositories of a rich tradition of natural resource-based health care. This is under threat, on the one hand from modern mainstream medicine, and on the other from the degradation of the natural resource base.

Traditional medicine in combination with modern medicine must be promoted while ensuring conservation of the resource base and effective protection of IPRs of traditional knowledge. Developing countries should also strive to strengthen the capacity of their health care systems to deliver basic health services and to reduce environment-related health risks by sharing of health awareness and medical expertise globally.

Mainstream education must now be re-aligned to promote awareness, attitudes, concerns and skills that will lead to sustainable development. Basic education which promotes functional literacy, livelihood skills, understanding of the immediate environment and values of responsible citizenship is a precondition for sustainable development. Such education must be available to every child as a fundamental right, without discrimination on the basis of economic class, geographical location or cultural identity.

Private investment cannot replace development aid as it will not reach sectors relevant for the poor. Such investments and other mechanisms can at best be additional to, not replacements for, development assistance. Conditions attached to financial assistance need to be rigorously scrutinized, and the assistance accepted only if the conditionalities are acceptable.

Financial support for sustainable development programmes must not be negatively influenced by political considerations external to the objectives of the assistance.

Trade regimes, specifically WTO, are sometimes in conflict with sustainable development priorities. Imperatives of trade, and the concerns related to environment, equity and social justice however need to be dealt with independently.

Environmental and social clauses which are implicitly or explicitly part of international agreements must not be used selectively to erect trade barriers against developing countries. Developing countries will suffer a major trade disadvantage if the efforts to put in place globally acceptable Process and Production Methods (PPMs) are successful. Instead, existing disparities between the trade regimes and multilateral environmental agreements, such as those between Trade Related Intellectual Property Rights (TRIPS) regime and the Convention on Biological Diversity (CBD), should be thoroughly addressed. Mechanisms to resolve such conflicts between multilateral agreements should be set up.

Developing countries need not follow the conventional path to development with regard to technologies but must use to their advantage the cutting-edge technology options now available to 'leapfrog', and put the tools of modern technology to use.

Mechanisms must be put in place to make available to developing countries the latest technologies at reasonable cost. Technology transfer must be informed by an understanding of its implications in the social, economic and environmental contexts of the receiving societies. Technologies must be usable by and beneficial to local people. Where possible, existing local technologies must be upgraded and adapted to make them more efficient and useful. Such local adaptations should also lead to the upgradation of local technical skills.

Local innovations and capacity building for developing and managing locally relevant and appropriate technologies must be encouraged and supported. Integrating highly-sophisticated modern technology with traditional practices sometimes produces the most culturally-suited and acceptable solutions, which also makes them more viable. This trend should be encouraged.

The paramount importance of education in effecting social change is recognized.opment are essential. An understanding must be promoted among key decision makers of the potential of education to promote sustainability, reduce poverty, train people for sustainable livelihoods and catalyze necessary public support for sustainable development initiatives. The empowerment of women and girls must be supported by actions to improve their access to basic and higher education, training and capacity building. The emphasis should be on gender mainstreaming.

With India's population crossing a billion in the year 2000, the National Population Policy announced in that year has special significance. Its change in focus from merely setting target population figures to achieving population control through greater attention to socio-economic issues such as child health and survival, illiteracy, empowerment of women, and increased participation by men in planned parenthood, gives it greater breadth and depth, thereby holding forth better promise of achieving its long-term objective of a stable population by mid-century.

There is need for a better and more widespread understanding that the number of children desired by any couple depends on a large and complexly interrelated number of socio-economic and cultural factors, and that any policy action seeking to control population must seriously take all these variables into account. An important part of empowering women in matters pertaining to population, is to explicitly recognize and respect their rights over their bodies and their reproductive behaviour.

This recognition must permeate society in general, and religious, judicial and law-enforcement institutions in particular, through continual campaigning and dialogue.

Effective management of resources requires participation by all stakeholders. At the local level, strengthening democratic institutions generally leads to better and more sustained management of natural resources. To enhance effectiveness of people's participation in local governance, committees comprising both elected and executive members of local bodies and representatives of community groups, must be formed.

There are many traditional systems and practices whose value and validity needs to be recognized and brought into the mainstream of governmental development thinking and policy. Appropriate mechanisms for integrating them need to be created. Many policies were framed either before sustainable development became a major concern or in a sectoral perspective. These need to be reviewed from the point of view of sustainable development.

All future policies must be guided by considerations of sustainable development. Areas lacking policies should be identified and adequate policies compatible with the imperatives of sustainable development framed, taking into account successful examples, of policies and initiatives in similar areas. There is both a need and a scope for regional and global cooperation in sustainable development.

Some of the areas of common concern are marine and riparian issues, transboundary environmental impacts, management of bioresources, technology sharing and sharing of sustainable development experiences. Efforts must be made, especially by developing countries, to work towards synergizing experiences and raising shared regional concerns as a strong united front in international forums.

During 1990's, in Andhra Pradesh, there is significant improvement in literacy level of the rural population. But the employment opportunities have not improved. As a result, there is huge stock of educated unemployed constituting both male and female in rural areas of Andhra Pradesh. Although, the state has achieved remarkable progress in establishing schools, Junior Colleges and Degree colleges during 1980-81 and 2000-01, most of them were in private sector.

The number of high schools increased from 4106 to 10,359, Junior Colleges 398 to 2449, Degree Colleges 450 to 1157 during the same time. There is marketisation of education in Andhra Pradesh in recent years. Only the elite class children could reap the benefits of private education. The economy of the state is basically agrarian in character. The percentage of irrigated area is very low i.e., below 40 percent. The plan allocations by the state Government for irrigation had been declining from plan to plan.

Though the state is well endowed with natural resources and minerals, it is lagging behind other states in the country with regard to per capital income, literacy level and other parameters. There is no significant improvement in the number of hospitals/ dispensaries available in the state during 1980-81 and 2000-01. But the availability of government doctors improved compared to availability of infrastructure, medicines and other facilities.

However, in most of the hospitals, appointed doctors are on long leave or even on lien, causing hardships to the rural people, particularly Scheduled Castes, Scheduled Tribes and socially backward Sections of the society. Though there is an increase of 20 percent of irrigation facilities through canal irrigation during the last 47 years of state formation. The tank irrigation declined from 10.68 lakh hectares in 1955-56 to 9.00

lakh hectares in 1980-81, to 7.47 lakh hectares in 1995-96 and it remained at 7.47 lakh hectares in 2000-01, while well irrigation increased by more than three fold during the same time.

The Gross area irrigated has been on the increase from 26.56 percent in 1956-57 to 44.12 over the years due to increase in dugwells and borewells. The percentage of area under food crops is higher in Coastal Andhra when compared to Telangana and Rayalaseema. However, the proportion of area under non-food crops has been increasing over the years. This is due to the changes in cropping pattern as a result of commercialisation of agriculture.

Major irrigation projects were kept pending due to several reasons lack of finances and clearance from central government, inter state and intra-state disputes over the allocation of river water etc. At the same time, due to indifferent attitude of the successive governments most of the age-old irrigation tanks were prone to siltage and ultimately decline in irrigation potentiality from 10.68 lakh hectares in 1980 to 7.27 lakh hectares in 2000-01.

With the introduction of massive public distribution system and 2 rupee rice scheme by the T.D.P. government in 1983. There was state assurance of minimum support price for paddy. This has mostly benefited the big farmers from Coastal Andhra. As a result, farmers in dry areas of Telangana and Rayalaseema also switched over to paddy cultivation from cereals. A significant proportion of area under dry cropping have been converted to paddy cultivating lands with the help of dugwells and subsequently tubewells.

Paddy cultivation assured minimum returns while other crops could not. The mad competition among the big, small and marginal farmers to produce paddy led to going for energised tubewells. This has increased the number of tubewells and dugwells up to

24 lakhs. Consequently, there was depletion of water table in both regions Telangana and Rayalaseema. Most of the dugwells and tubewells are dried up. Now people are suffering even for drinking water in most of the districts during the drought effected summers.

In view of the non-availability of water in wells and tubewells due to depletion of water table and drought followed by drought, farmers are now forced to keep major part of their dry lands as current follow lands in Telangana, Rayalaseema and North Coastal Andhra. As a result, the area under follow land is increasing year after year. It increased from 7.00 lakh hectares in 1955-56 to 14.17 lakh hectares in 2000-01. There is a shift in cropping pattern also in the state. At the same time, the total area under jowar, bazra, caster and cereals decreased significantly, while the cultivable area under rice, maize, groundnut, oilseeds, cotton, pulses increased proportionately.

The yield and production of these crops also increased. It is a definite change in favour of commercial crops. Initially, the Green Revolution package seed fertilisers and assured irrigation technology provided to some districts like Krishna, West Godavari, East Godavari, Guntur and Nellore. This has resulted in increase in productivity and also promoted commercialisation and mechanisation.

Big and progressive farmers of these districts have reaped advantages of new agricultural technology and generated surplus in agriculture. The surplus of some of these rich farmers have also converted into entrepreneurs in industrial sector and service sector transport, cinema, real estate, business and trade, finance were some of the important areas they have promoted other regions like Telangana, Rayalaseema and North Coastal districts are lagging. This type of lopsided development has resulted in the widening of regional imbalances in the state resulting in unrest and leading for separate state of the backward region i.e.,

Telangana state.

Due to recurring drought conditions, most of the borrowers in rural areas of Telangana and Rayalaseema regions could not repay the loans borrowed earlier. In view of this, financial institutions kept those villages as de -faulted borrowers, included in the black list closing their chance of borrowing again. This has become a stumbling block to majority of the rural households in all the regions in the state particularly in Telangana and Rayalaseema regions.

Consequently, the dependency on money lenders and private financiers is again on the increase lending to increase in the cost of production, unremunerative cultivation and increasing indebtedness. The State needs to give priority for agriculture particularly, in the field of irrigation sector and cheap and assured credit facility. The focus should be on dry land farming, extension services and provision of quality seeds and fertilisers and timely assistance.

In recent years the plan allocations to the priority sectors such as agriculture, irrigation have been declining from plan to plan. Irrigation sector was neglected during 8th and 9th plan periods. Earlier, governments have made adequate allocations for irrigational projects like Nagarjuna Sagar, Srisailam, 420 TMCs (390 TMCs) Pochampad (90 TMCs) (SRSP) major irrigation projects. These allocations have created assured irrigational facilities to Coastal Andhra leaving Rayalaseema and Telangana regions. This also caused in regional imbalances in the state.

Allocations for other agricultural and allied activities also declined significantly due to populist and wasteful schemes found by Telugu Desam Party government. In recent times the allocations for transport, communications social and community services increased during the same period. Agricultural sector in Andhra Pradesh still contributes to more than one-third of Gross

State Domestic Product. It supports more than two-thirds of the rural population.

The development of agriculture is an essential pre-requisite to the state. The state could not make use of potentiality of water resources allocated by Bachavath Tribunal. Many of the proposed projects in Telangana and Andhra region could not be undertaken. While total canal irrigation through canals remained stagnant, tank irrigation declined during the last two decades. Similarly, cultivation under dugwells and borewells has increased significantly leading to power problems, and depleting water table below 600 feet in certain areas like Rayalaseema.

The increase of electricity charges and gradual withdrawal of subsidies to agricultural sector also increased cost of cultivation unremunerative cultivation. This has led to unrest among the farmers resulting suicide deaths especially in Telangana region. Andhra Pradesh state is lagging behind many other states in the field of industrial development. The index numbers of industrial production is self-explanatory. With regard to employment in factories the total number of workers remained stagnant during the period 1995-96 and 2000-01.

The number of industrial workers increased only from 8,23,979 to 8,25,827 during the same period recording only a marginal increase. It is argued that whatever the industrial growth taking place in the State it is without additional jobs. The state has achieved significant progress in the field of establishment of financial institutions including urban and rural banks. Public investment in industrial sector has been reduced. The growth of industrial sector declined from 7.36 percent to 6.2 percent between 1980s and the post-liberalisation period 2000-01. With regard to power sector, the installation capacity, power consumption pattern also witnessed significant changes. But the power consumption by the industries could not be increased.

The power sector is undergoing structural reforms and increased the tariff to all types of consumers including farmers since 1996-97. Farmers who depend on dugwells and tubewell in Telangana and Rayalaseema have been demanding subsidised power supply in view of the increase of cost of production in agriculture due to increased power tariffs charges. Village and small industries also could not benefit due to liberalisation policies. On the other hand, whatever the artisan units were existing earlier, they also succumbed to the onslaught of liberalisation and globalisation.

Lack of non-competitive nature of these units is one of the important reason for this crisis. Employment generation programmes and food for work programmes were snatched away by contractors, politicians and officials denying employment to the village labourers. As a result, employment and incomes have declined. Almost the entire state is witnessing unprecedented drought during 2002-'03. Most of the villagers from backward areas of Telangana, Rayalaseema and North Coastal Andhra have been migrating to nearest towns and cities in search of livelihood.

There are imbalances between the regions like Coastal Andhra, Rayalaseema and Telangana. Within each region patterns of development also varied. This can also be observed again within a district. Development is still linked with availability of assured irrigation water in all the three regions of the state. West Godavari and Karimnagar districts achieved significant levels of development, particularly, in those mandals where canal irrigation was provided. Drought prone districts like Mahabubnagar in Telangana, Ananthapur district in Rayalaseema and Vizianagaram district in Coastal Andhra still remain far behind the developed districts in respect of income, employment and living conditions.

The service sector has overtaken the agricultural and industrial sector producing more than 48 percent of Gross State

Domestic Product. As a matter of fact, major portion of this hike is being shared by urban sector. Again with in the urban sector, the major contribution is shared by 'knowledge sector' while Construction, Trading, Finance, Insurance, Real Estate also contribute significantly. Rural economy where 73 percent of the population is living has marginal role in this process of development.

However, this hype in service sector activities cannot be sustained in the long-run in the absence of development of agriculture and industrial sectors. In Andhra Pradesh the service sector is emerging as an important sector and contributes around 48 percent to the Gross State Domestic Product. In recent years, the government also has switched over to development of infrastructure for speedy development of the state economy in general and industries and service sector in particular.

The impact of liberalisation on the artisan households is also find devastating in nature. The small units hitherto surviving on a bare minimum have become vulnerable due to competition from multinational products. Occupations like weaving, tailoring, pottery, carpentry etc, are found in deep crisis. The suicide deaths of handloom weavers have become a common feature in Telangana region.

This is very important sector in the village economy supporting significant proportion of population is crumbling and falling on the other sectors like agriculture and petty business sector, which can not bear any more burden. There is a total decay of this age-old industry without proper development of alternative. As a matter of fact, majority of the households in villages are considered to be labourers.

Real development of villages can only be achieved if the labour households' employment, wages and incomes are improved. It is observed that employment, wages and other living conditions of labour households are further deteriorated in recent times.

Non-agricultural employment is found to be significant in those areas where canal irrigation is provided. With the development of agriculture, non-agricultural employment was also generated in the command areas. In other regions with the backward agriculture, frequent droughts in most of the mandals labour households find it difficult to get employment during lean seasons and prefer to migrate to far and near places.

The process of migration has accelerated in the current year which is in recent years. Due to lopsided developmental strategies pursued from time to time, balanced development of the state has become a casualty and regional imbalances went on widening. These imbalances have become stumbling blocks for the emotional integration of the people of all the three regions of the state.

The state government has borrowed about Rs. 57,000 crores from internal and external sources but no irrigational projects were takenup. Public investments in both agriculture and industrial sectors have come down. Further, the process of implementation of economic reforms including privatisation is taking place at an accelerated pace in the state. The policies of liberaliation, privatisation and globalisation have been displacing the masses from their opportunities. The benefits and subsidies meant for weaker sections are reduced year after year even these meant for the Scheduled Castes and Scheduled Tribes. This is not followed by a corresponding support in alternative occupations or opportunities.

With introduction of labour saving technology in the field of construction of roads and buildings, wage labourers have been badly effected in the state. In view of the lopsided pattern of development, the state has been witnessing agitations, movements, rural unrest, farmer suicides and hunger deaths in recent years. The village economy is facing economic and social crisis.

Agriculture is unable to absorb the over increasing working population. The growth rate of agriculture is recorded as 2.47 percent in 1990's, below the all India level. It is significantly lower than projected in much published Vision-2020 document of the State government. Further, the cost of production per unit of agricultural output in Andhra Pradesh now is higher compared to major agricultural States in India. The area under canal irrigation system declined in 1990s due to deceleration in public investment. In nutshell, the agricultural sector is neglected by the State government.

There is a need to review this policy. Though the state is providing planned allocations to infrastructure such as power, roads, communications and other services, still this needs accelerated efforts. State investment in the field of education and health may be further improved. Panchayat Raj institutions may be strengthened to eliminate rampant corruption in government departments. Corruption has become common in every public work leaking major proportion of government expenditure, showing little improvement in the conditions of poorer sections of people.

Small and marginal farmers have been worst effected. Majority of the small and marginal farmers still depend in informal or non-institutional sources of credit, particularly, money lenders private financiers at higher rates of interest, consequently, high cost of production and indebtedness. Liberalisation and Privatisaion process was initiated in the state with firm determination during 1996-'97. But it's impact is not well received by all section of the people.

Agricultural growth rates have gone down drastically. Employment situation in rural areas were not improved rather deteriorated. Whatever the employment opportunities have been created so far, they are largely low paid and casual in nature and insecure. Non-agricultural employment could not be generated to the levels of expectations. Villages have become markets for products of multinational, and big industries.

Whatever the industries, or small scale industrial units were available earlier, they are unable to compete with global products either in quality or prices. Backward areas like Telangana, Rayalaseema and North Coastal areas could not attract either domestic or foreign direct investment. Only coastal districts and Hyderabad and it's surroundings could attract 'limited' investments which could not provide employment as promised by protagonists of LPG era.

There is an exodus of young persons from villages of backward and drought effected districts to towns and cities in search of livelihood. People from Sreekakulam and Vizianagaram districts migrate to Visakhapatnam, Vijayawada, while Chittoor people migrate to Bangalore and Chennai, Ananthapur people to Bangalore, Nalgonda, Warangal and Medak people to Hyderabad to get some livelihood or other. Only old age people keep staying in rural areas Rural people in some of the districts and parts of districts migrating like those from Mahabubnagar.

The Information Technology could provide jobs to a few thousands of educated young people. The highly publicised and the pet scheme DWCRA, the Self-help Groups for women could not provide work as expected. This programme could enlighten rural women groups in political and social aspects. These groups could mobilise savings out of their hard earned income besides State/ Central assistance. As far as employment and income generation activity of this programme is concerned, very little is achieved.

Whatever the products are produced by these groups, they are decorative and artistic, unable to compete with global multinational products. Mostly they are neither mass consumption oriented nor essentials. Hence, they suffer from lack of demand. The scheme has become 'political wing' of ruling party for vote bank. The state is over burdened with domestic and foreign debts to the extent of more Rs. 57,000 crores with annual interest payment commitment of nearly Rs. 7,000 crores. This is effecting the budgetary allocations to priority sectors like major irrigation projects, health and educational needs and industrial development.

Role of Sustainablem Energy

The world faces a crucial decision at the beginning of the 21st century. For our own survival and the planet's, it is essential to cut back greenhouse gas emissions in order to reverse, or even slow down, the current rate of global warming, and to dramatically cut the current obscene levels of poverty. There must be a commitment to both.

There are internationally agreed targets on poverty reduction, the Millennium Development Goals, and greenhouse gas emission reductions, the Kyoto Protocol. But neither will be achieved if the right decisions are not taken at the World Summit on Sustainable Development. Central to all this is the use of energy in all its forms. The rich industrialised countries burn fossil fuels at a phenomenal and unsustainable rate and are primarily responsible for causing global warming.

Meanwhile nearly two billion of the world's poorest people never get to switch on a light bulb and are suffering the worst impacts of climate change because poverty means they are least able to cope. There is no need for developing countries to follow the unsustainable fossil fuel patterns of industrialised countries. A long term view is required and urgent action needed so that developing countries are not locked into unsustainable, and ultimately more expensive, energy paths, but are able to harness local indigenous sustainable energy resources which can help tackle poverty.

Energy is crucial to reducing poverty and hunger, improving health, increasing literacy and education, and improving the lives of women. Energy is central to reducing poverty, providing major benefits in the areas of health, literacy and equity. More than a quarter of humanity has no access to modern energy services. However the first energy priority of people living in poverty is how to meet their household energy needs for cooking and heating. They depend almost exclusively on burning biomass - wood, charcoal and dung.

Poor people spend up to a third of their income on energy, mostly to cook food. Women, in particular, devote a considerable amount of time collecting, processing and using traditional fuel for cooking. In India, two to seven hours each day can be devoted to the collection of fuel for cooking. The World Health Organisation estimates that 2.5 million women and young children in developing countries die prematurely each year from breathing the fumes from indoor biomass stoves .

The UN Commission on Sustainable Development (CSD) identified access to sustainable energy services as an essential element of sustainable development. The Commission stated that, "to implement the goal accepted by the international community to halve the proportion of people living on less than US $1 per day by 2015, access to affordable energy services is a prerequisite."

Although the Millennium Development Goals to reduce poverty omit any specific reference to the role of energy, access to energy services is a crucial element in achieving the goals. The goal of halving poverty by 2015 will not be reached without energy to increase production, income and education, create jobs and reduce the daily grind involved in having to just survive. Halving hunger will not come about without energy for more productive growing, harvesting, processing and marketing of food.

The world's greatest child killer, acute respiratory infection, will not be tackled without dealing with smoke from cooking fires in the home. Children will not study at night without light in their homes. Clean water will not be pumped or treated without energy. Poor people are most vulnerable to global warming because they lack the resources to cope with crises resulting from climate change.

Climate change is a direct threat to sustainable development itself, especially in developing countries that are the most vulnerable, yet least able to cope. Thousands have already died and millions more made into homeless refugees due to extreme weather events caused by the changing climate. The impacts on millions of poor people living in the developing world are harsh and "Africa is the continent most vulnerable to the impacts of projected changes because widespread poverty limits adaptation capabilities". Poverty limits their capacity to cope adequately to climate changes such as increased drought, famine, floods, threats of epidemics, cyclones, and other catastrophes.

The poor people are least responsible for climate change and efforts to combat the problem must be taken in the first place by the industrialised countries. In the future, developing countries will also need to take measures but without compromising their rightful aspirations to achieve sustainable economic development. Most governments and politicians in the industrialised world now acknowledge the global impact of climate change.

However, industrialised countries are selling to developing countries the same sources of energy which are increasingly being rejected in the North. Furthermore, the expansion of large power generating capacity has not been able, and will not be able in the coming decades, to supply the much needed energy services of the poorest people.

Expanding renewable energy is a win-win objective - cutting greenhouse gas emissions in the industrialised world and getting cheaper energy in the long run to the world's poor. Fossil fuel and nuclear energy sources are polluting and expensive and, because of local, regional and global impacts, they are unacceptable sources of power for sustainable development. But new sustainable renewable energy sources are developing and prospering, even if they are in an unfair market fighting against huge subsidies, estimated at between US $250 billion and US$300 billion a year, to fossil fuels and nuclear.

For the billions of mainly rural poor without access to basic energy services and with no prospects of getting such access under 'business as usual' scenarios, renewable energy can often be the cheapest option in the long run, even when the social and environmental costs are currently not included in the costs of fossil fuel technologies. For immediate sustainable purposes, there is clearly a need for public financial support to get these technologies to the places where they're most needed: rural communities and the urban poor.

World leaders at the World Summit on Sustainable Development have a historic opportunity to tackle the greatest threat to our collective survival - our unsustainable use of energy. The world leaders can and must decide to answer the needs of the two billion poor people who lack access to sustainable modern energy services.

Women and children can spend up to seven hours a day gathering firewood, leaving less time for other activities such as child-care, education and income generation. Smoke from the burning of biomass on open fires kills 2.5 million of women and children a year. Smoke is a major factor contributing to the contraction of acute respiratory infection, which kills more children under five than malaria or TB.

At the moment the majority of these people live in rural areas. However, urbanisation is one of the defining trends in the developing world today. In 1950, 29.7 per cent of the world's people lived in cities; by 1999 the figure was 47 per cent. Nearly four times as many people now live in cities, with most of this growth taking place in developing countries. Many poor people living in cities in the developing world are still dependent on traditional fuels for their principal energy needs.

Over 1.6 billion people do not have access to electricity. People need the services energy provides for lighting, studying, processing of food. These services will help halve poverty, reduce hunger, improve health, increase literacy and give women more choice. Energy services are currently provided by a wide range of sources including fossil fuels (diesel, gas, oil), large scale hydro, nuclear and renewable energy (biomass, solar, wind, small scale hydro).

Halving the number of people living with hunger. Approximately 95 per cent of the food we eat has to be cooked, and most foods need energy for processing of some kind. Hunger is related to poverty, so efforts to eradicate poverty should help eradicate hunger. Energy is needed to process food and to produce food. Poor people will use electricity for lighting, battery charging, radios and running small domestic appliances. They are unlikely to use electricity for cooking and heating as the high cost is prohibitive. In the short term improved use of wood, charcoal and biogas will be the main alternative for cooking.

UN Commission for Sustainable Development 9 Session (CSD9) acknowledged that access to sustainable energy services is an essential element of sustainable development stating that "To implement the goal accepted by the international community to halve the proportion of people living on less than US$1 per day by 2015, access to affordable energy services is a prerequisite." The European Union Initiative on Energy for

Sustainable Development (ISED) aims to contribute to providing the access to energy necessary for the achievement of the MDGs.

The EU proposes to work with developing countries towards creating the necessary 15 economic, social and institutional conditions in the energy sector to achieve their national development goals, in particular by providing and improving energy services for the 'energy poor'. Organisation of Economic Co-operation and Development (OECD) has issued a statement of intent to participate in a global effort to provide energy services to those currently without access and to encourage the involvement of private finance.

The World Bank's new Energy Strategy proposes direct help to the poor by providing finance and technical assistance for:

i) facilitating access to modern fuels and electricity;

ii) supporting energy needed for social services (education, communications, health);

iii) improving the macro and fiscal balances by replacing inefficient application of public funds by more directed subsidies for the poor;

iv) encouraging private investment; and

v) improving regulation of the energy industry

For the areas of the world with the most acute problems of access to energy services, the World Bank will focus on demand-driven infrastructure investments through such mechanisms as "Community-Driven Development" (CDD), Social Investment Funds (SIF), reform and privatisation of transmission and distribution, and investment in rural energy and renewables. However, this very positive World Bank Energy Strategy must be balanced with their on going financial support to huge traditional fuel projects.

Currently, the way the World Bank is encouraging private energy investments is largely facilitating the increased use of conventional fuels instead of developing the use of renewable sources. There is very little private investment going into distribution, which is the major requirement from most countries for increasing access by the poor, both in urban and in rural areas. The dispersed population in rural areas, with low spending power does not present an interesting opportunity for international private investors, but can represent a market for local investors and local small companies which understand the market and can provide cost-effective services.

Each of the major international development institutions, finance institutions, national governments, NGOs and the private sector energy developers, equipment suppliers and service providers has a role to play. The development organisations and national governments can provide leadership of ideas, targets and timetables for achieving them, applying renewable energy sources to their own facilities, facilitating the basis for leveraging private sector finance and enabling the private sector providers to operate in transparent, competitive markets.

There is a new consensus emerging on the actions that are needed to deliver improved and clean energy services to poor people: Creating mechanisms to respond to demand-driven development priorities, such as the Social Investment Funds (SIF) and Community-Driven Development (CDD) programmes, to provide finance directly to poor communities. This will enable them to control how they invest in their own priorities for improved services, such as water supply, health, education and production. Clean energy services have an enabling role to play in the delivery of these services, and the SIF and CDD mechanisms provide a means for financing a significant part of the initial capital costs, and creating markets for local service companies to deliver equipment and services.

Even poor countries such as Nepal are showing that there is local finance available, in local currency, to fund local projects. This in turn reduces the foreign exchange risk element. Prioritising knowledge sharing on best practice internationally is essential. Private Sector Delivery is also a key mechanism. This includes building the delivery capacity of local private sector service and equipment suppliers.

Decentralisation of government services and finance can go a long way to empower local government services and municipalities to provide support in response to the needs of communities in their districts. National governments can also provide an enabling legal and regulatory environment. This should ensure that utility plans are realistic and affordable, and must enact legislation to allow the local generation and sale of electricity. Governments can also provide an enabling fiscal environment through setting appropriate fuel taxes to provide the right messages and import duties on energy equipment which do not act as a tax on poor people.

Sustainable, clean energy can play a key role in reducing the huge burden of poverty and environmental degradation around the world. In order to maximise the role of clean and renewable energy in poverty reduction significant steps forward must be made to:

— Implement strategies which will allow access to clean energy for the world's two billion poorest people in 10 years.

— Greatly expand global renewable energy markets particularly in the North to cut greenhouse gas emissions and create economies of scale.

— Stimulate clean and renewable energy markets in developing countries to increase energy options available for sustainable development. Clean renewable energy is defined as modern biomass, geothermal, wind, solar, small scale hydropower and marine energy.

Participatory Watershed Development min India

During the 1970s and early 80s, the evaluation of watershed initiatives was based primarily on biophysical criteria. Large amounts of money for instance were invested in monitoring soil losses, changes in vegetative cover and changes in depth of water tables. The late 1980s saw a growing awareness that WSD is about more than maintaining or improving the productivity of natural resources. The guidelines issued by the then Ministry of Rural Areas and Employment for example cover multiple objectives including:

— productive (optimum utilisation of the watershed's natural resources);

— social (employment generation and development of other economic resources in the village);

— ecological/environmental (easy and affordable solutions that build on indigenous knowledge);

— equity (emphasis on improving the economic and social condition of the resource poor).

WSD is fundamentally about the creation of new opportunities for all sections of the community, which should be sustainable beyond the rehabilitation period. These included principally the National Watershed Development Project for Rainfed Areas (NWDPRA) under the Ministry of Agriculture and Cooperation, and under the Ministry of Rural Areas and Employment, the Drought Prone Areas Project, the Desert Development Project, the Integrated Wastelands Development Project (IWDP), and part of the Employment Assurance Guarantee Scheme. These early large-scale approaches to WSD exhibited a number of flaws:

— They were primarily evaluated according to biophysical factors. Thus success was related to changes in yield, land use, livestock productivity etc. There was no attempt to understand what changes this brought about in people's livelihoods

— The approach adopted in different projects WSD projects largely reflected the primary mandate of the responsible Ministry;

— They operated in a top-down fashion, implementing 'models' developed through research, with little attempt to take into account the needs of local users of watershed resources, nor to adapt to local biophysical or socio-economic conditions;

— Practically no contribution from beneficiaries was required, even on private land, so that there was little local ownership of the new works, little commitment to their maintenance and a syndrome of dependency on government was strengthened.

NGOs are widely diverse in terms of size, professional qualifications, geographical and sectoral areas of work, and in approaches, scales of financial support, networks and linkages. NGOs typically attempt initially to support the formation of 'focus groups' of various kinds on the principle that groups which are moderately homogeneous in economic and social terms allow skills to be developed for the much more difficult negotiations over the management of CPRs in a WSD context.

Such groups may centre on economic activities such as milk production, poultry rearing or the collection and processing of various non-timber forest products (NTFPs). In many cases, they will not be related at all to natural resource management, for instance in cases of groups formed for "woman and child health" activities. Groups are typically also encouraged to develop savings and small-scale local lending schemes to assist in breaking the control of local money-lenders, and are given training in the basic skills necessary to manage funds.

The major difficulty with NGO approaches to date is that they require lengthy periods of face-to-face interaction. NGOs can allocate the resources for this since they simply mandate themselves to work in limited areas. By contrast, government supported programmes necessarily aim for wider coverage. In the Indian context, the importance of donor-supported efforts lies less in their overall financial contribution than in their flexibility to experiment with and 'pilot' new approaches - a flexibility which government norms and procedures do not easily permit. Donors have also placed a strong emphasis on developing partnerships between stakeholders in the WSD process.

The approach of the Swiss Agency for Development and Cooperation (SDC), for instance, is characterised by efforts to share responsibilities between NGOs and the public sector according to their comparative advantage, in ways which are mutually reinforcing. They also seek to achieve collaboration among government departments and search for coherence and complementarity between participatory appraisal methods and 'scientific' measurement and planning techniques used by government.

They embody approaches to WSD intended to be:

— implemented on a wide scale, in ways which:

— enhance the productivity of the resources;

— ensure a degree of equity in the distribution of benefits;

— and are ecologically and institutionally sustainable.

WSD and Impact on Livelihoods

Recent history, it is difficult to make a detailed assessment of the performance of WSD programmes. Anecdotal evidence and impact assessments of individual projects suggest several positive trends:

— Increase in cropping intensity and yields of both irrigated and dryland crops

— Reduction in the threat of drought to crop and livestock production

— Increase in milk production (livestock systems move from open grazing and towards cross-breeds)

— Recharge of ground water

— Decline in sedimentation downstream

— Improved fodder production

— More livestock managed under stall-fed conditions

— Year-round availability of drinking water

— Creation of employment opportunities for landless labour

— Diversification of the village economy into artisanal and other activities as people gain the confidence to approach banks for credit. WSD is not an end in itself, but it is a means to an end: 'reducing the incidence of rural poverty'. The SL approach provides a framework for analysing the 'fit' between WSD activities, rural livelihoods and ultimately poverty reduction.

WSD has enabled rural communities to build up their capital assets and the extent to which these gains have been equitably distributed. It pays particular attention to CPRs, which have long been an important focus of WSD and are an important asset for the poor. As WSD approaches have evolved from primarily externally imposed biophysical interventions towards more participatory approaches encompassing a broader range of activities so the potential impact of WSD on household assets has increased. WSD has implications for all five types of assets defined in the SL framework, for example:

— *Human capital* - through capacity building activities; participation in new institutions and processes;

— *Social capital* - through the formation of watershed committees, user groups and new or strengthened institutions;

— *Financial capital* - through the establishment of credit groups, the establishment of a WSD fund;

— *Natural capital* - through increases in trees, livestock, irrigated area, more productive land;

— *Physical capital* - through increase in irrigation facilities, soil and water conservation structures.

There is a growing awareness of the links between different capital assets. Investments in physical capital such as bunds, check dams and the re-vegetation of common lands for instance are relatively easy to achieve. The returns to physical investments of this type however will rapidly decline if appropriate investments in social and human capital are not also made to develop sustainable and equitable institutions to manage these assets. Similarly the idea of sequencing is important.

Some NGOs argue strongly that the local institutions which determine access to natural capital (e.g. common land) need to be regularised before WSD activities are undertaken. Although WSD can no doubt have quite significant positive impacts on the natural resource base, there are growing concerns over the distribution of these benefits. The principle of the ridge to valley approach for instance may work against the interests of the poor who often rely on the commons in the upper slopes much more heavily than do the better-off.

To begin with water control structures in the lower slopes would privilege those (i.e. the better-off farmers) having reliable access to agricultural land. The notion that the poor, who are denied access to the commons during the rehabilitation period, can benefit from casual, unskilled employment opportunities created by construction requirements in the lower slopes is appealing, but requires close monitoring; and there are important questions surrounding the sustainability of any of these gains.

WSD envisages the construction of a wide range of physical assets principally for soil and water management, such as bunds, checkdams, gullyplugs, ponds, shallow wells, and so on. However, there remain questions over access and sustainability for the longer term, especially if joint responsibility for maintenance is not clearly agreed. The better-off, being landholders, generally benefit disproportionately from an increase in groundwater levels brought about by soil and water conservation.

Information on how any agricultural intensification impacts on employment opportunities for the poor remains sketchy. Common pool resources (CPRs) such as grazing or forest land constitute an important form of natural capital and joint action is generally required to manage these. Spending pressure under government programmes means, however, that the formation of resource user associations is hasty, and that the views of the poor and women are rarely taken adequately into account. Long standing problems, such as encroachment remain unsolved. After rehabilitation, the increased potential offtake of timber, fuel and fodder often attracts the attention of the better-off to CPRs, which, in degraded form, had generally been the preserve of the poor.

Social and human capital is being strengthened through the formation and capacity building of focus groups, watershed associations etc.. However, the short period allowed for preparatory activities, together with the lack of social organisational skills among (especially government) project implementing agencies (PIAs), means that careful approaches to human and social capital development are rarely implemented on a larger scale.

In terms of financial capital, most forms of rural investments in India suffer from a 'handout' syndrome, in which rural people have long been regarded as the recipients of government munificence, with the consequence that they distinguish clearly between 'government projects' for which the government has planning, implementation and (in their view) maintenance responsibility from activities they undertake privately.

CPRs represent a form of natural and social capital that individuals and communities can draw on in pursuit of their livelihood strategies. A study by Jodha concluded that CPRs make a key contribution to rural livelihoods and are critical for sustainable agricultural production in semi-arid areas. They form a part of rural peoples' strategies for adjusting to the harsh and stressful environment. The role of CPRs is particularly important in lean times, acting as a buffer in times of drought or other crises.

During droughts, the collection of tubers and wild foods from the forest is an important coping mechanism. CPRs also provide independent sources of income to women, through, for instance, goat rearing, broom making, leaf plate making and collection of tendu leaves and tamarind. All of these occupations depend upon CPRs, either for fodder or raw materials. WSD in India has its roots in the widespread concern over land degradation - with approximately 170 million hectares classified as degraded.

Large areas of this land are classified as CPRs. 'Before and after' pictorial comparisons of WSD efforts often compare areas of barren rocky common land with productive pastures and shrub cover. The assumption is generally that management regimes have deteriorated into open access in a 'tragedy of the commons' scenario. WSD projects have invested considerable efforts in establishing both the rules for access to such areas and in creating collaborative agreements for community management of such CPRs.

Watershed project in Andhra Pradesh had different impacts on households of different socio-economic status. Landowners were able to compensate for the loss of grazing, through the substitution of crop residues, the availability of which had increased due to improved irrigation facilities. Landless livestock owners on the other hand were forced to sell their livestock raised similar concerns.

WSD can open up new opportunities for households to both intensify and extensify production, for example through:

— Increasing the frequency of cultivation - increased groundwater recharge often permits cultivation of a second crop, or 'life-saving' irrigation of a main crop; and

— Adopting new technologies, such as improved varieties of staple crops, higher levels of input use and higher yields; shifts to the cultivation of higher value crops in some areas;

— Expansion of cultivated areas - soil and water conservation and irrigation structures can bring new land into production.

Some of the most striking evidence of intensification in rainfed areas in India comes from the livestock sector. Restrictions on access to CPRs - often promoted through WSD - have encouraged the move towards stall-feeding systems for both large and small ruminants. In the shorter term -when restrictions are most strict - households may become more dependent on crop residues. Some studies have also highlighted the importance of private resources, with increased numbers of trees on farmland

and the cultivation of range grasses and legumes in niches such as field boundaries, private wastelands, terraces and bunds.

In the longer term as access restrictions are eased and their productivity improves, CPRs can become an important fodder resource for cut and carry systems. Overall this suggests a diminishing role for CPRs in grazing systems, but an increasing role as a source of cut fodder. There are also important intra-household dimensions to intensification strategies. While increases in agricultural productivity might occur as a result of WSD, men usually appropriate on-farm gains and the increased drudgery is disproportionately borne by women.

With an increase in land productivity, men frequently choose to increase the production of cash crops such as sugarcane and cotton. It is important therefore that women are included in decisions over land use and crop planning, to ensure that household food requirements (vegetables, fruit and a variety of grains) are provided for adequately. It seems that WSD can support strategies of intensification if careful analysis of the livelihood strategies of different households and individuals precedes decisions on project activities. But in countries such as India, rigid socio-cultural relations at village level may work against the poor.

For poor groups (usually the low-caste and/or women) to assert their rights over resources as these become more productive through rehabilitation requires careful initial development of skills and confidence, robust and transparent procedures for decision-taking, monitoring of any departures from what has been agreed, and awareness among all concerned that, if necessary, resort to an external agency continues to be feasible. These conditions are difficult to put in place on a wide scale. Serious policy attention therefore also needs to be given to alternative strategies of diversification and migration.

In the past decade recognition has grown that agricultural production is only one of the strategies that contribute to livelihoods. Rural households - particularly the poor - engage in a wide range of activities. In India there are important traditions, often underlain by formal and informal institutions, which dictate the types of activities that households and individuals may pursue. For instance, villagers' participation in many non-farm activities such as carpentry or basket making is dictated by strong caste-based institutions.

WSD has supported these diversification strategies in a number of ways. NGO projects have paid specific attention to providing opportunities to the poor to diversify their livelihoods, often through the formation of self help groups for women, the landless and other marginal groups. These groups undertake a number of activities ranging from traditional crafts (such as leaf plate making; weaving and basket making), mushroom cultivation, forestry activities and so on.

Western Orissa Rural Livelihoods Project demonstrated, the prospects of such enterprises tend to be assessed on the basis of historical production and sales levels. Certainly, the evidence points to some prospect that local people could benefit if restrictions on their access to or sale of NTFPs were lifted but over the longer term, artisanal products generally face inelastic demand, so that the scope for any increased contribution to livelihoods is likely to be limited.

Migration is one of the most important means of diversifying rural livelihoods. Migration strategies in India vary widely: one or more family members may leave the resident household for varying periods of time and in so doing are able to make new and different contributions to its wellbeing. Migration may be seasonal or permanent; it may be point-to-point or circular in fashion; it may vary in distance of destination from within province, to within country or, occasionally, cross frontier. The contribution of migration to livelihoods will depend on various factors, including the seasonality of movement, the length of time spent away, assets and social structures and institutions allowing for women (if men migrate) and others to pursue activities previously reserved for men and household heads.

A starting point in assessing the role and implication of migration for livelihoods in any location is an understanding of the rationale behind migration. In large areas of tribal India, migration occurs as a defensive coping strategy to cover existing debts and seasonal variability. Households have little choice if they want to survive. Migrants leave their villages after crop harvest and migrate to towns. Many travel long distances often to the same place each year.

Migration is especially important for tribal groups and generally the livelihood strategies of poorer households with little or no land depend more heavily on migration. Whilst it has long been accepted that migrant remittances constitute an important component of rural livelihoods, increasingly in many areas, earnings from migration form the primary source of cash income. Migration is often highly formalised and involves complex sets of relations between building contractors, village recruiters and workers. These involve arrangements for securing work and providing for travel and accommodation expenses. These relationships are often highly exploitative in nature.

For instance in western Orissa, labour contractors are also villagers' only source of loans. Highly indebted to the contractors, migrants have little bargaining power and are trapped in a vicious circle. Migration is likely to become an increasingly important livelihood strategy for the rural poor. In relation to WSD there are several key issues which need to be addressed:

— Migrants' absence from villages tends to marginalise them from the decision-making process;

— Migrants' dependence on CPRs is highly seasonal and management strategies should accommodate this;

— Migrants may be absent at key points in the year and may lose out in the sharing of benefits from common resources;

— Migration often leads to the absence of the most able-bodied working population - often males - this has key implication for women's roles and decision making.

— Migration has an important impact on participation in local level decision making processes. WSD involves the establishment of new institutions such as user groups and watershed committees.

— Migrants - generally the poorest - are often absent from villages and so tend to be marginalised from decisions on resource use.

In the context of WSD in India, most NGOs and several donors see seasonal migration as a negative phenomenon, largely on account of its exploitative nature and its disruptive effect on family life and wider social relations. This view clearly has some validity, but, whilst policy interventions should be sensitive to these requirements, they should not be unduly influenced by unrealistic ideals. WSD offers an opportunity to address migration issues: to promote intensification under WSD in employment-creating rather than in labour saving modes, so that substantial employment is created beyond the construction phase of rehabilitation; the second is to support migration processes so that labourers' conditions are improved, and they are gradually released from exploitative contractual arrangements.

A livelihoods perspective can reveal why certain groups fall out or do not participate in WSD, and how participation can be enhanced. For example, activities may fit badly with livelihood strategies of the poor if involvement is particularly risky, requires access to specific assets, or occurs at a time when other livelihood activities are a priority for them. Some barriers may be insuperable, but in other cases, participation can be encouraged by adapting procedures to suit the livelihoods of the poor.

Livelihoods analysis for an Indian watersheds project highlighted many obstacles for the poor in attending community meetings, relating to migration, lack of time, and power. As a result, the second phase of the project is paying careful attention to timing and developing alternative mechanisms for participation, including informal sub-watershed associations, and 'livelihood - support teams' to work with the most vulnerable.

In terms of the overall impact of WSD - as a means to rural poverty reduction - watershed-based approaches have been demonstrated to lead to substantial improvements in rural livelihoods. However, they are not a panacea: productivity gains in pilot projects have not been achieved to the same extent on a wide scale and the links between productivity gains and livelihoods is complex and poorly understood.

The conditions necessary for successful WSD are becoming clearly-established, and include:

— adequately sloping topography; adequate rainfall; high contribution of land-based activities to livelihoods;

— the willingness of landowners to allow the landless adequate access to the benefits of rehabilitation;

— adequate prospects for long-term ecological sustainability, including restrictions on the distribution and volume of groundwater extraction; adequate prospects for long-term institutional sustainability, including market links, and strong community commitment to joint action in resource management.

6

Challenges and Opportunities of Rural Poverty Reduction

Poverty in all its forms is the greatest challenge to the international community. In many developing countries, the poor struggle at the margin of the formal economy. They lack political influence, education, health care, adequate shelter, personal safety, regular income and enough to eat. Worldwide the number and proportion of people living in extreme poverty declined slightly through the mid-1990s.

Most of the decline was in East Asia, notably China. But progress slowed temporarily in some Asian countries in the late 1990s, and ground to a halt or reversed in others. In the rest of the world, while the proportion of people in poverty declined, population growth meant that the number of poor people increased.

And in the countries of the former Soviet Union, undergoing economic and social transition, the proportion of poor more than tripled. The numbers of poor are greatest in South Asia, but the proportion of poor people is highest in Sub-Saharan Africa. Most of the poor live in rural areas, but urban poverty is growing faster. Women are more likely than men to lack rights to land and other assets.

They also have difficulty getting access to credit. And they lack adequate employment and economic security in old age. Malnutrition is a symptom of poverty. Today there are 150 million underweight children in the developing world. But the proportion is falling everywhere except Africa. Being underweight, even mildly, increases the risk of death and inhibits mental and physical development.

The problem perpetuates itself from one generation to the next, because malnourished women are more likely to have low-birthweight babies. Poverty rates can be cut in half by 2015 if countries follow policies that reduce social and gender inequalities and create income-earning opportunities for the poor.

Pro-poor growth

Economic growth is not a guarantee of poverty reduction - but it is absolutely essential for sustaining poverty reduction over the longer run. And it needs to be pro-poor. It has to generate more income-earning opportunities so that poor people can engage in productive and well-paid work. It has to give poor people more access to assets to help unleash their productive potential and allow them to feed themselves. And it has to be fair in creating better opportunities for poor women. This will require measures to strengthen women's land rights, increase their bargaining power and broaden their access to credit, training and new technology.

Many countries today need substantially faster pro-poor growth, among them the 30 developing countries whose real per capita incomes are lower today than they were 35 years ago. That growth will be built on increased production among the poor themselves: by productivity increases among small farmers; by small enterprises, both rural and urban; by informal producers and by the many women and men providing a host of small-scale services.

Economic policies must also be sound, well balanced and sustainable. This requires strengthening national institutions to build the capacity to implement the right economic and social policies. In all this is a concern for equity, so that all groups in society progress. But the concern for equity also extends to future generations. This means that economic growth must be sustainable -so that what we do to the environment today leaves the natural resources to support life on our planet for future generations.

Policies have to go beyond the purely economic to focus on the needs of the poor -to ensure minimum social standards and universal access to basic social services. Countries have to invest in education -especially girls 'education, which produces one of the highest payoffs in development. They also have to deliver high-quality and cost-effective services to the poor -health care, water, sanitation and other basic services. Part of this is ensuring action to reduce malnutrition, with a special focus on women of child-bearing age and young children. Countries also have to provide safety nets for the vulnerable -in times of crisis, whether global, national or local.

Globalisation offers enormous opportunities to the developing countries -better ways of tapping the world's knowledge, better technology for delivering products and services, better access to the world's markets. But taking advantage of the opportunities requires action .Countries have to lower their tariffs and other trade barriers and streamline their systems for the flow of imports, exports and finance. They also have to manage their inflation, interest and exchange rates-to be seen as good places for doing business.

And they have to maintain consistent policies -to be credible to investors, both domestic and foreign. The high-income countries have their part to play too -reducing tariffs and other trade barriers to imports from developing countries and providing assistance to build the capacity to trade effectively. Not all countries are enjoying the possible benefits, however. With a legacy of poor policies and poor performance, too many of them are being left behind in trade, in finance, in technology, in ideas -in precisely the things that could help them grow and reduce poverty.

Effective and equitable use of resources for development costs money. Much comes from the investments by people -and much, from the investments by government. What has spurred the growth of many East Asian countries is their high savings rates, often more than 30% of gross national product. That's allowed them to invest in infrastructure and social services. Many African countries, by contrast, have had savings rates of only 10 -15% of national income, too low to sustain growth fast enough to lift more people from poverty.

It 's important for countries to spend wisely -on basic services for the poor, not on subsidised services for the rich, and on sound investments for future development. How governments spend their money matters as much as what they spend it on. Instability and unpredictability in government expenditures make progress in poverty reduction more difficult. The quality of people that governments recruit also makes a difference.

Governments that hire and promote based on merit perform better than those that give the best jobs to friends and political allies. External aid plays an important part in supporting development, especially in poor countries. There is a growing consensus that country ownership of development policies and country leadership in development programmes are essential for success -and that donor procedures and reporting need to be co-ordinated and harmonised to reduce administrative burdens.

Donors and international financial institutions are now working more closely with developing countries on strategies for poverty reduction, formulated through a participatory process and driven by countries. They are also being more selective in the kind of aid that goes to a country, better ensuring that it is tailored to country priorities and local needs.

Challenges and Opportunities

Most of the world's poor are rural, and will remain so until at least 2035. The urban-rural gaps in poverty, health and literacy are large and, on the whole, not narrowing. These gaps are not only unjust but also inefficient: shifting resources, assets and access from urban to rural, and from rich to rural poor, often advances economic growth.

Now that most donors and developing countries are reorienting their policy towards poverty reduction, one would expect investment and aid to concentrate substantially on the poorest countries, and on support for agricultural and rural activity. The poor themselves report distress that stems not only from low consumption but also from illhealth, lack of schooling, vulnerability, lack of assets and disrespect from officials. Those who suffer from one of these conditions tend to suffer from others as well.

Disproportionately many are rural women, ethnic minorities in remote areas, landless, casual workers, or children: poverty and lack of education are inherited conditions. Breaking the 'interlocking log-jams of disadvantage' may require attacking several barriers. Lack of these human assets stops children from learning, compels parents to send them to work, and perpetuates poverty. Fertility decline and the dramatic rise in worker-dependant ratios in 1990-2030 can help the poor to escape poverty, if the extra workers can find decent work. This was achieved in East

Asia through early gains in farm yields, smallholder incomes, and hence farm employment —soon followed by increases in employment and growth in the non-farm sector.

South Asia and Africa can follow this path if their agricultural and rural policies can be set right, and if right policies can be translated into favourable outcomes in terms of the assets and opportunities of the rural poor at the local level and their livelihoods. Women's disadvantage and exclusion in education, landholding and, in some countries, nutrition and health care reduce their security and esteem; in some countries they slow the fertility transition. These disadvantages are greater in rural areas: they can be reduced by redressing the underallocation of rural resources.

The extreme poor spend almost three quarters of their income on food. They receive over two thirds of their calories from staples, and earn perhaps half their income from growing them. So the control of farmland by the poor tends to be a safeguard against extreme poverty. 'Classical' land reform has transferred more land, and with more success in reducing poverty, than is widely believed; but it has run into many problems.

Consensual and decentralized land redistribution is a promising way forward, with the largest farmers attracted to sell land in small amounts to the poor; but it requires some land fund in support. This is in tune with the policy preferences of many donors, recipients and civil-society organizations, as well as those of many of the poor.

However, especially with the new requirements of global markets, post-reform smallholders require access to competitively marketed inputs and services and to research, roads and other resources that normally only governments can supply. Water-yielding assets are also increasingly important to the rural poor as more areas are affected by water scarcity and diversion.

Removal of water subsidies is desirable, but caution has to be exercised against further transfers of water away from rural areas, which will endanger the already inadequate farm water control (and drinking water) of the rural poorest. The heavy biases against rural people, the poor and women in acquiring 'human assets', especially health and education, are inefficient as well as unjust, and in most cases not shrinking. Reducing these biases, and providing the poor with access to land and improved farm technology, are complementary; each increases the economic gain and poverty reduction from the other.

The value of human, land, water-yielding and other assets depends on the technologies that turn those assets, together with labour, into adequate incomes. The poor's shortage of assets compels them to live mainly by selling their labour-power. So increasing the market value of that labourpower, through choices in asset-building and in technology that are employment-intensive, is vital for poverty reduction. But subsidies to farm equipment, such as combine-harvesters and weedicides, displace human labour and ultimately harm the poor.

There are also positive requirements of pro-labour policy. If the poor have some farmland, their bargaining power in labour markets is increased. Agricultural researchers need to perceive that the use of labour itself, while a cost, has social advantages for poverty reduction. Rural technologies face two tasks: to reduce poverty through more and better distributed output and welfare; and to improve resource sustainability.

On the whole, the former has been best achieved by bio-agricultural research, and the latter by improved land and water management technology. The two are strongly complementary, though separated by fashion and by barriers between researchers and institutions. Poor farmers can seldom afford to buy into conservation technology unless there is a production gain. And all types of formal research are complementary with farmers' own research and succeed best with participatory methods.

But the lack of progress in the spread of water control and the slowdown in historically fast rates of food-crop yield improvement are serious causes for concern. The stagnation or decline in many areas of public agricultural research must end. The increasing locking-in, or patenting, of agricultural research results by a few private companies, with few incentives to structure their work towards the needs of the rural poor, has to be replaced by appropriate public-private partnerships and by new incentives for scientific endeavour.

Just as rural poverty reduction, growth in staples yield and farm income expansion in developing countries have slowed down, before the gains have spread to many areas, exciting new scientific prospects have been opened by transgenics. These have produced intense debate and polarized arguments. Careful consideration of trade laws, environment and safety regulations sympathetic to developing countries are important to ensure that neither the poor, nor the world, are exposed to undue risks.

However, from the perspective of ending poverty, a greater risk is that gains from transgenics will not reach the poor and the hungry. Decisions must not be confined to the world of business and politics, but should be open, drawing on the experience of professional research, the rural poor themselves (labourers and consumers as well as farmers) and organizations in direct contact with them.

Poverty, Liberalization and Globalization

The poor need technologies to increase output from their assets, and they also need markets to exchange that output freely and to best advantage. Yet the poor are dogged by the market power of others, market failure, bad distributional outcomes from market 'success', and barriers to market access. Rural areas are dispersed: in remote areas, market access problems are most serious, and competition and information least adequate. Action by civil society, government, donors and often the poor themselves can greatly improve their relative access and strength in markets.

Globalization can bring significant benefits to the rural poor. But it will bring most benefits if attention and support are directed towards helping small producers to make the best of their marketmediated relations with vastly more powerful and international private-sector operators. Access to information is an overlooked area for the rural poor; more information would enable farmers to take better decisions on markets and services.

Investment in rural roads brings striking returns in both GNP and poverty reduction. It is less affordable in remote or sparsely populated areas, but here, more imaginative solutions can improve physical market access or reduce the cost to the poor. 'Getting the prices wrong' is seldom sensible, but getting them right often does nothing to solve the market access problems of remote areas, and can even make them worse. Liberalization and globalization are changing the landscape of many poor rural areas. Despite their economic advantages of labour intensity, poor farmers have difficulty meeting exacting supermarket or export standards. Donors can work with ...s and cooperatives, as well as governments, to provide support and to increase the bargaining power of the poor through trade and marketing associations.

Pro-poor Rural Institutions

The poor are largely excluded from the institutions and partnerships that can enable them to share and control the decisions that affect their lives. This is because institutions often tend to be controlled by the powerful non-poor. Channeling appropriate assets such as land and education, technology to raise the productivity of assets, and markets to improve sales and purchases, improve the poor's 'exit options' that over time may also help them alter institutions for their sustained benefit.

Decentralized institutions for natural resources management and financial services have not always been successful in reaching the poor, although they have been important in helping the poor, through increased efficiency and sustainability, as the local elites are driven to recognize their shared interest with the poor. Poverty reduction is a complex task, requiring sustained commitment to consistent, yet flexible, joint action. There are no quick fixes and no easy solutions. No single institution, national or multilateral, public or private, and no single strategy can hope to deal effectively with the different contexts and causes of poverty.

Coherent anti-poverty strategy therefore requires stable partnerships, based on trust as well as self-interest. It is important to recognize the need for sustaining the management of change towards pro-poor institutions and programmes through support from below. The coalition of the poor among themselves and with others provides the best hope for the poor to get integrated with a process of sharing wealth and development more equitably than before. The best guarantee of good policy is effective accountability.

Macro-partnerships provide the overarching global framework for anti-poverty strategies. An important purpose of the macro-level partnership is enhanced aid effectiveness through improved donor coordination.

Thus, there is a paradox: an ambitious target for poverty alleviation with fewer resources to achieve it. If the target of reducing extreme poverty by half by .... is to be achieved, overall development assistance must be raised and the share going to agriculture should reflect its importance in generating livelihoods for the majority of the poor. Once that condition is met, the challenge is to develop and foster genuine cooperation, good governance and a policy framework in which the rural poor in developing countries can participate.

Developing country governments and donor agencies need partnerships to ensure a costeffective attack on poverty; the rural poor need partnerships to support their own initiatives, but free of the intrusiveness for which donors are sometimes criticized. Hence donors are emphasizing partnershipbuilding to improve the efficiency and effectiveness of poverty reduction efforts and to build a consensus on:

— setting development priorities;

— reforms necessary to pursue these priorities;

— the programmes and/or projects in support of the reforms; and

— the successful implementation of these programmes and projects with better definition of the responsibilities of the stakeholders in the process.

One response to the scarcity of development resources has been efforts to coordinate available aid funds around shared initiatives against poverty. Effective coordination among donors is of increasing importance to reduce duplication and avoid placing too great a burden on the host country's administrative and management capacity. Multiple donors and programmes may also cause confusion within the government.

Grateful as they may be for assistance, governments might come to see donor activities as more of a hindrance than a help, given the extra burden on government personnel in trying to manage different overlapping activities. The global initiatives to forge coalitions and partnerships among and with developing countries donors are welcome. However, success requires the substance to be made 'bottom-up' in two ways.

— Each government has to be responsible for country policy. History shows that imposed conditionality in aid, and anti-poverty planning from Northern capitals for the Asian or African poor, seldom works.

— The poor themselves have to take responsibility, as agents, for their own development; the poor, not just an abstract 'civil society', which can be biased towards the rich and strong.

Even where the poor can overcome that bias, civilsociety institutions are underdeveloped in some countries and repressed in others. The key issue is whether the poor have room for manoeuvre by capturing particular local or central institutions, or by coalitions with some of the strong. If poverty reduction is to reach the poorest, often linguistic minorities in remote rural areas, the problem is more difficult.

The future outcomes of rural poverty could be worsened such as increasing war or civil violence, or worsethan-expected effects of AIDS or global warming. Success in reducing mass poverty in low-income countries initially depends on progress in farm yields and employment, and later on a transition towards employment-intensive non-farm products, alongside a fall in the number of people engaged in agriculture, and increasing urbanization.

Improved small-scale agriculture in developing countries is essential for meeting immediate poverty reduction targets, and can contribute decisively to the overall development process, including the emergence of quite new opportunities for income and employment in other sectors. It is a stepping stone to larger solutions, but it is not itself the whole solution.

Several East Asian countries, following breakthroughs in farming, have made the transition to broad-based non-farm growth. This tends to make urbanization faster, not slower, creating new problems, but problems that are more soluble because migration is spurred by rural success rather than by desperation. However, widespread labour-intensive rural non-farm growth appears to have been central to East and South-East Asian success. We know that such growth is, in its early stages, fastest when there is demand, especially for consumer goods, from a not-too-unequal, fast-growing local farm sector.

Such rural non-farm growth readily broadens to wider markets later. Hence, the strategies of labour-intensive technical progress, and wide distribution of land and human capital, not only reduce poverty in the short run, but also ease the transition from agriculture-based to more broadbased poverty reduction. Periods of faster growth, overall, are associated with faster poverty reduction, but there are big differences among countries in their success in turning growth into rural and urban poverty reduction.

The failure of African rural poverty to fall is surely explained mainly by agricultural stagnation; recent exceptions to stagnation, such as Uganda, Ghana and parts of Ethiopia, appear to show some poverty decline too. It is hard to believe, especially with the fertility transition so that poor rural people have fewer and better-educated children, that the slowdown in rural poverty decline in India will continue if agricultural growth is maintained. It is, unfortunately, plausible however that poverty will persist in much of rural Africa if agricultural growth does not speed up, especially where land distribution is also very unequal.

The sources of progress lie in getting assets, appropriate technologies and market access to the poor, and in their obtaining more influence on decentralized and national-level institutions. Some of the old effective solutions, like classical land redistribution, the Green Revolution and irrigation expansion, have run into limitations. Yet the reasons these solutions were effective remain valid: the poor still need access to labour-intensive, securityenhancing assets and technologies.

The institutions, the required local and global partnerships (linking the poor especially with scientists and with the private sector), and the market forms best suited to obtain such access for the poor, have changed. But the need for the poor to participate in their own emancipation remains the same.

Rural Poverty Reduction Policies

Today we have witnessed rapid change in policies to reduce rural poverty. Greater emphasis is now placed on devolution and local management of common property resources and the extension and strengthening of partnerships with civil societies to nurture and develop human assets. These new approaches emphasize local participation, supporting the construction of social capital and linking the poor to dynamic sectors of the economy.

Participation allows the poor a voice, and through a transfer of responsibility gives them the power to discover and determine ways to improve their lives. Empowering the poor is the foundation of rural poverty alleviation. This policy shift thus involves a new emphasis on institutions: on the organizations (for example, families, banks and trade unions) that mediate the access of the poor to assets, technologies and markets, and on the rules (laws, customs and administrative practices) that determine whether the poor benefit from such access.

The poor's chance to influence rules, and to help control organizations, depends on their power and influence. These, in turn, depend on their knowledge, access and, perhaps above all, whether alternative courses of action are open to them. This matter recognizes the paradox that, while we want institutional change to help the poor, institutions, including the state and NGOs, tend to be controlled by the powerful non-poor. Often, those who control one institution also control others.

For instance, even after land redistribution, the large farmer may continue to have better access than the ex-landless labourer to production, credit, information and marketing networks, and the capacity to diffuse and insure against risk. How can the poor and weak use and benefit from those institutions, which were initially controlled by the rich and powerful and run mainly in their interest? It may be necessary for the poor to seek empowerment at the centre to restrain both the non-poor from arranging things to their own advantage and the rural elite from wielding 'decentralized' power over rural financial institutions or over natural resources.

In some cases, the poor may benefit by uniting with some of the rich in a coalition to raise their income shares at the expense of others. In most developing countries the poor can vote. Many non-poor, for whatever reason, often support forms of insurance or universal coverage amounting to pro-poor redistribution: to provide basic health care or social safety nets. In all these cases, much depends on whether the poor use their resources and power jointly, or are fragmented by distance, caste, ethnic group or gender. It also matters whether the poor can afford the time and cost of political mobilization.

Institutions may often persist, but they are not immutable. Channeling appropriate resources such as land, education, and technology to raise the productivity of assets, and markets to improve sales and purchases for and from asset use, improve the poor's 'exit options' that over time may also help them alter institutions for their sustained benefit. For instance, by changing the political structure in the village, land redistribution gives more voice to the poor and induces them to get involved in local institutions and management of the local commons. There are three institutional approaches to empowering the rural poor in their quest for poverty reduction:

a) a blend of devolution and collective action for natural resources management;

b) delivery of financial services to the poor to enable them to access and secure financial assets; and

c) developing linkages with NGOs and the private sector as partners for service delivery.

Decentralisation

Decentralization is redefining the boundary between state and market. It is an umbrella term for a number of related policy reforms, in which central government agencies transfer rights and responsibilities to local institutions. Decentralization's merits include easier access to local information, greater sensitivity to local needs, and accountability to the local community. In theory, as the decentralized system becomes more attuned to local preferences it becomes more transparent and accountable. But in practice things may not always turn out that way. The result depends on the context of decentralization. Recent Indian legislation granting rights of ownership and management over categories of natural resources to gram sabhas (village assemblies) of forest villages is a step that can be used by disadvantaged local minorities to assert rights to their share of resources. But whether at local, provincial or even national level, such devolution of powers and revenues has inevitably been linked with struggles of the concerned minorities.

Devolution of powers to the village has also worked well in making possible high rates of accumulation and elimination of poverty in some Chinese villages where there has been a reasonable level of agreement between the leaders and the village as a whole on the development goal of raising incomes. In the absence of mechanisms of public debate, the ability of these villages to meet crises could be limited. When conscious and aroused, the rural poor are more likely to be able to influence decisions at the local level than in distant metropolitan centres. Supporters of decentralized targeting claim that information about who is poor is more readily available at the local level than at the centre, and that as local institutions tend to be more accountable to local people, they have an incentive to use information to improve programme performance. That may be so in a few cases, but, by and large, the claim that local institutions are accountable to the poor is con-troversial, as decentralized institutions may be controlled by powerful elites that reduce the efficacy of programmes. Viable alternatives are few, however, since non-local institutions have often proved to be even less accountable to the poor.

The case for decentralization depends partially on the extent to which the local programme has been free from capture by the non-poor. This status is also likely to influence the actions the centre may need to take to set the 'rules of the game' for efficient and equitable local operation. This was successful for drought-relief operations in Brazil. Again, the relative success of decentralized government in Karnataka, India, is attributed to the effective system of democratic accountability. Anecdotal evidence exists of local capture of decentralized anti-poverty programmes and development projects. Rich local farmers in Bangladesh captured a World Bank-funded local irrigation facility intended for poor farmers. More recently, the World Bank's participatory poverty assessment in Bangladesh suggests that the rich in the community tend to dominate the local power structure; they tend to be the first, and possibly only, people consulted when a development programme is undertaken in the community.

Such observations warn against assuming that local communities are homogeneous, whether in terms of class, ethnicity, age, or gender, and point to serious accountability problems with antipoverty programmes.

Differences in the relative power of the poor, and marginal groups particularly, in local decision-making can make a big difference to the distributional outcomes of programmes within villages. Thus, while there are many benefits from decentralization, local institutions will not necessarily be more accountable to the poor than centralized ones. Analogous to the risks of centralized alternatives, the poor face a real threat of capture of decentralized social programmes by local elites unless some safeguarding measures are deliberately introduced. It is therefore necessary, in implementing institutional interventions to reduce poverty, to examine the interaction between central government, civil society, and NGOs and popular institutions, and the options for intervention. The issues are whether these institutional arrangements reach, benefit and empower the poor to enhance their capacity to benefit from economic growth; and whether participation in these institutions enables the rural poor to increase their welfare and bargaining capabilities.

Natural Resources Management

The daily livelihood of many of the rural poor depends on the success with which common property resources CPRs. are managed, and on the environmental consequences of their management. The poor depend more on CPRs for income than the rich, but rural income from CPRs is falling sharply as they are privatized or statized. Recent years have witnessed an increasing trend towards devolution of control over natural resources from government agencies to local communities. These resources include farmland, water (especially irrigation), and other common pool resources such as rangelands, forests, fisheries and wildlife. Experience has shown that centralized and technocratic 'top-down' conservation is effective only with large expenditures on enforcement or under undemocratic circumstances. Usually the rich evade top-down conservation laws, e.g. by poaching from national parks in Africa and exploiting reserved forest resources in Latin America, while the poor are effectively excluded from livelihoods without compensation.

On the other hand, participation of different types of local stakeholders—an effectively enforced condition prior to IFAD funding of many projects—has proved essential for effective and sustainable management and conservation of natural-resource systems, and, in general, is fostered by a significant degree of decentralization to local communities. Privatization of CPRs is, however, seldom a sensible alternative if poverty is to be reduced, since this may create problems of access for the poor, as documented in India. Moreover, community programmes aimed at protecting forests against overexploitation by restricting access could be harmful to the rural poor. Where the poor are heavily dependent on CPRs for survival, there is little hope for poverty reduction if access by the rural poor to these dwindling resources becomes less certain.

Devolution of management of CPRs to local communities can, however, greatly reduce poverty, both directly through sustaining or enhancing food security, and through empowerment, and increased capacity for local management, which should occur as a result of the institution-building required to manage the resources. Yet the rationale behind many efforts at devolution of CPR management to local communities continues to be sustainability of resources for use by all, including the non-poor, rather than poverty reduction through securing livelihoods for the poor per se.

Poverty reduction is too often a secondary goal: the poor, who are the main users of CPRs, are in the most strategic position to conserve them—yet, unless proper incentives are provided, also under most pressure to use them. In short, it is essential to question two assumptions when decentralizing CPRs, or to take action to validate those assumptions. The first assumption is that community CPRs management will automatically give the rural poor better control over, or access to, those resources and thus help them become less poor. The second assumption is that it will make sense for the decentralized CPRs managers, especially poor ones, to give high priority to conservation, given that this depends largely on affordable techniques for making conservation methods quick income-yielders.

Devolution of natural-resources management has two sets of advantages. For the users, devolution leads to increased accountability of those responsible for its management. Local users may have a comparative advantage over government agents in managing resources. Being nearer to the resource and having a greater understanding of its importance to users means that more efficient rules can be designed. In addition, the monitoring and enforcement of such rules are easier at the local level.

Close scrutiny of resource use by the users themselves leads to greater accountability. For the government, devolution helps to reduce the cost of delivering these interventions. The active involvement of beneficiaries may lower the informational costs associated with anti-poverty interventions. Devolution also helps government to overcome lack of knowledge of local conditions. Local participants have the advantage of local knowledge necessary for the conservation of natural resources, and maintenance of resources requires considerable local knowledge and inputs. This is important where the cost of the acquisition of such knowledge by outsiders is high. Irrigation systems are a good example of this.

Local factors such as soil conditions, water velocity and shifting water—courses are important considerations in their design; external planners and engineers often lack detailed information. Through devolution, government can get a sense of user preferences. Beneficiary participation offers the potential for the design and implementation of interventions that reflect the preferences of the population they are designed to assist. However, since communities are rarely homogeneous, it is important to examine whose preferences are being voiced. Devolution of natural resource management enables the local community to take account of local costs (external costs) that are ignored in higher-level decisions. These local costs can be balanced against the incomes and overall livelihood impacts to get more balanced natural resource management decisions.

Further, such local management can be designed to link investment with returns: for instance, fishstocking and infrastructure maintenance with the returns from selling fish. Such a link between investment and returns, secured by assured user rights, is likely to result in higher levels of production, as observed in the Oxbow Lakes Small-Scale Fishermen Project in Bangladesh. But although there is the potential to lower the costs of implementing interventions, it does not necessarily follow that beneficiaries will always be the lowestcost providers. Because their benefits cannot be withheld from anyone, and also because of their size, most irrigation systems, forests, rangelands and fisheries cannot be managed individually or by the household, and require coordinated regulation.

Programmes to devolve natural resources management are generally based on the assumption that users will take on the roles formerly assigned to the state. This requires some form of collective action to coordinate individuals' activities, to develop rules for resource use, to monitor compliance with the rules and sanctions against violators, and to mobilize the necessary cash, labour or material resources. Moreover, natural resources have multiple uses and users. Many of these uses have high economic value or are essential to the livelihood of different households.

Local collective action can be instrumental in finding rules and allocation of the resource between different users in a way that is seen as equitable by the users themselves. There are therefore equity as well as productivity arguments for collective action in natural resources management. Small groups have lower negotiation costs, are better able to recognize illegal users of the CPR and are less prone to free-riding by members. On the other hand, because relationships within a small group are highly personalized, there is more potential for conflict, and as there are fewer people to monitor CPR use, poaching by non-members may go unnoticed.

The latter difficulty was experienced in a community forestry programme in Almora District, India. For these reasons, a precise specification of the appropriate group size is difficult. However, several IFAD funded projects have been successful in reducing conflict between group members through a conscious choice of more marginalized people and areas and with a special focus on ethnic minorities and women. Such groups enjoy a considerable amount of homogeneous and shared sense of both deprivation and expectations.

In some situations, traditional patron-client relationships are sustained during the development of viable CPR management institutions. For example, in the High Atlas Mountains of Morocco, senior members of society have full rights to any part of the range for a greater length of time than other members who must negotiate with the local council for access. Indeed, cooperation can develop under unequal conditions in some situations. Confidence and trust among members of user groups are not ruled out even when there is inequality of endowments.

In landlord-initiated and funded irrigation projects in Tokugawa, Japan, collective action was possible because of existing patron-client relations. IFAD's experience in the Oxbow Lakes Small—Scale Fishermen Project in Bangladesh, however, shows that it is possible to create trust where strong traditions of collective economic action did not previously exist. The preconditions were the granting of secure, long-term user rights to the fishers and cooperation incentives in the form of substantially higher incomes.

The fishermen set up systems of equity in income and cost sharing, democratic rotation of leadership, and monitoring by group members, which themselves depended crucially on the acquisition of relevant knowledge by members. The costs and tangible benefits of participation have long been at the heart of the collectiveaction debate. One aspect of participation that is often not recognized is that people often choose to participate in natural resources management because it offers them an opportunity to socialize and form stronger relationships.

Such networks contribute to greater livelihood security, especially in situations of poverty and vulnerability, where mutual support among family, neighbours and community becomes vital. In Haiti, even landless households would contribute labour to watershed management activities, in part to strengthen networks with landowners who might later offer employment or other help. Such social capital could be an important survival strategy of a poor household.

An examination of the effectiveness of community based water projects in Central Java found that in villages with high levels of social capital—in particular with active village groups and associations household participation is likely to be high and monitoring mechanisms are more likely to be in place. But, village leaders and outsiders do not necessarily represent the preferences of households: household participation in service design and decision-making led to different— typically more expensive and convenient—water technology choices in Central Java.

For local users to be willing to take on responsibility for CPR management, the rights and responsibilities must be transferred from the state to users. Property rights play a central role in the management of natural resources, conveying authority and shaping incentives for management. They give necessary authorization and control over the resource; and can enforce collective action. However, privatization of these common resources often implies disenfranchisement of the poor.

A community institution for natural resources management is not inevitably or necessarily pro-poor. A study of four watershed development projects in India that were designed primarily to promote eco-restoration and improve the natural-resource base, with poverty reduction as a secondary concern, found that their (direct) benefits to the poorest were relatively small. While significant improvements were achieved overall in crop yields, diversification, income from farming, and women's participation in meetings, the benefits to the poorest (through higher employment) were much lower.

Community management of resources can lead to improvements in productivity and sustainability of the resource. In Nepal, a study of 86 community-managed and 22 government managed irrigation schemes found that community managed schemes were more efficient in terms of crop yield, cropping intensity, and so forth. Similarly, Oxbow Lakes in Bangladesh managed as CPRs of poor fishermen showed much higher rates of investment and yield per hectare than both privately leased and government-managed lakes.

A study of Ugandan forests found that state-owned forests were heavily exploited due to lack of incentives to staff to enforce the law. State and private forests which allow villagers to use their traditional rights to access forest resources in return for monitoring duties are much less over-exploited. The condition of forests in Nepal varies with the presence of community institutions for monitoring use and restricting harvesting. Similarly, the Aga Khan Rural Support Programme's work with natural resources management institutions in Gujarat, India, found that where programmes were managed by local institutions, farmers were willing to make greater investments in resource conservation, and agricultural productivity increased by up to 100% within three years.

All this makes a strong case for encouraging and strengthening local-level institutions for the management of local commons. Extreme diversity and inequality among the potential appropriators of a resource may inhibit cooperation, whereas equality may promote it. Across a number of countries, greater equality of endowments among the irrigators was associated with a higher degree of rule compliance and good maintenance. The relatively egalitarian structure of the community was an important factor in the farmers' willingness and ability to organize irrigation projects in Gujarat.

Similarly in the Indian State of Meghalaya, villages with greater equality of ownership of land, including forests, showed a greater propensity to overcome collective problems in regulating both distribution of ownership and methods of harvesting of forests for timber. On the other hand, in villages with greater inequality of landholding, even investments in land improvement were not forthcoming because of problems in combining the interests of large landowners and those of numerous tenants. The absentee landowners suspected that land improvements by tenants would lead to claims over land and blocked such investments.

In South India, inequality of landholding among the irrigators generally reduces cooperation on water allocation and field channel maintenance; but at very low and high levels of inequality, conservation is possible, while for some, at middle range of inequality it is not. An analysis of 54 farmer-managed surface irrigation systems in central Mexico yielded similar results. In general, however, the relationship between inequality and collective action is complex. There are distinct but opposite effects of inequality.

Those who benefit most from collective action are more willing to bear the costs involved and thus to make collective action possible. But those likely to benefit least have little incentive to participate in the collective effort: free riding then may be the more lucrative option for them. Besides, the transaction and enforcement costs for some cooperative arrangements may rise with inequality.

Although self-managed irrigation schemes may yield an equitable distribution of water among participating farmers, the criteria for membership in these irrigation groups tend to exclude women. Weaker categories of users are frequently excluded by dominant groups in order to achieve efficient use of resources. Although a number of forestry and drinkingwater projects have been aimed at women as primary users of the resources provided, most CPR institutions exhibit a virtual absence of women.

In several IFAD funded projects it was commonly observed that women are invisible farmers. As a result, women's needs are less likely to be taken into account. The impact is two fold. In addition to the disadvantages faced by women themselves, the overall productivity of the CPR system is often impaired. Water users' associations have been particularly dismissive of women's needs due to the misconception that only men require water for irrigation.

Both Joint Forest Management (JFM) and Community Forest Management (CFM) in India have tended to ignore the demands of women and the poor in general. When communities closed their forests for regeneration they prevented poor women from collecting firewood, whether for consumption or for sale. Cultural taboos such as fear of ritual pollution in Nepal stop women from contributing labour for irrigation system maintenance. In Malolo, Tanzania, women are prohibited from maintaining canals, so that they feel they cannot complain if they do not get their fair share of water.

Government policy in the Philippines excludes women from construction work. Not surprisingly, female participation in water user associations in Sri Lanka, Nepal, Pakistan and India is lower than that of men. Women often refuse to provide labour to, or participate in, agricultural development projects because they believe that the benefits will accrue only to male household members.

In India and Nepal, fewer than 10% of community forest group members are women, perhaps because, in almost half of Indian States where the JFM Programme exists, only one member of the household may become a member, which tends to be the man as head of the household. Women may be worse placed than men in their ability to attend meetings. In the Ambewelar irrigation system in the hills of Sri Lanka meetings are held at night to accommodate men who work all day, but it is not thought to be suitable for women to go out at night.

In Nepal, women gave their illiteracy as a reason for not attending meetings. They thought they would not understand what was being said and would not be able to contribute. Women seldom speak at forest management meetings and their opinions are rarely listened to. Given that so few women are members of natural resources maintenance groups or attend meetings, it is not surprising that more women are not present on executive decision-making committees.

The few women who are involved in forestry committees often participate because it is mandatory for the committee to include one or two women. As a result, and as there are few female members to represent, women on such committees tend to have 'nominal rather than effective presence'. Despite these barriers to women's participation in CPR management, in India and Nepal women are active in protecting the forests as they feel that men's patrolling is not effective; but their inability to take part in decision-making has consequences for equity and efficiency. Several times more forest resources can be extracted sustainably than is actually permitted. An important implication is that knowledge about resource levels is lacking, as the most regular and frequent users are excluded and gender differences in preferences for forest species are not taken into account. To overcome this problem, the IFAD funded Tamil Nadu Women's Development Project has been encouraging women to take a greater interest in watershed management projects. Participating NGOs such as MYRADA and OUTREACH have now adopted an approach of facilitating the emergence of women's self-help groups (SHGs).

One of the typical discussions is about the management of the natural resources around them. The women group members then try to help men to organize activities for natural resources management. Once this is achieved, women SHGs leave it up to the men, but they do have a representative in the decisionmaking group. Sometimes women are fully included in management of irrigation systems. In the Provincial Irrigation Unit, Nyanza Province, Kenya, women's contribution to rice farming is recognized and, accordingly, a minimum of 50% attendance by women is required at the preparatory meeting of new water users' associations, where women are organized in order to articulate their needs. Similarly, in Dodoma, Tanzania, the Water Supply and Health Project in Marginal Areas encouraged allocation of water rights in quantities sufficient for irrigating one acre to both men and women.

In Nepal, 3% of community-forest groups consist only of women. Women directly bear the cost of poor participation in community institutions designed for natural resources management. Village forest protection committees regulate forest access for its sustainable use. The cost of foregoing forest use is disproportionately borne by the women through a larger amount of time spent in fuelwood collection. Women's collection time increased from between one and two hours to between four and five hours for a headload of firewood, and journeys of half a kilometre lengthened to eight or nine kilometres soon after the start of protection in the Indian States of Gujarat and West Bengal. Wherever possible, women shift to alternative fuels such as twigs, dung cakes and agricultural wastes. While some of these hardships have been alleviated in some areas, they have not been eliminated entirely. The persistent shortages women face in these contexts thus appear to have more to do with their lack of voice and bargaining power in the, than from a lack of aggregate availability.Yet the various JFM and CFM initiatives show that where women and the poor do organize they are able to make some impact on the agendas of the community institutions.

In Meghalaya, for instance, the strongly male-dominated village assembly, after continuous pressure from the IFAD project, has begun to include women in its deliberations. Women's issues of access to fuelwood and fodder have also been included within the forest management programmes. The inclusion of women and other poor does not come about as a matter of course. Changing age-old traditions is a matter of struggle to change gendered or caste-based norms of behaviour, a struggle involving mainly the local participants but also facilitated by external agencies, NGOs and government legislation and orders. The various laws and rules in different South Asian countries, including most recently Pakistan, mandating a certain proportion of women members in village committees create a strong climate in favour of women's public and community roles. While such representation of women often starts out as nominal, over time it also tends to become more real and effective; but, of course, not without struggle.

Participation is necessary but insufficient by itself. It needs to be built upon improving the livelihood security of the poor. The poor who live at the edge of subsistence necessarily place a high value on their time: if conservation of natural resources comes into conflict with meeting the immediate need for survival, then they will disregard the concern for conservation. For instance, in northern and western Senegal, immediate safeguarding of the food supply has become the first priority of ordinary peasants because of the low fertility of land, insufficient rainfall and incidental swarms of locusts.

Long-term investment in soil or trees is not undertaken because it would in fact endanger the food supply. For the poor to be interested in conservation, a mechanism has to be devised that incorporates it into the livelihood security of the poor. This is especially true in a differentiated society where the poor might be tempted to free ride in the hope that the wealthier section would make the necessary investments for conservation. Of course, the wealthier section may not oblige, especially if increasing links with the external economy allow them alternative opportunities for investing their surplus. In that case, depletion of resources would become inevitable. The solution is to take advantage of links with the external economy in a way that simultaneously promotes conservation and improves the livelihood security of the poor.

Conservation has also been linked with security of livelihood with the JFM programme announced in 1988 in the Indian State of Madhya Pradesh. The policy accepts that the biotic pressure from villagers seeking fuelwood, fodder and timber, both for their household needs and for generating cash income, is the main cause of forest degradation. But, unlike previous policies, which tried to prevent degradation by depriving the villagers of their traditional right to forest produce, the new policy recognizes that the life of tribal people and other poor communities living within and near forests revolves around those forests, and that their domestic requirement of fuelwood, fodder, minor forest produce and construction timber should be the first charge on forest produce. An integrated village resource development programme is now an important aspect of the JFM programme, which presumes that if forests support village development, then people will appreciate their forests and help protect them. In other words, if resources outside forest lands become more productive, people will give up gathering from forests.

Institution-building must be just, genuinely participatory and inclusive. If the poor are to benefit from cooperative arrangements for resource management, they must participate fully in setting them up. Such arrangements can be built on the basis of patron-client relationships, but these are unlikely to advance the living standards of the poor much beyond the level of survival. The alienation of the clients from the residual income accruing from their labour makes it difficult and costly, even impossible, to monitor their performance effectively. This alienation within patron-client relations would reduce productivity itself; while a more inclusive situation is likely to enhance productivity.

As traditional hierarchies are being eroded everywhere with the spread of education and democracy, a new basis of cooperation must be created so that the appropriators can themselves devise viable institutions by mutual consent. Even in this case, however, the poor might be excluded. It is essential that the poor are encouraged and welcomed to participate in the decision-making process. Today, this is a fundamental requirement of most IFAD funded projects. Evidence from Mexico shows that successful management requires vigorous, regular and well-attended community assemblies, and the existence of accounting and reporting practices that provide community members with a healthy flow of accurate information.

Outside agencies interested in institutionbuilding for the poor will need to adopt special measures to ensure that participation is genuinely all-encompassing. In The Sudan, the state-run water supply services are in the process of being privatized. In many villages, water shortages are severe and prices high; families can spend up to half their income on water alone. Communities themselves selected individuals for receiving training in system operation and maintenance, while legislation was passed providing for the transfer of ownership to the community groups.

The communities now manage most of the water stations. Living conditions in the villages have improved greatly, reducing migration from them: a clear indication that the poor have benefited. IFAD's Special Programme for Africa has revealed some difficulties. This programme was launched in 1986 to assist governments in sub-Saharan Africa in responding to the devastating droughts of the 1980s. A sub-programme on Small-Scale Irrigation and Water Control (SSI/WC) was a major component of this programme. Its objective was two fold:

1) to increase the productive capacity of smallholders and improve household food security, and
2) to build the capacity of the farmers to take over operation and maintenance responsibilities of the scheme by involving local communities or beneficiary organizations.

A participatory demand-driven approach was considered a prerequisite for ensuring sustainability. Beneficiaries were expected to be key partners involved in selection, design and implementation. The strategy was to construct small-scale irrigation schemes which farmers would own and therefore take responsibility for their subsequent operation and maintenance. The water users' associations did reasonably well in operating and maintaining the schemes, especially in view of the complexities involved. As a result, participation was limited to consultation with village chiefs, local farmers' leaders and individual farmers.

This experience emphasizes the importance of devoting time and resources to building organizations of the poor if genuine participation is to become a reality. But it also has to be recognized that in most rural societies it would be practically impossible to ignore or bypass the traditional power structure altogether. The power base of the traditional elite may be eroding, but it still exists, and no largescale project of common property resource management can possibly be undertaken without their involvement, even if that implies agreeing to hand over portions of community assets to the poor. The difficulties well-off lessees face in instituting 'social fencing', whether of forests or water bodies, and thus in securing their investments can itself be an important factor in persuading them to agree to such redistribution.

Both the Oxbow Lakes Small-Scale Fishermen Project in Bangladesh and the Hills Leasehold Forestry and Forage Development Project in Nepal are examples of successful redistribution of community assets to coalitions of the poor. The latter project in Nepal selects the marginalized members of the community, families below the poverty line, women, small and marginal farmers, and landless and deprived ethnic or tribal people, and forms them into groups that are then given a 40-year lease of designated forest areas, which often amounts to a lease for life. It was found that targeting marginal groups would not produce positive results unless the agreement of the whole community was obtained. These leases were given out on what had been de facto community land, used by the richer as well as poorer farmers. A long period of time was spent persuading first the officials and then the rest of the community—in particular the village leaders—that the project would benefit everyone and not just the leasers.

In the same way, in the Oxbow Lakes Small-Scale Fishermen Project in Bangladesh, the local elite could see that fish culture by the poor increased local availability of fish, both reducing price and improving freshness. But at the same time, the success in large-scale aquaculture has also made the lakes attractive targets for takeover by local vested interests. In the present economic and political climate it may be necessary to present the case for equality in terms of its contribution, or likely contribution, to efficiency in use of resources.

Egalitarianism needs to be cast in terms of asset transfer rather than outright income transfers. While income redistribution may have no effect on productive efficiency (though the experience of East and South-East Asia shows that income redistribution in terms of higher public spending on health and education can have positive effects on productive efficiency), asset redistribution would link labour and investment with returns and income. For instance, the granting of property rights in forests to local communities and families, as in China or in North-East India, could improve micromanagement of the forest and link investment with returns.

Thus, a generalisation of this equalityenhancing property reform is likely both to be more just and to increase productivity of forest for products, including ecological services such as flood control and carbon sequestration, for external stakeholders. At the same time, we should also consider restrictions on property rights, in terms of excluding absentee claims or of excluding the right to sell or otherwise transfer forests. Asset redistribution can contribute to sustainable poverty reduction only if it increases the productive capacity of the poor and of the economy as a whole. The generally superior yields on small farms vis-à-vis large farms makes an important case for land redistribution to the landless.

Similarly, even in the case of common pool assets, like forests or water-bodies, the success of the Nepal Hills Leasehold Forestry and Forage Development Project and the Bangladesh Oxbow Lakes Small-Scale Fishermen Project shows that coalitions of the poor can increase the productivity of community resources. Inclusive local community institutions are inconsistent with the exclusion of women from effective community roles. The question of enhancing women's roles in public and community affairs is critical even in matrilineal and forestbased communities, let alone in patriarchal ones. Women have gender-specific knowledge of local resources and processes, and have gender-specific economic and other household responsibilities. Men tend to dominate inclusive community organizations; encouragement of separate public and community organizations for women would promote their greater participation in the management of the community.

Finance for Rural Poverty Reducation

Credit helps the poor to smooth consumption, and later to acquire assets greater than the value of the liability. Consumption smoothing is especially important for the rural poor; agricultural incomes and rural health fluctuate widely and will destabilize consumption if households cannot fall back on savings or access to credit. Once poor households feel that consumption is safe, they are more ready to risk borrowing for investment in physical, natural or human capital assets. But the poor can sustainably service credit only if the new asset yields more than enough to repay interest and, eventually, the capital element of the loan.

Thus finance for investment can reduce poverty, but not

while basic consumption remains at serious risk or if technology (or market access) does not enable the poor to earn a decent return on assets. Yet investment by the rural poor is often constrained because they cannot borrow. At the same time, if formal lenders are to reduce moral hazard and adverse selection to affordable levels, they must avoid high unit transaction costs on tiny loans; especially if they cannot effectively screen poor borrowers (who lack collateral). Informal (local) lenders are put off providing loans to the poor (again lacking collateral) by high co-variance (a bad harvest means loans fail together)— and often it does not pay to price-discriminate, charging more to poor/risky borrowers, because that stimulates even more risk-taking.

The rural poor often lack reliable access to financial services as a whole—including not only competitive credit, but also savings and insurance services—whether from public, formal private, or informal sources. From the early 1950s, developing-country governments and international donors provided massive doses of credit to the agricultural sector at concessional interest rates, often negative in real terms, through either cooperatives or state-run banks. This approach achieved little in reaching the poor, raising output, using credit efficiently, or developing sustainable rural financial institutions. Subsidized interest may even have destroyed competitive private lending and stimulated low-yield investment.

There is now a widespread consensus that problems in state intervention in rural financial markets arose as much from interest-rate ceilings as from distorted incentives and weak governance structures of the public-sector financial institutions. Yet the international development community recognized that, if state monopoly was bad for growth and poverty, untrammeled markets alone were unlikely to do the job either. Increased access of the rural poor to financial services was achieved by rapid increase in microcredit provision during the last 20 years. Targeted microcredit programmes seek a strong anti-poverty focus, and aim to increase incomes and smooth consumption.

Enthusiastic and large-scale support for these innovations from multilateral and bilateral donors has ensured a rapid growth of microfinance institutions across the world. The predominant financial product offered by most microfinance institutions (MFIs) is an advance of a lump sum of money, with capital and interest to be repaid in regular instalments. To ease collection and enforce repayment, individuals are often federated into groups that are collectively responsible for loans extended to its members ('peer monitoring'). Further incentive for regular repayment is provided in the form of quick, easy and increased access to repeat loans. The repayment by—instalment arrangement provides an opportunity for clients to take the maximum advantage of fungibility of cash by managing regular instalments from existing income sources.

The financial product is insensitive to seasonal demand and risk (which can be a disincentive for poorer clients using credit as quasi-insurance substitutes), and does not take into account the cash-flow cycle of client enterprises. Nevertheless, in sharp contrast to subsidized and loss-making state-backed rural credit, many (though not all) of the new microfinance agencies achieve sustainability by combining high repayment rates with interest at the market rate, thereby confirming that 'the poor need credit, not cheap credit'. But this is not costless.

Though part of the package is that the state (and donors) phase out subsidies of interest rates, initial administrative subsidies to create sound microfinance intermediaries for the rural poor have been huge. They are incurred, in part, because of the belief that poor populations can implement income-generating economic activities, and that the main limitation on their initiative is the lack of access to capital in contexts where:

1) financial markets are not well developed;
2) commercial banks are reluctant to commit themselves because of the extent of the risk, and also because of their lack of familiarity with the sector;
3) development projects and banks have most often failed; and
4) the informal sector is neither sufficiently large nor capable of responding to the challenges of development.

Initially, then, the challenge for microfinance was to demonstrate that, once financial tools specifically adapted to the needs and constraints of 'poor' populations were developed, then people would be able to use these tools for productive purposes and incorporate themselves into the financial milieu, repaying the loans and accumulating savings. Based on this assumption, many microfinance systems have been developed in South and Eastern Asia, with different institutional forms, and often giving preference to disadvantaged areas and to the most disadvantaged groups within these areas. In the second phase of the development of the microfinance sector, the need to create sustainable financial markets became evident, and the legal and financial sustainability of microfinance systems became a priority.

Microfinance systems were set the goal of breaking even, and thereby being able to liberate themselves from grant-funding within a reasonable period of time, and this very rapidly became the fundamental orientation of microfinance 'best practice'. The emphasis was on providing small loans, often focused on women entrepreneurs, as a means of reducing poverty. These loans have three objectives: to generate productive income streams; to reduce poverty; and to support sustainable rural financial institutions.

There is no reason to expect that these three objectives will point to the same set of loans or even of lending institutions, or that they will be consistent; and where there is no sufficiently productive/profitable safe opportunity that the poor can take up, the objectives will not be achievable. In short, production-oriented credit success needs assets and/or technology, usually with market access. While many agree that microfinance can make a difference to people's lives, the extent to which it contributes to poverty reduction remains uncertain.

The relationship between microfinance and poverty reduction is fairly complex: just as poverty is multidimensional, so there are many pathways to its reduction. Welfare indicators relate not only to income, but also to human, physical and social capital. The existing evidence of the impact of microcredit is not clear-cut. Some research suggests that access to credit has the potential to reduce poverty significantly, but there is also research suggesting that microcredit has a minimal impact on poverty reduction. It is now increasingly recognized that microfinance alone is not a magic bullet for poverty reduction, but only one of many factors that may contribute to it. In fact, in an effort to dispel the impression that microfinance is a cure for poverty, it is argued that 'the claims that microfinance assists "the poorest" and "the poorest of the poor" are unfounded within national contexts.

In many cases, the poor face significant structural challenges, which marginalize them not only in economic terms but also in social and political terms. This makes them 'invisible'. Many very poor people migrate seasonally for wage employment; some consciously avoid joining the mainstream, such as the banjaras in parts of India; some households, such as the 'Kamaiyas' in Nepal, are 'attached' to other households in semi-bonded relationships. Such 'invisibility' makes targeting difficult. It is hard to arrange loans or repayments from short-term migrants. Further, microfinance agencies (and members of peer groups) emphasize regularity in attending meetings and depositing savings—which penalizes employees in general and migrants in particular.

Poorer participants are less able to sustain benefits from these programmes and might drop out disproportionately, perhaps because the products offered are not appropriate to their needs. The rural poor need a range of financial services, including savings and insurance, not just credit. The poor operate in a micro-economy in which production, consumption, trade and exchange, saving, borrowing and income-earning occur in very small amounts, which increases the per unit transaction costs and makes it unattractive for them to borrow from the formal sector.

They are also exposed to high levels of risk arising from violence, natural disasters, health, harvest failure, and price and labour market fluctuations; the different forms of these risks weaken the capacity of community-based social security networks to provide support. These features mean that the poor must devise ways to spread risk, by economic diversification and the development of informal financial networks. Savings and credit mechanisms are used by the poor as substitutes for insurance, so savings, credit and insurance have to be treated in a unified way. Under these circumstances, the provision of microcredit has been found to affect crisis-coping mechanisms positively by allowing the diversification of income-earning sources and building assets. Even where there may be no evidence that access to microcredit leads to increases in consumption, it does contribute to reducing household vulnerability.

According to estimates, consumption variability is 54-47% lower for eligible microcredit borrowing households than for the control group. Such consumption smoothing is driven by income smoothing, which is shown by the significantly lower laboursupply variability experienced by households using microcredit than by the control group. This is important as poverty is so closely associated with risk and vulnerability. These results suggest that programme participation by the poor is driven largely by the benefits of risk reduction rather than the benefits of greater consumption levels.

In Sri Lanka, SANASA's poorest clients use savings services more than credit services and small, high-cost emergency loans more than large, low-cost investment loans. Designing financial services for the poor must focus on risk and vulnerability if they are to extend their outreach and prove more useful. One obvious response is insurance. However, quasiinsurance can be built into existing products, such as more frequent, but also more flexible, repayment; giving the opportunity to use savings for loan repayment; more flexible repayment schedules suited to client preferences; and purposespecific contractual savings products for events such as marriage, death and so forth.

Recently, the emphasis has shifted from the link between microcredit and poverty alleviation to the intrinsic importance of building sustainable financial systems offering wide-ranging services comprising microcredit, microsavings and insurance facilities. This is because the poor need access to financial services, particularly: deposit facilities for accumulating and safekeeping their savings, consumption-smoothing and self-financing of economic operations; credit for consumption-smoothing and external financing of their operations; and insurance for social security and loan protection. Provision of a wide range of financial services will not only serve clients' needs more effectively, but also improve outreach depth and improve access to external sources of funding.

Improved access to financial services can enable the poor rural household either to augment income generated by the production process or to reduce the cost of smoothing consumption at sufficient levels. Smoothing disposable income generated by borrowing for consumption, or by saving in highly liquid but less remunerative assets, is expected to be relatively more important for households that face the risk of transitory or chronic food insecurity. This perspective of financial service allows us to understand the difficulty that poorer households face in participating in and sustaining benefits from some of the current innovations.

The importance of financial-service provision to the poor is of intrinsic value, irrespective of its promise as a poverty-alleviating tool. Viewed thus, the issue is the design of suitable financial-service products that the poor would find useful. This in turn warrants an understanding of the financial behaviour and preferences of the poor. Households all around the world have always saved: as insurance against emergencies, for religious and social obligations, investment and future consumption.

The importance that poor people attach to saving is also demonstrated by the many ingenious, but often costly, ways they find to save in addition to keeping small amounts of cash secreted at home. These methods include investing in assets that can be sold in case of emergency, participating in local initiatives such as Rotating Savings and Credit Associations or funeral funds, or lending between family and friends. But these mechanisms can often fail to meet the needs of poor people in a convenient, cost-effective and secure way. If a poor household is given a safe, accessible opportunity, its capacity to save and the amounts it manages to save are remarkable.

There was a notion that 'the poor cannot save', and compulsory savings systems often required members to deposit small token amounts each week as well as levying more substantial amounts at source from loans. These compulsory savings were then often 'locked-in' until members left the organization, thus denying them access to their own money. Until recently, compulsory, locked-in savings systems, in one form or other, were a prevalent model for MFIs throughout the world.

However, compulsory savings systems have come under increasing pressure not only from the professionals involved with financing, managing and reviewing MFIs but also from clients themselves. Poorest has stressed that possibly the greatest challenge in microenterprise finance is to expand the provision of savings services to the poor. This is driven by the fact that 'there is substantial evidence from many parts of the world that:

1) institutional savings services that provide the saver with security, convenience, liquidity and returns, represent a crucial financial service for lowerincome clients; and

2) if priced correctly, savings instruments can contribute to institutional selfsufficiency and wide market coverage'.

Nonetheless, for MFIs with a history of creditdriven services that have levied compulsory savings as part of a package, the shift to flexible financial services, including savings products, is often hard to effect. MFIs need to acquire more sophisticated management capabilities to manage liquidity, risks and cost, as well as develop a more complex organizational structure and information systems in order to act as financial intermediaries. Furthermore, several other factors often provide significant impediments to promoting savings. These include macroeconomic problems such as high inflation rates as a result of political turmoil and/or economic imbalances, and financial repression through interest rate controls and subsidized credit schemes.

In addition, in many countries there are no appropriate systems of regulation and supervision for MFIs leaving them either operating outside a legal framework or pinned down by traditional formal-sector banking laws. Thus, despite the huge demand for savings facilities for the poor, the supply of such services is inadequate, in terms of both quantity and quality.

Insurance can complement the provision of credit services for institutions seeking to help their clients to smooth their consumption. Insurance is a powerful poverty-reducing tool, as well as a means for the institution to reduce risk. As institutions mature they are in a good position to provide insurance to smooth consumption of the poor and to enhance institutional profitability. Insurance goes even further than savings to minimize dips in basic needs consumption. It also gives the poor a sense of security that allows them to dare to pursue profit-maximizing income strategies, and hence to borrow, because they know that an income shock will be minimized when the claim is settled.

With the repayment rate of a lending institution closely linked to clients' return on investment, insurance has considerable potential as a complement to an institution's credit programme. Insurance provision in the semi-formal sector is still not viewed as a policy goal: hence the large surplus of premiums over claims that MFIs' insurance products typically generate. Resources attracted by MFIs through insurance provision are generally used to build up capital for smoother operations rather than to improve upon the insurance services provided to clients. While capital accumulation is certainly an important advantage of providing insurance, neglecting to improve insurance products is short-sighted and keeps the institution from developing a valued service.

Developing insurance products will help address an institutions long-term profitability and protect members against larger, more destabilizing economic shocks. Insurance instruments are a profitable complement to credit delivery for a mature MFI. As the average loan size of an MFI increases, it becomes increasingly risky to disburse credit, since if a family's return on investment from borrowed capital is less than anticipated, the larger repayments cannot be mustered from the family's normal income. The opportunity for profits through lower-risk insurance instruments could significantly help keep microfinance operations profitable, even as default pressures increase with larger loan sizes. With increased profits from insurance services, credit disbursement could be more selective with respect to screening and follow-up. The likely result would be more efficient and profitable credit delivery for income generation.

From a social welfare standpoint as well, a more fully developed insurance market is desirable. Absorbed savings in the form of insurance premiums are disbursed when beneficiaries are most likely to spend additional income on basic necessities. For the institution, therefore, insurance provision means more effective poverty alleviation, improved loan repayment rates and improved profitability. Consumption-smoothing strategy is strengthened with insurance provision. Demand for savings services could in part be accommodated by insurance services that would have a more direct and positive effect on poverty.

Microfinance Institutions

The preceding discussion establishes that different types of financial institutions and strategies are required; there is no single best type. Institutions must be tailored to the potential of the area, the cultural environment and the requirements of the clients. There are marginal areas with a predominance of subsistence agriculture and low-return activities. Here, user-owned SHGs or small cooperatives which are savings-oriented and operate at nominal costs may be most suitable.

There are high-potential areas with high-return agriculture and profitable rural microenterprise activities. In these areas, credit-oriented rural banks with professional management, large financial cooperatives and commercial bank branches with individual or group technologies may be more appropriate. The choice of institutions that are suitable in a given situation will depend on the situation and environment specifics. The degree to which financial disciplines and cost-recovery principles can be applied will depend on the extent to which the local production environment is developed, that is, the rate of return from activities taken up through MFIs. It will also depend on the effects of various man-made and natural disasters on the normal flow of economic events. Large gains can be wiped out overnight, making recovery of loans difficult, if not impossible. Such circumstances will need provision of additional resources for supporting the development of MFIs. If such costs are to be internalized, many of the microfinance initiatives may cease to be viable.

The viability of MFIs will also depend on how far these institutions can reduce transaction costs. This is a major challenge. Informal financial markets in many parts of Asia and Africa have been demonstrated to be efficient mobilizers of savings and providers of financial services. They can often show the way for cutting down on costs and ensuring fuller recovery. Efforts need to be made to integrate the positive features of informal financial market behaviour into the formal MFIs.

Poverty reduction is a complex task, requiring sustained commitment to consistent, yet flexible, joint action. There are no quick fixes and no easy solutions. No one institution, national or multilateral, public or private, and no unique strategy can hope to deal effectively with the different contexts and causes that underlie poverty. So coherent anti-poverty strategy requires stable partnerships, based on trust as well as self-interest. The most fundamental partnership is with the poor. Poverty reduction is not something that governments, development institutions or NGOs can do for the poor. They can help create the conditions in which the poor can use their own skills and talents to work their way out of poverty. This requires putting the poor at the centre of the process, as full partners in determining the priorities and the directions of change, emancipating them from the constraints that trap them in poverty, empowering them. It is therefore misguided bureaucratic centralism to plan for the poor; partnerships for poverty reduction should, wherever possible, start with the agency of the poor themselves, with their preferences and potentials. The evidence of the success of partnerships with the poor even in such apparently unlikely areas as plant breeding—not passive farm trials but farmers' active varietal selection and development—is telling. Whatever kind of resource is involved—technologies for plants; animals; housing; asset choices among skills; types of rural road; forms of consensual land distribution— involving the poor through the institutions of partnership assists success. The problem is that doing this locally with decentralized systems means opening opportunities to the articulate, the strong, or the unscrupulous.

Microlevel partnerships are institutional arrangements - formal or informal organizations and rules—among nearby people, e.g. to manage common property resources. Meso-level partnerships—of government with civil society, NGOs or the private sector—are increasingly used for service delivery, with the NGOs implementing government projects, often working jointly for lobbying and advocacy, or with donors. Micro- and meso-partnerships are necessary not only to deliver services, but also to identify and develop demand for them. Macro-partnership, the overarching global framework for anti-poverty strategies.

NGOs as Service Providers

National government institutions and external donors have long collaborated with NGOs and other civil-society institutions as service providers in the context of development projects and programmes. Currently, NGOs in developing countries reach directly an estimated 250 million people. These organizations now supplement, and in some cases have displaced, state agencies in the provision of relief and welfare, social services and development projects. The delivery of international development assistance has also been transformed with increased NGO involvement in various projects. Resources disbursed for development projects increased steadily from USD 0.9 billion in 1970 to USD 6.3. billion in 1993 (in constant 1970 dollars). In an international finance institution like IFAD for example, virtually every project in recent years involves civil-society institutions and NGOs.

In several Latin American countries, the responsibility of providing a number of social and development services has been delegated to NGOs. In some cases the state has withdrawn from financing as well as delivering services, such as rural credit and agricultural extension in Peru. The involvement of NGOs has often been found to enhance the prospects for successful project implementation. Such organizations have a comparative advantage in reaching the poor. Often they have better information about the poor because of local contacts, and they reduce the leakage in delivering benefits that results from corruption in government bureaucracies. NGOs typically work in communities or settings where the reach of the government is weak. In the West Bank and Gaza an estimated 1200 NGOs provide 60% of primary health care, up to half of secondary and tertiary health care, most agricultural services, low-cost housing, and microcredit. The same is true of primary health care and education in many African countries in remote rural areas where NGOs run by Christian missionaries are often the only service agencies operating.

In many regions, development programmes have in effect been captured by vested interests, with either the active collusion or the passive acquiescence of state elites. Lack of people's organizations that actively promote the coalition of the poor is usually a major contributory factor in capture by powerful interests. Although there is a risk of being over-optimistic on the basis of limited evidence, the temptation to rule out a strong coalition of the poor on the grounds of ethnic, religious and caste differences must also be resisted. A recent synthesis draws attention to key factors in promoting coalitions of rural poor.

Cooperation depends on whether cooperative action was successful in the past. The latter may be associated with the shared norms of trust in a community. There is some evidence that if the gains are large, these could overcome the disadvantages of a socially heterogeneous membership. The problems of social heterogeneity are nevertheless compounded by those of economic inequalities. Capture of local organizations by the rural elite often remains unchallenged by the poor, who are trapped in a dependent role.

An agricultural labourer, in debt to his regular employer, will be disinclined to cooperate with other labourers to demand an increase in the agricultural wage. It is commonly believed that the only reliable way to achieve an increase in participation and the collective action potential of poorer groups is to increase the resources available to them through redistributive policies. For instance, access to land through a market-mediated land redistribution programme could weaken elite dominance and induce more effective participation by the poor in local bodies. However, while earlier land reform helps facilitate later success, decentralized institutions have also worked well in areas where land reform has had little success, such as in Bangladesh or in the Indian State of Karnataka.

7

Assessment of Rural Poverty

Poverty is defined as the situation of households or persons with the lowest incomes or expenditures, and the poverty line is determined as a proportion of the average income per person, usually one half to two thirds of Gross Domestic Product (GDP) per person. The difference between the concepts is that the absolute measure ignores distribution aspects of poverty. In some cases, absolute poverty may be reduced while at the same time inequality is rising. This appears to happen more frequently in sub-Saharan Africa than in other regions.

It is generally recognized that poverty is not just a matter of income or expenditure shortfalls. There are other contributing factors, but which are the most relevant is a matter of extensive debate, although access to education and health is mentioned most often. In addition, a growing literature stresses the importance of local perceptions and attitudes in defining poverty and its characteristics. Aspects not commonly included, such as dignity and being part of a social mutual-help network, turn out to be as important as the income and social parameters usually considered. Others have developed vulnerability approaches that focus on the dynamics of poverty or vulnerability. In these approaches, vulnerability is defined as the probability of an acute decline in access to food or consumption, which leads to the inability to meet minimum survival needs. Vulnerability includes two main elements: the exposure to risk and the inability to cope with it, which need to be simultaneously present.

The most commonly used definitions of poverty are designed by outsiders and focus mostly on income or expenditure. Other outsiders have realized and shown that noneconomic considerations are often more, or at least equally, important to 'insiders' and therefore need to be integrated into the poverty concept. Gender aspects of poverty are rarely taken into account, nor have insider concepts so far been made operational. It would appear consistent for those who give a high priority to participatory development to base their poverty concept on insider perceptions of poverty and deprivation.

Sub-Sharian Africa (SSA) is one of the poorest regions in the world, and poverty seems to be increasing, at least when measured by the poverty line of USD 1 per day and during the period for which incidence data are available (1987-98). By 1998, all developing regions together accounted for about 1.2 billion poor persons, amounting to 23.4% of the total population in these areas. Since 1990, both the absolute number of poor and their proportion of the total population seem to have declined.

In SSA, on the contrary, the total number of poor has risen from 217 million to 302 million persons, and by 1998 the poverty incidence had reached 48.1% of the total population. SSA has the highest poverty incidence among all developing regions. While the incidence of poverty has declined since 1990 in all developing regions taken together, primarily due to progress in Asia, in SSA its incidence has continued to increase. The number of poor in all developing regions decreased during 1987-98 by 0.5% per year, in spite of a total population growth of about 1.5%.

In sub-Saharan Africa, a reverse trend can be seen: poverty

increased faster than the population. Another disquieting factor is that, contrary to all developing regions together, the poverty gap in sub-Saharan Africa remains constant at about 20%, while it dropped to 7.2% for all developing regions together. This implies that the African poor are remaining on average at 20% below the poverty line, while in other areas the poor are moving towards the poverty line income.

Poverty is, however, not only a matter of low incomes; it also relates to social conditions. These are usually measured through outcome indicators in health and education, most frequently the infant mortality rate (IMR), life expectancy, gross enrolment in primary schools and female illiteracy rates. The disadvantage of these measures is that their improvement over time does not necessarily mean that the conditions for all the poor have improved.

The overall literacy rate for women or life expectancy, for instance, may improve nationally, while the conditions of the poorest portion of the population remain the same or even become worse.

Table 1: Poverty Incidence and Poverty Gap, 1987-98

	Number of Poor (millions)			*Poverty Incidence (%)*			*Poverty Gap (%)*		
Region	*1987*	*1990*	*1998*	*1987*	*1990*	*1998*	*1987*	*1990*	*1998*
Sub-Saharan Africa	217.2	242.3	301.6	46.6	47.7	48.1	20.0	20.0	20.1
All developing regions	1 227.1	1 276.4	1 174.9	28.3	29.0	23.4	8.6	9.0	7.2

Progress in IMR reduction brought the region to the level of SSA. On the other hand, the decline in life expectancy since

1990, both in Western and Central Asia (WCA) and SSA as a whole, reflects the growing impact of the HIV/AIDS epidemic. By the end of 1999, according to official estimates, 25 million persons in SSA had HIV/AIDS, of which 5.9 million in WCA. Another disturbing development is the decline in gross primary enrolment rates. This trend, also occurring elsewhere in Africa, suggests that improvements in social conditions are not necessarily also benefiting the poor: it is in fact most likely the poor rather than the better-off, who are sending fewer of their children to school, mainly because they cannot pay for school fees and other education expenditures. A similar reasoning applies to improvements in indicators such as access to health services.

The social indicators thus show a mixed pattern of improvements and stagnation or declines. It is impossible to determine how these trends have an impact on the conditions of the poor and who has benefited from any improvements. Social indicators are not established by income group, and a generalized improvement in, say, primary school enrolment should not be taken as an indication of reduced poverty because the beneficiaries may be wholly or largely the non-poor. Using average national social indicators to further understanding of poverty, therefore, may increase the risk of conceptual confusion, taking overall social improvements for the non-poor as reductions in poverty.

The Human Poverty Index calculates the percentage of the total population affected by one or more of the four elements that constitute the index. Within rural areas, however, poverty is often localized. In Cameroon, for instance, 45% of all poor live in the Far North and Northern Provinces which is a savannah-type agro-ecological zone. Farming systems in the provinces are based on millet, sorghum, cotton and groundnuts and/or livestock raising. Droughts are frequent and periods of food shortages occur. Similarly, in Ghana, poverty incidence is highest in rural savannah areas and somewhat lower in rural coastal areas.

In several countries with a savannah in the north and a forest in the south, rural poverty tends to be significantly higher in the north. There are often, of course, differences in the socio-economic and demographic history of the two regions. Generally, however, the north depends for its economy on cereals, cotton and livestock, while the south produces several tree crops for export. The latter suffer from fluctuating terms of trade, but on the whole seem to generate more household resources than the savannah systems. Poverty and household size are positively related, and larger households tend to be poorer than small families.

The sex of the household head is an important factor in poverty: the probability that a household is poor is much higher when a man heads the household than when a woman does. Contrary to conventional wisdom, available data consistently show that the poverty incidence among woman-headed households is lower than among man-headed ones.

In rural areas of Nigeria, the incidence of poverty among woman-headed households declined from 42% in 1985 to 22% in 1992. Compared with man-headed households, woman-headed households not only had a lower poverty incidence, but also reduced the incidence faster. Apart from their (poverty) income level, when women have more control over the use of household incomes, expenditures tend to be more focused on meeting the basic needs of the family and those of children. In comparisons of woman-and man-headed households with similar resources in seven sub-Saharan countries, the children in the former have higher school enrolment rates and better completion rates.

Education is fundamental for human development and poverty alleviation. However, while improved education levels may be a positive factor in poverty alleviation, they are certainly not the only or sufficient ones. The main explanation for this difference is that urban education improves access to the urban labour market, while the rural labour market is much less stratified and demands relatively less skilled labour.

The education level of the household head is an indicator for the income-earning potential of the household. An analysis in Niger, where overall education levels are low compared to all other WCA countries, shows that poverty incidence is highest among households where the head has no education; when she or he is literate, the incidence is 65%; while a completed primary level further reduces the incidence to 56%.

Studies in Ghana have confirmed that location is an important factor in enrolment: school attendance is lower in rural areas than in urban ones. Gender and income are other determining factors; together with location, they make for stark differences. In Niger, for instance, enrolment is 6% for very poor girls in rural areas, and is 13 times higher, at about 80%, for non-poor boys in urban areas.

Within the rural area, there are important differences: in the poorest 20% of rural households, the primary enrolment of girls is about 40% that for boys, while in the richest 20% of rural households, it is 55%. Individual factors with a strong impact on primary enrolment in the household are the education level and sex of the household head, woman-headed households recording higher enrolment rates.

In Mauritania in 1990, primary net enrolment rates in rural areas for the poorest 20% of households were 21% for boys and 14% for girls, compared with, respectively, 58% and 28% for the richest 20% of households. Parents in the Central African Republic, where gross primary enrolment in the rural areas in 1995 was 74% for boys and 42% for girls, stated that the most important factors constraining primary school enrolment were the high cost of school materials, the various fees to be paid, the distance to schools, and the incompatibility between the school calendar and the agricultural calendar.

Moreover, the content of education had little relevance to pupils' needs and was unlikely to improve their earning capacities. Parents gave as main reasons for low school attendance of girls the risk of sexual harassment in school and the practice of early marriage. While the overall health situation in WCA countries is generally worse than the average for sub-Saharan Africa, little information on the health status of the poor is available.

In Ghana, 16% of persons in the lowest income group reported an illness during a two-week reference period, compared with 29% of those in the highest income group. Reporting on the importance of seeking treatment from outsiders also needs to be interpreted with caution. A large proportion of reported illnesses and injuries are selftreated, irrespective of household income level. In Ghana, 42% of the poor and 57% of the rich obtain treatment from outsiders when sick.

In Benin, about 20% of the urban poor use traditional therapy, not only because it costs less but also because it is thought to be more effective than modern medicine. When sick, the poor resort first to self-medication; if this fails, a healer is consulted. The most common illnesses, such as diarrhoea, measles and chickenpox, are considered the domain of traditional medicine.

Healers are not only cheaper, but they also accept credit and the fee does not need to be paid in advance as it does in the formal system. In Niger, household surveys revealed similar attitudes and practices among poor families. In the absence of health indicators by income group, it is not clear whether the poor are in a worse health situation than are the rich. Also, at the macro level, the health situation is only partially explained by income.

A quick regression analysis between Gross national Income

(GNI) per person and IMRs in the poor WCA countries in 1998 revealed that only 15% of differences in IMR can be attributed to different income levels. Similarly, the mortality rate of children under the age of five (U5MR) was only very partially determined by income levels. The same weak degree of correlation was found in 35 poor countries in SSA, but income levels still only explained one fifth to one fourth of the health situation.

At the household level, however, the appearance of a serious illness presents a major risk; and when it affects an income-earning member of a poor household, it can constitute a dramatic drain on resources. In the extreme, this situation can even render the household destitute, as treatment costs may need to be covered by selling off assets such as small livestock or consumer valuables.

In 2000, an estimated 25 million people had HIV/AIDS in SSA - representing an alarming SSA-wide infection rate of about 8% of the adult population. Since the epidemic began, 17.2 million people have died from AIDS. The number of new infections in 1999 alone was about 4 million. In the 35 highly affected African countries, the life expectancy at birth in 2000-05 is estimated at 48.2 years, a whole 8.9 years less than it would have been without AIDS.

In Nigeria alone, some 2.5 million people are affected. While the ravages of the disease in the subregion are not yet as devastating as in other parts of Africa, the situation is about to 'erupt' in several countries. A major factor fuelling the epidemic is the pattern of male labour migration - both the long-distance movement of rural men and boys to coastal areas in search of better livelihoods; and their short-term seasonal migration from rural to urban centres within the same country.

In both scenarios, it is usually men heads of households who migrate from poor rural communities leaving behind their families (mostly women, children and older members) to manage the subsistence farms. The men are away for extended periods of time, increasing their risk factors for HIV/AIDS infection because of the high probability that they will seek the services of commercial sex workers who in most cases are among the first groups to be infected. The 'second wave' of infection is the result of the spread of the disease among other household members, including women and children.

In the past, the spread of infection seemed slower because most infected men returned to their families in rural areas only when they were seriously ill and needed the care and attention of other family members. The disease has now entered many rural farm households, and its multiplier effects are beginning to be felt, with prevalence rates increasing alarmingly.

Caring for the sick depletes household resources and reduces production capacity. This double impact results in a vicious cycle of impoverishment and decline of the farm household. In West Africa, many cases have been reported of reduced cultivation of cash crops or food products. In many rural areas in these countries, the capacity of rural people to ensure their livelihoods has been dramatically curtailed. While cross-border conflict and refugee movements were often the rule in the past, civil war with massive internal displacement is now more common in WCA countries, making it more difficult to reach affected civilian populations. Civil war is devastating for all segments of a country's population, including rural people.

There is evidence that in cases of similar access to resources and decisionmaking, women and their households are less poor than men and man-headed households. Yet in poor households, the impact of poverty is harder on women than on men, although, again, poverty-specific data are not available. A first indication is the division of labour costs and time spent on productive activities, including domestic work. In the Centre

Province of Cameroon, men work an average of 32 hours per week, while women work twice as much. Of this time, women work 31 hours in domestic activities while men work only four hours. In spite of this, women also work more in agriculture: 26 hours per week against 12 for men.

The integration of households in the market is ensured by household transport activities, and it is in these that the division of labour is strikingly biased against women. Women generally transport more on their heads in volume than is transported in vehicles. The average time spent by an adult woman transporting water, firewood, crops and consumer goods ranges from little less than one hour to 2.5 hours per day. Village surveys in Ghana and the United Republic of Tanzania have shown that women spend about three times as much time in transport as men do, and they transport about four times as much in terms of volume.

In Burkina Faso, the total transport volume ensured by women carrying head-loads amounts to 10-15 tonnes (t) per kilometre (km) per year per woman, while men provide less than 5 t/km. Women and girls have lower education levels than their male counterparts, the result not only of poverty but also of social and cultural constraints and the policy environment. Illiteracy among adult women in Burkina Faso was 91% in 1995, while in Congo it was 33%. A pronounced negative correlation exists between women's education levels and infant and child mortality and fertility.

Primary school enrolment of girls is increasing faster than that of boys, but still stands at 30-60% of boys' enrolment. An important determining factor for primary enrolment is the availability of drinking water close to the household. Access of women to productive assets and investments such as land, finance and inputs is a major limiting factor despite the documented fact that women tend to manage such resources more productively than men.

The lack of decision-making authority of women outside and within the household has major implications for resource allocations, income levels, and also for fertility and the use of contraceptives. Studies have found that the ability of women to negotiate decisions that impact on fertility and population growth rates depends in part on their access to independent income sources and the choices that are created through access to literacy, numeracy and formal education. In general, women and men perceive poverty differently and tend to see their incomeearning roles as quite separate in the same household.

In Ghana, members of poor households indicated that the household is not seen as a unified entity but made up of individual women and men, each with his or her own responsibilities and each contributing in some way to household resources. In conclusion, a number of gender-specific patterns have emerged. Income poverty in WCA is primarily a rural phenomenon. In 16 WCA countries for which urban/rural poverty incidence data are available, 41% of the total population is classified as poor, of which the rural share is 74%. Based on these estimates, approximately 91 million people in the region can be categorized as rural poor.

Given the declining trend in income per person in all countries except those in the coastal zone, and the ambivalent trends in social indicators, it is probable that both rural and urban poverty are increasing in terms of incidence. Rural poverty, however, concerns on average twice or three times as many people as urban poverty does and therefore is more important as a phenomenon and in terms of the resources required to improve the situation. On the other hand, and intuitively speaking, the quality of living among urban poor is lower than in rural areas.

Social conditions contributing to vulnerability include the incidence of woman-headed households, primary school enrolment rates; and areas where a major proportion of the population has only access to surface water for drinking water purposes. On this basis, areas where vulnerability and poverty incidence are highest can be determined. Several participatory analyses have brought out aspects of well-being and poverty that are highly relevant for the poor themselves, but not always taken into account in other analyses.

According to the poor in Cameroon, poverty is characterized by the presence of hunger in the household; fewer meals per day and an inadequate diet; a high percentage of income or expenditures used for food; no or few cash income sources; and the feeling of being powerless and unable to make oneself heard. In Nigeria, the adequacy of the diet is also perceived as a poverty indicator, but probably more so in urban areas than in rural ones, where the poor have access to basic foodstuffs.

In Niger, the rural poor identified the difficulty of access to good land as a main economic factor leading to poverty. The traditional chief manages the land and assigns the best land to the most senior members of the clan. New land is of lower quality, and outsiders such as impoverished nomads who have to settle in agriculture after the loss of their herds, can only hold such land in usufruct. Other factors contributing to poverty are:

i) the number of small children and elderly dependants in the household unable to work in the fields or elsewhere; and

ii) inability to diversify income sources through livestock activities, off-season farming or gardening, and small trade.

Those unable to diversify activities have to migrate for labour, which is seen as another indication of poverty, as is working for others. The extended family and clan relations provide solidarity and help between urban and rural households and among households in rural villages. The institution of Muslim solidarity, zakkat, implemented by the local religious leader, provides, to varying degrees, a social safety net for the poorest households.

Safeguards are, however, limited if the whole community is subject to the same occurrence (for instance, a drought). Participatory poverty analysis in Ghana confirms the importance of the community, especially in rural areas.

Access to food is felt to be a main poverty determinant. Poverty in this sense is perceived not only as an individual or household condition but also as a state of the whole community. For instance, during part of the year, practically all community members in rural areas in the north suffer from food insecurity, and community mutual-help systems are unable to cope with such a situation. Participatory analysis in Nigeria classified several rural poverty symptoms as follows:

— The poor tend to be located in isolated villages with inadequate road and communications linkages. Most transportation of goods and produce is done through head-loading.

— Poverty is associated with cropping small areas, mainly with food crops, using simple tools. The labour available in the household is more than that required by the small farm, and often household members work on other people's farms. Few or no cash crops are produced; and where trees are owned, they are often pledged as security against debts.

— Food insecurity during the pre-harvest period is another symptom of poverty, and is often combined with a starch-based diet; sometimes stale food, normally used for animal feed, is consumed.

— Poor households lack linkages to influential persons or urban opportunities. They depend largely on income-generating activities with low productivity. They have little access to savings and credit, and own few or no valuable assets.

— External signs of poverty are, among others, the absence of a corrugated iron roof on the house; wearing one set of clothes continuously; and, for women, working in the fields rather than engaging in traditional women's activities such as crop trading.

Rural Poverty Alleviation

Despite major investments by governments and donors over the last 30 years, constraints to agricultural development and rural poverty reduction in Western and Central Africa remain formidable. Although conditions vary among countries and sub-zones in the region, the most important of these constraints can be grouped as follows:

— insufficient human and social capital development;

— lack of appropriate macroeconomic and sectoral policy frameworks;

— low farmer productivity and major challenges in natural resource management (NRM) in the face of steadily rising urban population and food demand trends;

— inefficient agricultural marketing systems, especially for food products;

— lack of access to financial capital;

— inability to fully exploit potentially remunerative and risk-reducing non-farm investment opportunities; and

— inadequate rural infrastructure development.

Several cross-cutting issues commonly appear within these constraints: lack of effective institutions (public, private and non-governmental) for supporting initiatives to energize rural development and reduce poverty; lack of legitimate beneficiary participation in the design, implementation, monitoring and evaluation of investment projects, despite donor and government rhetoric to the contrary; inadequate attention to the needs of women and to the design of appropriate measures to address their needs; and lack of coordination among donor agencies, which sends conflicting messages to host governments about appropriate policies and strategies, and stretches already weak project implementation capacity. Yet a number of positive developments have also occurred.

Many governments in the region have launched economic and sectoral policy reforms and begun to liberalize markets. Most exchange rate regimes now provide incentives to economic development rather than discouraging it. Financial sectors have been cleaned up. While it would be an exaggeration to say that the region has entered a 'post-adjustment' era, government has now withdrawn from many areas where it did not belong.

The challenge ahead is to define new and more appropriate roles for government to facilitate broad-based and pro-poor agriculture and rural development. There has been substantial progress in improving some important social indicators. Civilsociety organizations (CSOs) have rapidly developed over the last several years. The wave of democratization that swept across much of Africa in the early 1990s broadened economic and agricultural policy debate, formerly the exclusive domain of a small clique of government and donor technocrats.

Now there is greater civil-society participation, and many different actors take part in policy and project design and implementation. CSOs include, among others, producer associations and business groups, non-governmental organizations (NGOs), the popular press, opposition parties, parliamentarians and consumers.

Importance of Social Capital Development

If an iron law of poverty alleviation exists, it is that the way to escape poverty in the long run is through human capital development. The importance of social capital development for poverty alleviation has also been increasingly recognized. There has traditionally been a serious pro-urban bias to public expenditure on health, education, and water and sanitation in WCA—despite the overwhelmingly rural nature of poverty in Africa and the many pronouncements that increasingly acknowledge this.

Unfortunately, governments have been slow to correct imbalances where they matter—in budgets. The importance of investing in human capital in terms of the provision of education and health care has figured prominently in the literature of development economics. Regarding education, empirical evidence on its impact on poverty and economic growth can be grouped as follows:

i) general effects on economic growth;

ii) effects on productivity growth; and

iii) effects of women's education on long-term development and the quality of life.

The first evidence of education's impact on economic growth dates back to the late 1950s. The World Bank again emphasized this theme in the 1990s in its analysis of the causes behind the rapid income growth rates of eight east-Asian economies during 1965-90. Over this period, the eight economies grew at an impressive average rate of 5.5%, five times faster than SSA. The World Bank concludes that primary education is by far the largest contributor to this growth, with secondary education coming a close second.

Regarding poverty alleviation, the poor in particular benefit from free and universal primary education, and it is therefore at this level that government budgets in developing countries should focus, together with assuring quality standards. Education has a strong impact on the capability of people to adopt new technologies. However, secondary sources confirm the relationship between education and farmer productivity at least in Ghana and Uganda. If children are not nourished properly, their capacity to profit from extra years of schooling does not reach its potential.

Better nutrition improves a child's cognitive abilities, better equipping him/her to benefit from schooling. This in turn means that public investments in primary education will yield higher returns. If the last point is accepted, a strong case exists for investing in girls' education. There is a strong link between a mother's education and the health and nutritional status of her children. Women's decisions on fertility, for example, directly and indirectly affect children's nutrition and health.

Evidence indicates that health and family programming efforts are unlikely to substantially reduce fertility rates and IMR if they are not coupled with greater support to girls' education. Research based on simulations from 72 developing countries, for example, shows that doubling the mean level of secondary education from 19% to 38% reduces the average total fertility rate from 5.3 to 3.9, and IMR from 81 to 38 per 1 000.

Not only do the highest gains come from countries in southern Asia and sub-Saharan Africa, but if the chosen policy had simply been to increase the number of physicians, IMR would have been reduced by only 9.5%. Although boys' education with regard to fertility decisions is also important, data from Kenya suggest that a father's education has no significant effects on his children's nutrition. A recent World Bank publication on gender, growth and poverty reduction in SSA provides strong arguments in support of this statement.

Thus, the mother's role in the nutritional status of her

children seems to be confirmed. For this reason the gender disparities in primary school enrolment in WCA are all the more disquieting. The evidence presented in this section points to provision of education to girls as a key measure for poverty alleviation. Education not only benefits girls themselves, but also has great impact on the nutritional and health status of their eventual children.

Healthier children have better cognitive capacity at school and can therefore gain more from education, which in turn equips them to take advantage of future income-earning opportunities and/or produce at higher productivity levels. Education should not be interpreted here as solely formal education. Informal education, and in particular functional literacy, are important means of empowering the poor to take charge of their lives.

Such training is essential for building self-confidence, increasing the transparency of intra-village decision-making and leveling the playing field in interactions with marketing agents and service providers. Where literacy is severely limited, it is difficult to manage funds for community projects and credit and savings programmes since those who are illiterate are blocked from full participation.

Often when rural people are asked what keeps poor people poor, the first thing they say is, "The poor are alone". When asked what they appreciate most about a successful development project in their community, before mentioning monetary or technical benefits, poor participants frequently remark on how the project helped them to stand together. Strong social organization makes it possible for the poor to gain access to resources and knowledge within their communities and to develop links with external partners.

In many ways, the region leads the developing world in the blossoming of civil society that has occurred over the past decade. Examples at the 'macro level' include the various national conferences of the early 1990s, the fall of a number of long-standing dictatorial regimes, more widespread and increasingly fair electoral processes, and the peaceful electoral-based transfers of power to opposition parties in Benin, Ghana and Senegal.

At the more micro or sectoral level, these developments are reflected in the rapid growth of local NGOs, farmers' associations, producer federations and a general opening up of dialogue at sectoral policy and project levels to the importance of consulting with civil society in areas where they are legitimate stakeholders, and in investing in capacity-building of grass-roots organizations.

Things were not always this way. Through the late 1980s, many groups and associations were 'empty shells'—top-down structures imposed by the state. This characterized nearly all farmers' cooperatives and pre-cooperatives, which had been established to exercise state control of crop marketing and input/credit distribution. Governing parties frequently used them as tools for political mobilization in rural areas.

If many of the recently emerged WCA grass-roots organizations appear vibrant, it is because they are indeed popularly based and not so only nominally. This is a radical break with the past. Rural activities are often characterized by market imperfections, such as weak information systems, the geographic dispersion of market agents and poor transportation and communications infrastructure. These problems are generally worse for the rural poor than for others.

They have also become more severe in many countries as a result of state withdrawal from productive activities as part of structural adjustment processes. Private-sector agents either have been slow to fill the void or have little incentive to share information with competitors and farmers. Collective action by grass-roots organizations is an important means for overcoming these obstacles and reducing transaction costs. In the context of globalization, rural actors also need to increase their competitiveness, productivity and agility in taking advantage of potential market opportunities.

The public sector has a crucial role to play in creating enabling conditions necessary for grass-roots organizations to function effectively. Popularly based grass-roots organizations have numerous functions: economic, social, representation (advocacy and voice), information sharing/capacity-building, and coordination. Today, donors increasingly recognize the importance of building institutional capacity and strengthening governance mechanisms.

A wide array of associations are found at the village and inter-village level, including but not limited to: traditional community associations; village associations; specialized producer organizations; cooperatives; economic interest groups; associations des ressortissants (migrants to urban centres who have maintained strong links with their villages and fund development projects and mosque construction there) in Sahelian countries; and credit and savings clubs throughout the region.

In some countries, traditional groupings are very strong. There is considerable scope for working more closely with existing informal groups. The focus of public and donor-financed support services has tended to be on formal institutions such as cooperative unions, cooperatives and pre-cooperatives. Ultimately, more formal cooperative or pre-cooperative structures can be perfectly consistent with traditional means of organization if people are free to form their own groupings and a degree of flexibility is allowed.

In Cameroon and Senegal, among other countries, simple legal mechanisms for formal recognition of GIE have been established. Due to its flexibility, the GIE structure has considerable potential to allow small cohesive groups access to training and other forms of assistance for income-generating activities. Successful grass-roots organizations often follow a recognizable evolutionary pattern as they mature over time. For capacity-building efforts to be effective, it is important that stages of maturity are carefully identified so that appropriate training and related assistance can be given.

Policy Environment and Rural Development

Throughout the 1970s and 1980s, macroeconomic and agricultural policies were generally inhospitable to rural development in the region. Factors discouraging the development of dynamic food and export crop markets included overvalued exchange rates, state trading monopolies for domestic marketing, external trade of agricultural commodities and high tariff and non-tariff barriers on manufactured inputs.

Partly because of power disparities between highly concentrated and vocal urban pressure groups (civil servants and trade unions) and dispersed, rural small farmers, the implicit over-arching objective of governments at that time was to transfer wealth from rural to urban areas. Export revenues from agriculture and mineral wealth were used to fuel the growth of the civil service while not necessarily creating the conditions for sustained rural-sector growth.

In countries with substantial mineral resources, agricultural development was grossly neglected. The net effect of pricing, exchange rate and trade policies in many countries was to favour food imports over domestic production of food and export crops. In all countries in the CFA franc zone, extended periods of exchange rate overvaluation reduced competitiveness of locally grown food and export crops. Because of the lack of an enabling policy environment, the World Bank and other donors began in the early 1980s to make structural adjustment a condition for lending to SSA.

At the macro level, reforms generally consisted of trade and exchange rate liberalization; financial-sector reform, including restructuring/liquidation of poorly performing public and commercial banks; public expenditure reform and civil-service downsizing; and privatization of state-owned enterprises. Trade and exchange rate liberalization has been widespread. The majority of countries outside the CFA franc zone have adopted market-determined exchange rate systems and freed up foreign exchange allocation systems.

The 1994 CFA franc devaluation provided a long-needed boost to competitiveness, to which many of the countries of the CFA franc zone responded with renewed economic growth (particularly in agriculture) and subdued inflation after the initial shock. In many countries, the banking systems are now in much better health; and this, in combination with the general withdrawal of government from productive investment and agricultural credit, has greatly reduced levels of political interference, which proved so damaging in the 1970s and 1980s.

International debt continues to loom large as a major constraint to mobilizing the resources necessary for human resource development, rural development and poverty alleviation. Launched with great fanfare in 1996, the Debt Initiative for Heavily Indebted Poor Countries (HIPC) initially moved at a very slow pace and with limited means. Three years after its initiation, only three WCA countries had approved Debt Initiative programmes and none had yet received debt relief.

Establishment of the enhanced Initiative at the June 1999 G-8 Summit improved the situation. Deeper and more rapid debt relief, and a much stronger focus on poverty alleviation via the poverty reduction strategy paper (PRSP) process, are the hallmarks of the enhanced Initiative. As a result, approvals and release of debt relief have accelerated substantially, debt relief is now strongly linked to appropriate poverty-reducing public investments in social sectors and rural development.

Many governments are putting in place decentralized decision-making systems as a way of bringing government services closer to the people concerned, to respond better to their real concerns and to be more accountable. But decentralisation is just beginning, and operationalizing local participation in decision-making, local fiscal autonomy and accountability still has a long way to go. The aim is to increase the effectiveness of local public service provision in rural areas.

More accountability to local populations holds the promise of more effective public services from which the poor may benefit. More local autonomy and popular representation, fiscal transfers and local taxation can lead to more local spending to eliminate key constraints on rural development. Current legal frameworks are often quite good, but fail to be implemented at the local level. Public actions at the local level can also largely bypass the poor.

For the voices of the poor to be heard, empowerment is imperative, which is one reason why access to basic education is of paramount importance to poor families. Only when their views and needs are heard and understood through policy dialogue can better governance, which helps the poor, have a chance of succeeding.

At the sector level, the basic policy mix in most adjustment-related agricultural reform efforts has included:

— reduction of agricultural taxation through domestic price liberalization, reduction of export taxes, and (at the overall macro level) reduction of implicit taxation by either reducing exchange rate overvaluation or, where devaluation was not politically possible, "mimicking" devaluation through imposition of export subsidies and import taxes;

— domestic food market liberalization through abolition of food crop marketing boards and removal of price controls and restrictions on purchase and sale arrangements, processing and interregional movement of produce;

— removal of input subsidies, including those on fertilizer, seed, agrochemicals, machinery and irrigation services;

— abolition of agricultural development banks that had become insolvent due to cheap credit policies, poor management, overpoliticization and unsustainably low repayment rates;

— abolition or restructuring of state marketing boards and agro-processing industries for agricultural exports, and privatization of selected agro-industries; and

— rationalization of public expenditure related to agricultural projects, and restructuring of ministries of agriculture and national research and extension agencies.

Progress in achieving market liberalization is now substantial, especially for food crops. With rare exceptions, domestic food markets for staple food crops have been almost completely liberalized, with generally favourable impacts on producers and consumers. The private sector has readily stepped into the vacuum temporarily created by state withdrawal from food crop marketing and processing.

The World Bank judged that, of 19 WCA countries where agricultural policy reforms had been initiated during the 1980s, in 13 countries, government intervention prior to reforms was either strong or moderate. After reform, in late 1992, only one country maintained a moderate level of intervention; the rest had no public intervention, with the possible exception of maintenance of food security stocks.

At that time, governments in several countries still exceptionally played a dominant role in setting food crop prices and controlling marketing and trade with respect to rice, edible oils, wheat and sugar, with only the first two bearing much relevance to small farmers. However, since then, with the exception of Burkina Faso, rice marketing has been completely liberalized. With regard to domestic production, governments that have heavily invested in irrigated rice continue to provide some support to the operation and maintenance of major infrastructure, but have liberalized most aspects of input and output marketing.

Liberalization has been uneven for crops predominantly geared to export, and there is great controversy over whether, and to what degree, liberalization has been beneficial or disastrous. The Government agreed to complete liberalization beginning in 1999/2000. Although viewed by the World Bank as a major adjustment success story at the macroeconomic level, Ghanaian cocoa sector reform has been minimal. In Cameroon and Nigeria, where liberalization of the cocoa sector proceeded quickly with little or no advance planning, the transition was rocky.

It is not clear, however, whether this was primarily due to how liberalization was carried out or rather to general conditions of political and economic turmoil in those countries at the time of liberalization. Liberalization has proceeded more slowly and unevenly for cotton. This subsector is characterized by strong vertical integration in all aspects of marketing and technology development and transfer.

Liberalization has been less rapid primarily because the integrated model has been successful in many countries in generating steady gains in production and productivity, and in developing and effectively disseminating new technologies for production and processing. Key ancillary services (extension, credit, and input distribution) have also functioned effectively despite their general collapse in many countries. Yet this success has sometimes come at the cost of a reduction in farmers' decision-making autonomy because of the monopolistic structure of the industry, buttressed by powerful national and international interests resistant to change.

Input markets have been partially liberalized, but this has been a source of major problems, with serious negative implications for sustained increases in agricultural productivity in the region. In addition, governments (with the tacit approval of donors) have been slow in creating a level playing field for private-sector importation and distribution of inputs. In addition, some donorsupported commodity import programmes for inputs are non-transparent and depend on public distribution, thus seriously impeding the development of private markets.

Tariff anomalies also have led to distortions and inconsistencies in many countries, although this is being addressed to some extent by the customs unions agreements of the West African Economic and Monetary Union and the Central African Customs and Economic Union. After a slow start, the rate of privatization of agro-industries has picked up. However, one point of particular relevance to IFAD's target population needs to be made: for agro-industries that have in the past been an important outlet for smallholder sales at pan-territorially fixed prices (cotton, groundnuts, palm oil), part of the general privatization formula concerns making potentially attractive investments in favourable zones (in terms of agricultural productivity, proximity to markets and existing infrastructure) to the private sector, while leaving farmers in more distant and less productive zones (i.e. poorer farmers) to fend for themselves.

The future of social services (including health, education, road maintenance and technology transfer) previously provided by public enterprises also remains unclear even in productive zones. Farmers living in remote, less accessible areas now probably receive lower prices than under uniform pan-territorial pricing. Perhaps even more important, they have lost guaranteed marketing outlets. This is especially a problem in the less populated areas, particularly in the forest zone in Central Africa.

Examples include cocoa and coffee in the south and east provinces of Cameroon. Yet more commonly, pan-territorial pricing (export crops in coastal countries; cotton, rice in irrigated Sahel schemes) was often not effectively applied by marketing boards or, when it was applied, products were often paid for with great delays. Market liberalization has increased price risk and has led certain farmers to speculate on prices, with sometimes disastrous results.

Thus, better market information, an explanation of how markets work, exploitation of alternative cropping opportunities, and developing market linkages with private traders within a competitive environment are opportunities that can be exploited. But the first priority for farmers living in remote areas is to improve market access through improved feeder roads, group action in produce marketing, contractual arrangements with a buyer, or a combination of the above. In areas where market linkages never really existed, for food crops in particular, physical infrastructure development may be a top priority, and policies to support sustainable funding of the rehabilitation and maintenance of road infrastructure is critical. This is especially the case in the forest zone of much of Central Africa. In certain cases, farmers in remote areas have to change their cropping system, replacing a low-value crop with a high-value one (such as horticulture, tobacco) or switching to livestock production.

By and large, however, most farmers have gained considerably by market liberalization since commercialization, like technology, can be the prime impetus for poverty-alleviating growth. Yet commercialization is not without problems, especially for women. Sometimes, they do not share equitably in the proceeds from commercialization; and some may have an undue work burden placed on them, leading to the neglect of household activities, including child care. In certain cases, commercialization can lead to child labour, neglect of schooling or eviction of tenants.

While liberalization has succeeded fairly well in removing governments from agricultural production and marketing roles best left to private actors, progress has been much slower in improving their capacities to handle a number of roles related to 'public goods' provision that only they can fulfill. Restructuring of public institutions related to agriculture has been slow. While many inefficient and overlapping extension agencies have been eliminated, the agencies established under the World Bank-led national agricultural services projects to replace them have not yet shown that they will improve the effectiveness of national technology development and transfer systems in a sustainable way.

With respect to general rural development and infrastructure investment, renewed efforts at decentralization are just beginning. It is hoped that decentralized decision-making systems will be more accountable to local populations, thus increasing the effectiveness of rural infrastructure provision. The choice of public agricultural investments—small versus large-scale irrigation; small versus large-scale crop processing; good areas or poor areas; food crops versus export crops; locally manufactured equipment or imported equipment; people-centered (health, education) or hardware-centered (infrastructure)—has significant implications for rural poverty, and decision-makers must be made aware of this.

Prioritizing public investments by taking account of their incidence on the poor, knowing that one dollar of income more for the poor has much greater weight than one dollar more for the average citizen, should become standard operating procedure if poverty alleviation is to be taken seriously. Regarding technology choice and technology development, the availability of appropriate technologies and poor people's access to them are key determinants of productivity and income. Together with commercialization, they can be the prime movers for poverty-alleviating growth.

But governments in WCA should be more aware of the possible benefits and costs of biotechnology applications in agriculture, and the risks and difficulties involved. An appropriate legal and regulatory framework needs to be set up for responsible use of biotechnology applications in agriculture. So far, none of the countries in WCA has developed any operational (molecular) biotechnology capacity, including a policy and regulatory framework. Within a few years at most, biotechnology applications will arrive in the region and will be applied, probably first for export crops (cotton, coffee).

Marker-assisted breeding and diagnostic probes are already being used. While there has been notable progress in achieving significant macro and sectoral reforms, it remains unclear the extent to which the rural poor have benefited or been harmed. On the one hand, claims that the poor have been severely hurt by adjustment are often exaggerated. They fail to acknowledge that the poor were largely bypassed by most public investment prior to adjustment (such as subsidized credit and inputs) and that a number of policy measures (such as overvalued exchange rates, fiscal and monetary mismanagement leading to rapid inflation, protection of infant industries, urban bias in social investments) were decidedly anti-poor and anti-rural.

On the other hand, it appears that supply response to reform has been far more appreciable for export crops than for traditional food crops, and the rural poor in many WCA countries tend to be more concentrated on traditional food crop production. More fundamentally, as mentioned above, reform has been more successful in getting government out of areas it does not belong in than in getting government to fill the roles it should be playing.

A number of these roles relate to appropriate social and physical infrastructure investments and institutional reforms to make public interventions more responsive to the needs of the poor. A major challenge exists in creating and nurturing grass-roots organizations that can effectively articulate the interests of the rural poor.

Rural Development and Natural Resource Management

A major challenge facing WCA countries will be to dramatically increase food availability by 2025 while maintaining the natural resource base and reducing poverty. The population of SSA will nearly triple, from around 500 million in 1995 to nearly 1.3 billion by 2025. The urban share is projected to increase from roughly 35% to 55%. According to the West African LTPS for 19 countries in the region, total population in 1990 was estimated to be 194 million, 40% of which was urban. The LTPS projected that by 2020 these figures will increase to 430 million and 63% respectively. During the same period, per capita arable land is projected to decline to less than half the current levels.

Land degradation as a result of extensive agriculture, deforestation and overgrazing is already alarming. The forest area is declining because of agricultural expansion and demand for fuelwood and timber for a growing population. For the entire subcontinent, forest cover has been disappearing at a rate of 3.7 million ha annually. Most of this disappearance is concentrated in the rainforests of Central Africa and the West African coastal countries that were once heavily forested in their southern regions. This degradation has implications for biodiversity in flora and fauna where the losses are irreplaceable. About 50% of farmland suffers to some extent from soil erosion; and as much as 80% of pasture and rangelands exhibit some form of degradation, with use exceeding carrying capacity.

On-farm socio-economic research has shown that there are

important regional differences in terms of land/labour productivity, depending on land/labour scarcities resulting from different resource endowments, population densities and market access. But even within what appears to be homogeneous resource endowments and farming systems, large differences exist among households in terms of farmer productivity and income.

This has to do with different managerial capacities, attitudes towards risk, different initial endowments, family composition, luck, etc., and is not different from agriculture in more industrialized countries. Farmers learn a lot from each other, but some farmers never seem to learn, or always seem to have a stroke of bad luck. It is therefore wrong to consider all farmers in a given setting as a homogeneous group. It is also for this reason that, for a given improved technology, certain farmers are early adopters, others are late adopters and still others never adopt.

Thus, in any poverty alleviation strategy, attention must be given to the most vulnerable farmers, to those least inclined to adapt improved technologies and to those who manage their resources the least optimally, without of course excluding the other farmers. In WCA, low labour productivity is a major constraint although land productivity is increasing in importance in the more densely populated areas, in marginal areas and in areas where inframarginal land scarcities are emerging. When land productivity is increased, labour productivity usually also increases.

But often, postharvest operations are a major labour bottleneck and increasing labour productivity of the total production and post-harvest system also requires improvements in the postharvest operations. This is particularly the case for root and tuber crops, where nearly all post-harvest operations are the responsibility of women. Often, too much research and extension is directed towards increasing land productivity (higher yields, improved fallow management) when labour is the real constraint.

Certain techniques can increase labour productivity greatly. Notable among these are animal traction, use of herbicides for weed control, mechanical grating of cassava and mechanical milling of cereals. Thus, special attention must be given to labour productivity, particularly of the poor, as Western or Western-trained researchers and extension agents often only look at land productivity in terms of yields per unit of land. Nevertheless, as land frontiers are closing rapidly in the coastal zone of West Africa and in the densely populated moist and dry savannahs, and to a lesser extent in Central Africa, agricultural intensification becomes a necessity in terms of higher yields per ha, and land-use intensification in terms of shortening fallows. This requires more inputs per hectare, particularly labour inputs.

Agricultural and land-use intensification help to preserve the environment, including nature reserves, wetlands, fragile areas, game reserves and mangroves. Without intensification, such areas will also be brought under cultivation. This is clearly the case in many parts of Nigeria. Agricultural intensification on the best soils, including irrigation in the drier areas, can help to preserve fragile soils and ecosystems elsewhere. This trade-off must be considered if NRM is to be taken seriously.

Agricultural intensification does not necessarily mean more external inputs, which may be damaging to the environment, especially pesticides. In all cases, use of indigenous knowledge needs to be optimized and new technology development needs to be more demand-driven. New technologies need to be adapted to local conditions and on-farm testing and adaptation is imperative before embarking on large-scale extension. This also means that farmers need to be intimately involved in technology generation and adaptation.

Particularly for the resource-poor farmers, biological control of pests, soil fertility management using on-farm resources and low external input in agriculture are indicated. Except for the shifting cultivation areas in the forest, particularly in Central Africa, fallows are shortening everywhere with often-decreasing soil fertility as a result. Improved fallow management and the use of legume cover crops, mulches (live or dead) or agro-forestry species show a lot of promise. Getting improved on-farm tested technology adopted by farmers is a key to productivity improvement and better NRM.

Although many farmers depend on livestock, particularly in the dry areas, not much progress has been made in productivity over the last decades. More veterinary services are now private and herders' associations have been successful in acquiring veterinary supplies and services. Maintaining good animal health is still a major constraining factor related to improved nutrition management, particularly during the dry season. Transhumant livestock farming is becoming more and more problematic in many WCA countries.

Many conflicts arise between transhumant livestock herders and sedentary farmers. Better integration of crop and livestock production is part of the solution, also in light of animal traction and more sedentary ways of livestock keeping. Transhumant and nomadic livestock herders are among the poorest farmers, and ways of alleviating their poverty have yet to be found. Only when they become more sedentary do existing solutions become feasible.

Agricultural Marketing

In general, food crop agricultural marketing in WCA is characterized by high marketing margins and lack of innovation. Large marketing margins (particularly so for perishable food crops) are caused by high transport costs, lack of economies of scale in marketing, lack of marketing information, high risk, legal and illegal taxes, too many intermediaries and serious physical losses, among other factors. Marketing margins are lower for export crops where competition tends to be greater.

Marketing costs are highest for farmers located in remote or less accessible villages where buyers can exert monopoly or oligopoly buying power. Donors and governments alike tend to neglect agricultural marketing for food crops. Because it is a private-sector activity in a liberalized environment, governments see no particular role except for general infrastructure provision (roads, communications).

High marketing margins are usually attributed to dishonest or 'extractive' traders who exert their buying power in making extra profits. These traders sometimes come from ethnic groups resented or distrusted by local populations and politicians. Taxing them or levying a variety of legal and illegal taxes is then seen as an answer. When donors and governments invest in marketing, approaches are often inappropriate.

Many projects equate marketing with providing credit lines, building warehouses and roads and, sometimes, supplying group managed processing equipment. While roads are essential, the provision of credit and warehouse and processing equipment often does not address the real problems. Simpler and cheaper solutions may be more appropriate. Farmers may only need to be reasonably assured that they will have an outlet for their sales.

In such cases, establishing links with traders so that produce is bulked at a pre-arranged delivery point may be all that is needed. Where reasonably competitive private agents are in place, donors and governments need to stop funding ill-conceived projects that attempt to substitute groups for private marketing agents. The African countryside is littered with empty or underused donorfinanced warehouse facilities whose intended purpose was to facilitate replacement of private-sector marketing by cooperatives.

In nearly all such cases, no effort was made to appreciate the private-sector function, and no rigorous constraints analysis was performed. Organizational complexities and risks inherent in group storage and marketing were ignored or minimized. The same can be said for donor investments in processing equipment. When visiting towns in rural areas, one frequently comes across defunct donorfunded grain dehullers sitting right next to bustling private mills, some of which strip the donor mill for spare parts.

In the wake of market liberalization, some donors have rushed in to finance small rice mills—without first asking whether lack of processing capacity was a true constraint to market performance and improved producer welfare. Creation of marketing cooperatives or producer associations marketing their products jointly is a good concept if approached from a business perspective. Successful group action is often the result of small-scale groupings in homogeneous structures with a particular purpose and where a sure market outlet is available.

In some cases, niche market opportunities can be exploited, such as fair-trade products, environmentally friendly products and organic products. Niche markets such as organics may represent a way to tap into premium markets and reduce reliance on agrochemicals. One key strategic issue is that there is simply not enough knowledge about how to support agricultural marketing operations affecting poor farmers, without introducing market distortions and going against economic liberalization.

The marketing of inputs and products affecting poor people often encompasses cases of market failure. But replacing market failure by state failure— government intervention that goes against the working of the free market and kills private-sector initiatives—is not the solution. Finding ways to support poorly working 'infant' or 'thin' markets without replacing the private sector by the public sector is not easy.

There is therefore a need for more action-research on agricultural marketing, including the setting up of small-scale pilot projects for improving marketing performance. Public market information systems in Africa generally do not have a good track record and are not a panacea. Public market infrastructure helps, but it is expensive and often underused.

Rural Finance

Often a major constraint to improving the lot of the rural poor is their lack of access to financial capital for financing income-generating on- and off-farm opportunities, paying school fees, meeting emergencies and fulfilling important social obligations such as funerals and assisting relatives. While informal credit and savings schemes are widespread in the region (and the potential to build upon them is too commonly overlooked), they present a number of drawbacks. Traditional moneylending occurs at extremely high rates of interest. This limits lending to emergency situations rather than investment, and will therefore serve only to increase indebtedness, not to escape poverty.

Rotating savings and credit associations are more benign in their effects but limit the pool of resources available for investment to existing levels and are used exclusively to finance short-term consumption and working capital needs. For significant agricultural and rural development to occur, it is necessary to go beyond these to identify ways of increasing the pool of investment resources for smallholders in the sector, while recognizing that the greatest source of such funds are savings that can be tapped within the sector.

Problems with traditional financial institutions. As is the case elsewhere in the world, commercial banks in WCA are not able to adapt their financial products to the needs of small, poor and remote clients. Therefore, they have no interest in becoming involved in microfinance or in agriculture in general. There is a long and disappointing experience in WCA with large formal agricultural credit institutions, and their legacy of political interference and non-repayment will make it difficult to rejuvenate similar institutions in the future.

While agricultural development banks still survive in several WCA countries, most are in a dubious state of financial health and have major problems servicing clientele on a timely basis—a crucial consideration given the seasonal nature of agricultural activities.

For a number of reasons, including an unfortunate historical legacy that leads many potential borrowers to equate credit with free money, WCA may be the most challenging region in the world for developing viable microfinance institutions (MFIs). This, of course, has limited the investment and employment opportunities that can be financed through microfinance programmes. Overall population densities in WCA are only about one quarter of those in other developing regions, which substantially drives up the unit costs of delivering credit and savings services to clients.

Another factor driving up the costs of financial services delivery in WCA is the high cost of qualified personnel. This is due not only to macroeconomic factors related to wage competitiveness, but also to a narrow human resource base that serves to bid up prices for educated loan officers. As a multiple of GNI per capita, the average loan officer's salary in WCA is nearly double that of the other regions. Because of low population densities, these loan officers also handle an average of 19% fewer loans than their counterparts in the other regions.

The daunting challenges of developing MFIs in WCA have not kept donors from multiplying such institutions in the region. In light of the exponential growth of MFIs in the last few years, numbers are probably now far higher, especially as virtually every donor and many NGOs have jumped on the microcredit bandwagon. Indeed, the microfinance fad has led to a situation where donors, and the NGOs they channel their funds through, may represent a problem for development of viable microfinance systems in the region.

Of course, it is ultimately the national governments that must show greater commitment to rationalizing the situation by tightening up criteria for allowing credit and savings deliverers to operate in their countries, while at the same time not overly discouraging the introduction of innovative approaches. In recent years, donors have invested heavily in credit unions in WCA with some encouraging results in terms of improved financial health and savings mobilization.

However, as a means of reaching the poor and mobilizing funds for rural investment, there are a number of limitations. Because short-term savings constitute the bulk of funds, credit unions usually adopt a conservative approach to lending. They normally allow only 50% of their deposits to be on-lent, while depositing the remainder in commercial banks. To the extent that rural members are the source of savings, this leads to a significant drain of rural capital to urban areas.

This, of course, is the opposite of what should occur if the agricultural sector is seen as a driving source of overall economic development in countries that are still overwhelmingly agrarian. To keep delivery costs low, few branches are established in smaller villages and hamlets, leaving the bulk of the rural population without financial services. Indeed, a key strategy for restructuring (assainissement) ailing mutualist systems in the 1990s was to radically scale back outreach by retreating from rural areas.

While challenges to developing pro-poor microfinance systems in WCA are formidable, there are also major opportunities.

- There is a strong entrepreneurial spirit in many WCA countries. Its origin was in pre-colonial trading patterns, and it was not radically circumscribed under colonial rule. Women are prominent participants in small commerce, actively involved in food marketing and long distance trade.
- But not unique to WCA, the rural poor have proved to be strong savers and decent credit risks, and there is a long tradition of informal credit and savings arrangements that can be built upon.
- If urban-rural linkages and population densities increase substantially in the long term as the LTPS predicts, and the informal sector becomes the single largest contributor to GDP by 2020, demand for financial services will increase, and economies in scale and increased population densities will lead to lower delivery costs.
- With adjustment, the macroeconomic environment has become much more hospitable to financialsector development in many WCA countries. Taming of inflation, financial-sector reform, and trade and exchange rate reform are specific policy areas where there have been improvements that augur well for MFI development.
- There is an emerging consensus among major donors and a number of governments in the region on what constitutes best practices related to MFI development.

The generally accepted approach is to develop appropriate specialized institutions, with strong emphasis on savings mobilization (or at least developing a savings discipline), deemphasizing targeting of credit to specific end uses (such as agricultural input provision or marketing credit), while instead emphasizing the development of appropriate financial products for poor savers and borrowers. It is also recognized that MFI development takes considerable time and subsidization.

Subsidies, however, should be applied in the form of support to institutional development and technical assistance—not in the form of subsidized interest rates, which are neither sustainable nor necessary/useful for reaching poor clients whose primary problem is access to credit rather than the cost of credit. Although MFIs have proliferated in recent years, most governments in the region have yet to develop coherent frameworks for determining what types of MFI practices to encourage and discourage.

Rural Access to ICTs

In this digital age, most Africans do not yet have access to the basic ICT services needed to make or receive a simple telephone call. As the 20th century comes to a close, one African still shares a telephone line with 99 others, compared to 10 lines per 100 people in Latin America and 64 in the United States. It is generally agreed that across Africa, ICT access unevenly favours urban and wealthy residents.

Within Africa, despite high demand for ICT services and a growing telecommunications market, rural access to basic ICT services, such as voice telephony, remains a major concern.

Information and communication technologies change and evolve, and individual projects do not last forever, but if our investments in rural ICT access are wise, they will enable long-term rural ICT access that evolves with new technologies, and contributes to sustainable improvements in health, education, social welfare, agriculture and the environment. There are very few substantive critical appraisals or evaluations dealing with rural ICT access and its impact on sustainable development. This in itself is an important finding.

Over the past several years, a great deal of attention and financial support has been focused on ICT access for rural areas. While there is a general belief that such investments achieve positive developmental results, concrete evidence to support these expenditures is sparse. Richardson suggest that the requirements for sustainability in ICT projects go beyond simply requiring partnerships in rural ICT initiatives, and that they must also include the components of "delivery of service and knowledge accessibility", and "the provision of electronic connectivity" to enable the transfer and sharing of information and knowledge to take place.

The importance of projects fulfilling the needs and demands of rural users is emphasized throughout much of the project documentation. Simply put, initiatives that neither meet the needs or demands of the communities they purport to serve, nor involve the target communities in the project planning process, will not survive and will not contribute to sustainable development. Senegal offers a strong example of the concept of 'keeping services simple' and then expanding the services according to the demands of the people.

Rural ICT project proponents should continue to explore multi-sector partnership possibilities in order to generate strong, collaborative efforts and ensure project objectives can be met. Through creating local, private and public sector collaborations, projects are able to better equip themselves with the human, technical and financial resources that are needed for ICT initiatives to become self-sustaining while also contributing to sustainable developmental results.

Unless ICT initiatives are established to satisfy the information and communication needs of the intended users, technologies will remain underutilized, and thus will have even less of a chance for achieving sustainable developmental results. Project proponents and planners must concern themselves not only with the ICT hardware and software, but also with the necessary capacity building activities which are necessary to ensure that both staff and clients will be in a position to utilize the technology and thereby have a stake in its future success and development.

Globally, studies of universal access indicate clearly that private sector participation and competition significantly increase the number of telecommunication access lines and ICT services, and that ICT competition lowers prices. "Increased competition and liberalization of telecommunications encourages infrastructure development, draws inbound investment, and assists in meeting universal service objectives".

Yet, in many emerging markets, including those in Africa, unfair interconnection & anti-competitive practices continue to hamper universal access. "Regulators have to create an ambience that attracts investment and makes it worthwhile for private companies to invest in telecommunications". When local entrepreneurs in unserved and underserved areas are allowed to participate, the network is extended even further. It seems the more barriers to market participation can be removed or reduced, the greater will be the network extension.

There is an urgent need for specific universal access and rural telecommunication policy strategies at the national level, strategies that include strong roles for independent regulators working to attract new entrants and encourage fair competition. There is also a related need for.African continent-wide dialogue and agreement on regulation, interconnection and tariff sharing among nations.

Policy needs to be developed with much greater participation from civil society and non- governmental organizations so that rural ICT access programs truly meet nationally recognized sustainable development objectives. Policy makers need to explore a range of alternative incentive packages for provision of rural service, and select those that are most appropriate to the local context and national development objectives.

These incentives can include universal service funds, public-private joint ventures, rural concessionary licenses, build-transfer schemes with international investors, cost-based tariff reform tied to interconnection agreements that favor rural operators, and special incentives for indigenous investments that support universal service.

Increasingly, the division between what are and what are not appropriate ICTs for developing nations results in a distinction between voice-only technologies and those advanced enough to transmit voice, data and video. While hi-tech, wireless technologies are being promoted as technologies to enable the Internet and other applications to reach rural and remote regions of the world, rural radio is still the most appropriate and most penetrating ICT from the perspective of rural residents.

A variety of satellite services can be employed to improve rural ICT access, however the jury is still out on widespread affordability of these services and the ability of regulatory environments to respond to satellite entrants. Global Mobile Personal Communications by Satellite (GMPCS) systems, for example, are touted as a large-scale solution to developing countries' poor rural access to ICTs.

Stationary satellite ground-station systems can assist in enabling both telephone operators and Internet Service Providers to deliver more cost-effective and widespread services to the African continents' widely dispersed population. The costs and effectiveness of using the various satellite technologies

(Geosynchronous (GEO) satellites, medium-Earth orbit (MEO) satellites, and Low Earth Orbiting (LEO) satellites) vary according to the distance of the particular satellite from the earth's surface, the range of the satellite as it passes through orbit, the quality of the transmission.available, and most importantly, the regulatory and tariff agreements in effect.

Jensen and Richardson point to the rapid deployment of very small aperture technologies (VSAT) in liberalized, African telecommunication markets, compared to the slow spread of VSAT in the rest of the continent, as evidence that liberalized telecommunication markets will lead to rural telecommunication services bringing new, effective, and lower costing technologies to rural and remote regions of the continent.

Countries such as Egypt and Mozambique are now utilizing VSAT technology as a key solution to their communication access issues. The impacts that satellite technologies will have on the African continent depend greatly on the regulatory environments existing in each country. Wireless Local Loop networks (WLL) Wireless local loop (WLL) networks are another option that are in some ways better suited for the rural clientele who seek access to telecommunications services.

WLL networks are able to transmit voice, data and video from one transmission tower to another, easily upgrade the networks to reflect changing network and user capacity and demand, and cover an area of several hundred square kilometers at a fraction of the cost of satellite technology. Jensen notes that the implementation of WLL networks in both rural and urban centers of developing countries has had a strong impact on the costs of telephony, reducing the average cost of installing a new fixed line from about $2,000 for the traditional copper cable system, to less than $500 for basic wireless telephony services.

Because subscriber lines are "fixed wireless lines," WLL

systems do not require hardware and software solutions to "track" mobile users, as is the case with mobile cellular networks. WLL systems can also be configured for broadband data services, together with voice telephony services.

Of all the technology options available to rural and underserved regions in Africa and other developing countries, perhaps none offers as rapid a "fix" as cellular networks, of which at last count there were 65 cell networks in 39 African countries. The popularity of cellular networks owes to the fact they require less fixed infrastructure and can generally be deployed more quickly than WLL and satellite; users can also take advantage of pre-paid telephone services.

Cambodia's cellular success, where 72% of all telephone lines are mobile cellular, enabling it to surpass 31 other countries in overall telephone penetration in the last 6 years, highlights the potential that mobile cellular telephony can offer for rural ICT access in Africa. Cellular coverage is expected to continue to improve with the ITU's mandate of achieving global standardization of Third Generation (3G) cell phones to enable data, voice and video transmissions via cellular technology.

GSM's competing standard, CDMA, is a packet shared medium for transmission and can be upgraded without requiring upgrades to all phones and all infrastructure on the network. CDMA mobile cellular systems are also compatible with a variety of WLL systems which tend to be based on the CDMA standard. To counter the problems associated with limited availability of cellular frequency, manufacturers are introducing lower frequencies normally utilized for television broadcasts.

This approach requires up to 90 percent fewer base stations in rural areas, and costs as much as 75% less than networks needed for GSM networks in the existing 900, 1800 and 1900 bands. Despite the push for broadband, digital technologies, analogue, copper-wire systems are still being pursued by national operators in developing nations due to the fact in more densely populated areas they can sometimes be implemented at a lower cost than wireless, digital systems. This is acknowledged to be a poor long-term solution in terms of enabling countries' ability to join the rest of the world in digital communication technologies.

Nations with a legacy terrestrial copper network may be able to take advantage of new generations of digital switching systems and new modes of broadband transmission such as Digital Subscriber Lines (DSL) that do not require any changes in the basic copper wire infrastructure that delivers service to the subscriber.

While many telecom experts are focused on deploying networks that are built primarily on one particular technology, such as WLL, VSAT or cellular, others suggest that the key to making rural connectivity profitable is through the creation of a hybrid mixture of wireless, copper and fibre services which fit with the geographic and economic contexts of the region.

Jensen states that the perception that low capacity voice-only systems will suffice for the needs of developing nations should be re-evaluated in light of the increasingly common perception that access to advanced services such as the Internet is part of the basic human right to communicate. Ultimately, the selection of available telecom services, and not the technical infrastructure to make it work, will be of most interest to the average user.

Local "dial-up" Internet access Encourage the provision of local "dial-up" Internet access in rural areas. Recent figures indicate that only 10 countries on the African continent have this service, meaning that the long distance costs for basic Internet access are passed on from the Internet service providers (ISPs) to the users of the technology, which does not encourage rural access and use at all. With local dial-up access, it becomes easier for those interested in the technologies to utilize them.

Encourage the creation of a regional backbone for connectivity within and among African countries in order to: a) facilitate the national deployment of services to rural and remote regions within a country through tie-ins between cellular, VSAT and fixed-line operators; and, b) eliminate the need to transmit intra-continental communications outside of the continent in order to facilitate the transmission.

Making communication and information sharing among African countries less costly will do much both for the private sector, which is attempting to encourage business development through communications, and the public users who desire to take advantage of the technologies.

Greater sensitization and education on emerging ICT infrastructure options for government policy officials and decision-makers. This is crucial given the rapid, continuous evolution of wireless technology solutions for rural and remote access.

Unless the policy leaders and government officials are able to make informed decisions about which technology is most appropriate for their contexts and their people, decisions on rural infrastructure investment will be left to the abilities of telecom manufacturers to convince clients that their technologies are the best for their respective needs.

More in-depth research on rural infrastructure options is needed. With the multitude of telecommunication solutions available for improving rural ICT access, it is imperative that project experiences with these technologies are documented and made available to the ICT and development communities. Universal access throughout the developing world will only become a reality if projects share their results with new and emerging technologies.

Due to the relatively high costs of implementing ICTs in rural areas, very few local organizations or entities can afford to proceed with such initiatives alone. Thus, in order to make rural ICT access a reality, a combination of different partners who each share similar project objectives are needed to work together to share their collective resources, experiences and knowledge to leverage greater ICT opportunities

Achieving the support of local politicians who support and understand the potential of the technology is vital to the spread and success of ICTs. Without local political support, the barriers to achieving community buy-in will more than likely remain in place. In order to facilitate the introduction of ICTs as smoothly and as quickly as possible, local champions who believe in the project objectives and methodology need to be incorporated in the process from the start.

As the utilization of a technology will depend heavily on the understanding of that particular technology, the sustainability of the ICTs and their effective use will depend on a large scale training of both the people who provide and maintain the ICT services, and the people who use them. Therefore, continuous training is critically important.

In order for the proposed technologies to be easily understood and implemented, the applications should be appropriate to the context of the region where it is to be utilized. At the same time the ICTs should be as user-friendly as possible. Communities need to be comfortable with the technology and what it can reasonably achieve. The information collected and disseminated through the use of ICTs should be available to or constructed by participants in a format that is comprehensive and meaningful.

Collecting the information and reorganizing it in a way that it can be easily understood and meaningful to the rural community will make it possible that ICTs will be seen as a means to an end (the general development of the rural community) and not as an end in itself.

The strongest evidence indicating the positive impact of planning gender-sensitive ICT services for rural women are found in two recent evaluation reports on the Grameen Telecom's Village Phone project. This project leases mobile cellular telephones through a micro credit initiative to women members of the Grameen Bank.

Communal telephone and Internet access project in Pondicherry, southern India, in which women primarily used the technology to obtain information related to family income supplements and public welfare schemes, low-cost insurance, and health issues.

In an examination of IDRC's ICT project experiences around the world, Graham reported that women involved in the projects believed that having ICT skills was an important way for them to generate income; that economic activities which utilized ICTs, such as their creation of "walk-in" communications centres, was successfully providing economic returns and linkages to community activities in some rural African communities.

More involvement of women needed in the development of ICT initiatives A number of sources identify how ICTs can enhance the lives of African women through enabling greater participation in civil society and democratic processes; however there is a crucial need for programs which target women for improved ICT access, training and use of Internet applications.

Women entrepreneurs who provide rural ICT services can not only advance their own social and economic well-being, but can also provide access to ICT services to other rural women.

Telecommunication agencies and ICT project proponents are urged to incorporate gender awareness policies into the planning, execution and evaluation of rural ICT projects. This can be achieved by encouraging greater participation of rural women leaders in policy formation, sensitizing and educating key stakeholders about gender-specific issues, and highlighting the different information and communication needs of men and women in rural areas.

Aim to increase rural women's socio-economic status through rural ICT interventions Utilizing the mass media to promote the role of women in ICT initiatives will help generate the necessary awareness and political intervention required to respond to the needs of rural women. Moreover, ICT proponents should attempt to enable civil society organizations and other representatives from marginalized sectors to participate in the formulation of ICT policies, which promote equity and access to information.

Assist the integration of ICTs with women's entrepreneurial activities Government policy makers and ICT project proponents can help enable women entrepreneurs to integrate ICTs with their businesses and business plans. These strategies can do much for helping women raise their communities' revenue generation opportunities, and can be accomplished, for example, through encouraging the involvement of rural women's NGOs in the development of key strategies to encourage women's participation in ICTs.

Such strategies could include encouraging rural women to utilize email discussion lists as a means of sharing information with a larger population of women ICT users. Alternatively, women can incorporate a mixture of media which will be most beneficial to rural African women, such as combining Internet use with low-tech dissemination networks such as community radio, newsletters, and popular theatre.

Bibliography

Barraclough, Solon L., "An End to Hunger? The Social Origins of Food Strategies", Zed Books, London, 1991.

_____________, "Towards Integrated and Sustainable Development?", *UNRISD*, Geneva, 2000.

_____________, and Krishna Ghimire "Forests and Livelihoods: The Social Dynamics of Deforestation in Developing Countries", Macmillan, London, 1995.

_____________, and Daniel Moss "Toward Greater Food Security in Central America Following Hurricane Mitch: Rethinking Sustainable Rural Development Priorities", *A Report Commissioned by Oxfam America,* Oxfam America, Washington, D.C., May, 1999.

Bromley, D.W., "Property relations and economic development: The other land reform", World Development, Vol. 17, No. 6, June, 1989.

Busch, Lawrence, "Biotechnology and Agricultural Productivity: Changing the Rules of the Game?", *paper presented at the International Conference on Agricultural Productivity and Economic Development,* Centre for Environment and Development, University of Trondheim, Michigan State University, East Lansing, MI (mimeo).

Coase, R.H., "The Firm, the Market and the Law", The University of Chicago Press, Chicago and London, 1988.

Dirven, Martine, "The role of agents in agricultural policies: Intentions and reality", CEPAL Review, August 1999, pp. 175-190, 1999.

Kurien, John, "Icelandic fisheries governance: A Third World understanding", Economic and Political Weekly, Vol. XXXV, No. 34, 19-25 August, 2000.

OECD, Agricultural Policies, Markets and Trade in OECD Countries—Monitoring and Evaluation, OECD, Paris, 1998.

Pretty, Jules "Sustainable Agriculture: A Review of Recent Progress on Policies and Practice", *paper prepared for UNRISD*, Geneva, September, 1999.

Singh, Ajit "Global Economic Trends and Social Development, OPG 9, UNRISD, June, 2000.

World Bank, "The Assault on World Poverty: Problems of Rural Development, Education, and Health", *published for the World Bank* by The Johns Hopkins University Press, Baltimore and London, 1975.

Index